THE ANGLO-IRISH

By the same author:

Biography
THE ROAD OF EXCESS—THE LIFE OF ISAAC BUTT
KEVIN O'HIGGINS
A LEAF FROM THE YELLOW BOOK—
THE DIARIES AND LETTERS OF GEORGE EGERTON
A FRETFUL MIDGE
THE PARENTS OF OSCAR WILDE

History
THE STORY OF THE ROYAL DUBLIN SOCIETY

Topography
LEINSTER
IRELAND

Fiction
AN AFFAIR WITH THE MOON
PRENEZ GARDE
THE REMAINDER MAN
LUCIFER FALLING
TARA
THE LAMBERT MILE
THE MARCH HARE
MR. STEPHEN

THE ANGLO-IRISH

by

TERENCE DE VERE WHITE

LONDON
VICTOR GOLLANCZ LTD
1972

© Terence de Vere White 1972

ISBN 0 575 00764 8

Printed in Great Britain by
The Camelot Press Ltd, London and Southampton

For Frank Mac Dermot

ERRATUM

Pages 218, 287, "As I was Walking Down Sackville Street" by St. J. Gogarty.

Acknowledgements

Senator M. B. Yeats and the Macmillan Companies have kindly permitted me to quote from W. B. Yeats's *Autobiographies* and *Responsibilities*. I have to thank Messrs Constable for leave to quote from a poem of Oliver St John Gogarty, Messrs Robert Hale for the quotations from Lt.-Col. O. Head's *No Great Shakes* and Maurice Headlam's *Irish Reminiscences*, the editor of *Apollo* for an extract previously published therein, Messrs J. C. and R. G. Medley for quotations from George Moore's *Hail and Farewell*, the present Lord Dunsany for his father's poem on A.E., the Authors' Society for quotations from G. Bernard Shaw, the National Gallery of Ireland for leave to reproduce the illustrations, Lord Fingal for the photograph of his mother, R. B. McDowell, F.T.C.D. for allowing me to pillage his Fitzgibbon letters, Perry Curtis of Berkeley University for help and quotations. Finally, I would like to thank the Director and staff of the National Library—old friends—Miss Hilda Mac Dermott, who typed and re-typed it all, and Mrs Sybil le Brocquy, who read the proofs.

Contents

		Page
	Preface	13
	Introduction	17

PART ONE

The Creation

Chapter		
I	Towards a Definition	31
II	Yeats as an Anglo-Irishman	39
III	Back to Swift	52
IV	The Lighter Side	67
V	The Eye of the Stranger	76
VI	Theobald Wolfe Tone	84
VII	The First Unionist	94

PART TWO

Decline and Fall

VIII	Thomas Drummond	113
IX	Drummond and the Royal Dublin Society	127
X	Philanthropists	139
XI	Thomas Davis and Protestant Nationalists	144
XII	Isaac Butt	155
XIII	Parnell	162
XIV	Social Life in Victorian Ireland	167
XV	The Irish Revival and Provost Mahaffy	185
XVI	Oscar Wilde	197
XVII	Emergence of a Middle Class	202
XVIII	Edward Martyn and the Kildare Street Club	211
XIX	The Optimists	224

XX	The Approach of Home Rule	235
XXI	The Unknown Unionist	246
XXII	The End of the Anglo-Irish	258

Appendix

A Potted History of Ireland	269
Biographical Notes	281
Bibliography	285
Index	289

List of Illustrations

following page 96

Jonathan Swift by Charles Jervas (*Courtesy of the National Gallery of Ireland*)
John Philpot Curran by Thomas Lawrence (*Courtesy of the National Gallery of Ireland*)
George Berkeley, Bishop of Cloyne, with his wife and friends (*Courtesy of the National Gallery of Ireland*)
John Fitzgibbon, Earl of Clare, by H. Douglas Hamilton (*Courtesy of the National Gallery of Ireland*)
James Gandon by Tilly Kettle and William Cuming (*Courtesy of the National Gallery of Ireland*)
Gandon's Custom House, Dublin (*Photo National Library*)
St Stephen's Church, Mount Street, Dublin (*Bord Fáilte Photo*)
Ely House, Dublin (*Bord Fáilte Photo*)
Fireplace from Ely House (*Bord Fáilte Photo*)
Plasterwork from the House of Lords, Bank of Ireland, Dublin (*Bord Fáilte Photo*)

following page 160

The Casino, Dublin (*Bord Fáilte Photo*)
The Irish Volunteers, in College Green, parading round the statue of William III, by Wheatley (*Courtesy of the National Gallery of Ireland*)
Thomas Drummond by Henry William Pickersgill (*Courtesy of the National Gallery of Ireland*)
Isaac Butt by John Butler Yeats (*Courtesy of the National Gallery of Ireland*)
Augusta Gregory by William Orpen (*Courtesy of the National Gallery of Ireland*)

Sarah Purser by Lilian M. Davidson (*Courtesy of the National Gallery of Ireland*)

George Moore by John Butler Yeats (*Courtesy of the National Gallery of Ireland*)

William Butler Yeats by Albert Power (*Courtesy of the National Gallery of Ireland*)

Sir J. P. Mahaffy by S. C. Harrison (*Courtesy of the National Gallery of Ireland*)

Charles Stewart Parnell by Sydney Prior Hall (*Courtesy of the National Gallery of Ireland*)

Grafton Street, Dublin, at the turn of the century (*Photo National Library*)

Daisy, Countess of Fingall (*Courtesy Lord Fingall*)

Preface

THE ANGLO-IRISH, if they had a history, lived it in the eighteenth century. Lecky wrote five excellent volumes on the period, correcting the crazy brilliance of Froude, whose theme was simple: in the struggle for existence the better bully wins. Because the Irish had allowed the English to walk on them they were, ipso facto, inferior. In so far as they had attempted to fight back they were treacherous and ungrateful.

Froude used the term Anglo-Irish a great deal, Lecky not at all. The reason for this is clear. Froude, having demonstrated to his own satisfaction the inherent inferiority of the Irish was in some difficulty how to explain their achievements in the eighteenth century. He could only do so by distinguishing these Irish as half English. Lecky was not under this necessity; he was one of the class Froude was referring to. But he did once speak of 'two nations'. And it would be perverse to pretend that there is not in Ireland, among others, two traditions: one deriving from the Gaelic past, one from British institutions. Scotland and Wales are in the same case. But Grattan, O'Connell, and every constructive statesman, everyone who wanted to bring the Irish together, has had the idea for which all the credit is now given to Wolfe Tone, that in the term Irishman should be merged all the interesting differences which, at some level or other, can be discovered in every people. What different strains must run in the veins of the Italians? How much of North Africa is eternally lodged in Spain? How many tribes have swept across Europe? Even in Ireland we do not know what, or how many races came before the Celts, and nobody would ever be able to unravel England's tangled skein.

There are, however, two fundamental differences in the history of England and Ireland. If both suffered (and gained?) from the attentions of the Norsemen, who, in their new guise as Franks, were eventually to conquer them, Ireland escaped the direct Germanic blood infusion which explains the origin of the Anglo-Saxon race. There is that diluted blood difference. And Ireland was never invaded by the Romans. To what extent that explains Irish social and political habits has always been a subject of curious speculation.

What we call the Anglo-Irish began when? When Strongbow landed his Norman knights and armed bands, many of them Welsh? Surely, not then. The Normans in Ireland, we are told, became more Irish than the Irish themselves. They adopted Irish names and manners. They spoke the Irish tongue.

In later struggles against English power, in the time of Henry VIII as in the Williamite war, the 'old English' made common cause with the Irish. What bound them together as well as neighbourliness and long association was religion.

John Fitzgibbon, Earl of Clare, of whom I shall have more to say, pronounced on one occasion that since Henry's time the division in Ireland was between Catholic and Protestant. And as regards Catholics he had this to say in a letter to William Eden, the first Lord Auckland. They were discussing the Catholic claims which led to concessions in 1793.

'The catholics are now distributed into three classes. The higher order, consisting of men of property and consideration who are few in number; the agitators who are much more numerous and are to a man rebels and republicans, and many of them infidels; and the mass of the people who are in a state of perfect barbarism and ignorance. The first class very naturally wish for a repeal of the laws which exclude them from the state and bear upon their religion, but they would not hazard a convulsion to gain the object, and I am confident if they could once be satisfied that it cannot be attained without convulsion, they would resist the project as warmly as any other description of the king's subjects ought to do. The agitators who have assumed to themselves the government of the whole body of the catholics now for five years look to separation from England, and, of course, to a subversion of the Monarchy, and if they were to succeed in their object of catholic emancipation, as it is most stupidly and wickedly called, it would only encourage them to proceed in their projects of treason.

And with respect to the mass of the people, they are perfectly indifferent and uninterested on the subject, except they are taught by the agitators to suppose that catholic emancipation means anarchy and plunder.'

Fitzgibbon, as his name betrays, was of Norman origin. His family had sunk to the rank of peasant farmers; but his father, an ambitious barrister, became Protestant; and he was himself a living example of his own thesis. He was the complete Anglo-Irishman.

As I am confining my book to a study of people, I would like to assume that all my readers had a rudimentary knowledge of Irish history. But this is possibly a pious hope. If it is, I have attempted in as brief a space as possible to make a rough sketch of that history from the Norman Invasion until the end of the Union with Great Britain. This may be found in the Appendix as well as in the Biographical Notes for those who may not be familiar with the Irish scene, but these are confined to names mentioned incidentally. There is an Index. The Bibliography contains only the sources actually drawn upon, and is in sequence. I have refrained from decorating the text with a rash of scholarly numbers.

Introduction

WHO ARE THE Anglo-Irish and what is their history? This book is an attempt to answer the first question and to cut a path through the thicket that has overgrown the second. In a sense the history of Ireland, since the Normans under Strongbow landed in 1170, is a history of the Anglo-Irish; and modern critics, following the lead given by Daniel Corkery in his *Hidden Ireland*, complain that in such works as Lecky's splendid *History of Ireland in the Seventeenth Century* the Irish are overlooked; all that is discussed is the fate of their conquerors in that period.

Let me attempt to give a short answer to the first question now in order to make clearer what the subsequent pages seek to establish.

In other countries there are local differences between the people of different regions. The Yorkshireman is not at all like the Londoner, much less the Cornishman; the Prussian is distinct from the Bavarian. In Ireland there are differences of accent and, indeed, of disposition among the people of the four provinces. There are also class differences as elsewhere. A Parisian lawyer has a great deal in common with a Londoner of the same profession that he does not share with a Breton peasant. Owing to Ireland's history and the establishment of a Protestant ascendancy the class divisions in Ireland are confused with racial ones and even with religious differences.

The privileged Irishman for three hundred years of English rule was a Protestant of English origin. There were some exceptions, some Catholics—very few—managed to keep their heads up socially, but their number was insignificant. Brendan Behan's definition of an Anglo-Irishman is as good as we have—'a Protestant with a horse'.

When you meet an Irishman who talks with no brogue or only

a slight one, who is educated and apparently well-to-do, you assume, even still, that he is Anglo-Irish. Because the better-off aped English manners and were very often sent to school in England, Irishness was a sign of social obscurity, or worse. The Gaelic Revival at the end of the last century was the first peaceful effort to combat this; but it is not surprising, when you find any small country ruled by a powerful neighbour, there will be an instinct either to take on the colour of the ruling class or to rebel. Most of Ireland's rebel leaders, until modern times, came from the Anglo-Irish.

Nowadays Irish children tend to go more to school in Ireland; and, on the whole, the difference of accent is tending to be less distinct. But this is in keeping with trends in Britain and the cultivation there of regional accents. Sir Samuel Ferguson, quite a rebel in his early Victorian youth, deplored in middle age, what he described as the 'plebianising of Irish life' by the nationalists of a later generation. That trend continued and is in keeping now with a universal social tendency.

The Anglo-Irish conception does, however, have a unique character. It is normal for men of talent, who rise in the world from humble beginnings, to acquire in different degrees, the manner of the ruling class. Dickens, we may be sure, at his dinners, when he liked to entertain celebrities in every field, comported himself like a man in society. He did not feel any necessity to establish his integrity by talking Cockney. Hogarth, in an earlier generation, married and settled for the way of life of a dignified citizen. The example of Shakespeare could always be cited to prove that a desire for social eminence was by no means incompatible with genius of the loftiest order.

This was certainly the case in England, and one must assume, elsewhere. Henry Moore, the sculptor, recalls that his father, on the outbreak of the 1914 War, advised him to join a Middlesex Regiment as a way of sloughing off his Yorkshire accent. It used to be the general practice among the better-off in Ireland to send their sons and daughters to school in England. The object of this was to preserve, if not to fit them out with, the manners and accents of the ruling class. I made myself unpopular on a public occasion by suggesting that the same ambition should now lead parents to inculcate in their young the accents heard in schools run by the Christian Brothers, from whom the majority of Irish Ministers of State have acquired their education.

Visiting Americans, in particular, regard the Christian Brothers' accent as normal for the Irish and anything less than a brogue as Anglo-Irish. Anglo-Irish has become a convenient label. But these are paths in which only a Proust is qualified to wander. 'Anglo-Irish' in many cases is a euphemism, designed to avoid raising hackles at a time when the subject of class difference is taboo. This diplomacy would be all very well if it did not tacitly attribute to people, less than racy of the soil in manner, political opinions which they do not necessarily possess. Richard Barton and George Gavan Duffy, two signatories of the Treaty with Britain in 1921, who afterwards dissociated themselves from their co-signatories, were completely anglicised in accent and manner. Their colleagues on that occasion, Griffith, Collins and Duggan, could never be mistaken for Anglo-Irish, and yet they—in the terrible months ahead—stood firmly by the treaty of accord with Britain and opposed the extreme nationalist and ultra-Republican attitude, which Barton and Duffy found it impossible to withstand. In this they were influenced by Erskine Childers, in whose veins there was probably not a drop of Irish blood. Yet, if accent and manner were the test, it was these, not the others,—one might assume—who would in a crisis adopt the more pro-British line.

Deprived of their natural leaders, after the aristocratic emigration to Europe at the beginning and end of the seventeenth century, the Irish—even in rebellion—had to find them among the Anglo-Irish; but that class did not supply the bulk of the rebel leaders in the final confrontation with England. It was inevitable that the people should eventually find their leaders among themselves. Again, no generalisation is water-tight. A very few of the Anglo-Irish—notably Barton and Childers—did give assistance to Sinn Féin during the period 1916–21, which saw the end of British rule and with it the end of Protestant ascendancy.

In 1920, before a treaty was signed between the Irish revolutionary leaders (or Sinn Féin) and the British Coalition Government, led by Lloyd George, a separate parliament was set up for six counties of Ulster (there are nine counties in the province). The area was sufficiently large to make a separate parliament a practical possibility and yet not large enough to make the danger of a greater Catholic birth-rate a foreseeable threat to a permanent Protestant majority.

I have not devoted any space to the Anglo-Irish in Northern Ireland because the type as it is established in the general imagination is not common in the North. There is something aggressively unaristocratic about the average northerner, in voice and manner. And the term Anglo-Irish, as Jane Austen bears witness, suggests a certain social gracefulness.

The Unionists in the North prefer to call themselves British rather than Irish; and they have not made use of the expression 'Anglo-Irish'. The history of Northern Ireland has, to a great extent, been governed by geography. Since earliest times that narrow sea passage to Scotland has led to periodic exchange of population. The Northern accent, even in Catholic Donegal, is more like Scots than Irish. But there is an exaggerated idea of the extent of actual plantation in Ulster. It has been more lasting in its effect because of the very drastic action taken after the Rebellion in 1641. That began in the North, and when its effects were redressed, good care was taken to get rid of all the ancient proprietors. The area around Belfast was never planted. Two Scots, Sir James Hamilton and Sir Hugh Montgomery, got possession of North Down and South Antrim and introduced the Presbyterians who now form the hard core of Northern Unionism. But the large and dour population, which appears in bowler hats at Orange processions, is as much, or more, the result of voluntary immigration from the lowlands of Scotland in the eighteenth and nineteenth centuries, when the Ulster shipbuilding and linen industries were growing so fast. Belfast was a small town until a few years before the Union in 1800; before half the century was over, it was the largest industrial city in Ireland. The size of the Catholic population in planted counties, Tyrone and Fermanagh (where Catholics are in the majority), show that plantation was no more a decisive or permanent factor in the North than in the rest of Ireland, most of which was planted at one time or another.

I have not followed the orthodox chronological course. Had I begun with the Norman conquest, and gone on to the plantations, from Mary to James I, recapitulated the confused history from 1641 to Cromwell's conquest and then led on through the Williamite War to Penal Days, I would have been treading the path worn out by eminent historians. When we come to the eighteenth century, the giant presence of W. E. H. Lecky blocks the path and dominates the scene. The history of the Anglo-Irish in the period that mattered—the eighteenth century—was written finally and splendidly by one of themselves. It would, of course, have been possible to try to follow Lecky and to write The Decline and Fall of the Anglo-Irish. I did not do that; but I have given that sub-title to the last part of this work.

I am interested in character and in people more than in politics. This is a study of people. Had I written a conventional history of the Anglo-Irish I would have had to enter a caveat at some stage in the proceedings. As the story unfolds it becomes increasingly evident that religious differences in Ireland were the ultimate dividing line. It is not of course a doctrinal contest of the kind that a St Thomas Aquinas engaged in. Religion in Ireland had the significance of colour in Rhodesia, South Africa, or the southern states of America. It was so for all Ireland, now it is true only of the northern counties; but that is because the Protestant minority in the rest of Ireland has kept quiet and sedulously avoided giving offence.

The expression 'Anglo-Irish' is used in a literary context with an exact meaning to distinguish the writings of the Irish in the English language. This is a new departure since the establishment of independence in Southern Ireland, where most of these writers came from. Until then the English treated Irish writers as part of their general stock. Since the distinction has been made critics have fancied that this Anglo-Irish writing has a special character of wit and feyness. This is an illusion. Nowadays, instead of blandly accepting the Irish contribution without separate recognition, every effort is made in Britain to identify what is Anglo-Irish. Miss Iris Murdoch, for example, is now so described. Her name is Scots, but she was born and spent some of her childhood in Dublin. The bizarre character of her writing sought definition;

and some critics categorised it as Anglo-Irish. Nobody in Ireland has ever written in her manner.

It would be absurd to claim a national monopoly of any sort of verbal facility. Alistair Cooke, the radio commentator, having taken samples universally, expressed the view in Dublin that the conversation he met with there was in quickness of wit second only to Hollywood, where unemployed intelligence had no other way to pass the time.

If the Irish are witty—is it an Irish or an Anglo-Irish phenomenon? Edith Somerville, who listened more attentively than others, decided that the special quality of the Irish peasant speech was its employment of an English that had been learnt only from gentlefolk—Irish being the vernacular. As a result it had a particular grace and elegance of phrase. She had the courage to attack the traditional patois in which Carleton's peasant stories are told—a manner which when outsiders use it is condemned as stage Irish. I think Edith Somerville flattered her own class; she knew only as much Irish history as was common among them—the subject was never taught. And what she may not have realised is that when Cromwell sent the Catholic proprietors across the Shannon to make room for English 'adventurers' and soldiers, some of them stayed behind as tenants and even farm workers on their own estates. Another factor in Irish life was the absence of Catholic schools; the devoted souls who tried to make up the loss gave a more classical education than primary pupils receive now from their teachers. The two languages in Ireland interbred, probably, to a far greater extent in times of limited transport than we realise; the result was an injection of fantasy into English. There is also in the Irish character—and some of it got through by intermarriage—a bravado, a recklessness of the sort with which Charles II is credited. He is the only King of England who *sounds* like an Irishman. Could it be that the conditions of his time—the insecurity—bred this quality that we like to call an Irish one, and that it explains the comedy of the Restoration stage? Farquhar had it, in its Irish form, more markedly than Congreve, who depended on perfection of style. Neither had very solid claims to Irish blood, any more than Sterne had—their connections with the country were fortuitous. Sheridan, whose family were long settled in

Ireland, had gracefulness and high spirits in a considerable degree. Is there of its kind anything more perfect in English than his 'beautiful quarto page, where a neat rivulet of text shall meander through a meadow of margin'?

But this is literary; too nice for common speech. It was his high spirits and fantasy that made Sheridan, as afterwards it made Wilde, so much funnier than their English rivals. The element of fantasy was also very strong in the speech of the writer, James Stephens, author of *The Crock of Gold*. People who knew him said he was the most entrancing of all conversationalists. But Stephens was hardly representative. His origins are largely a mystery. He had the Irish form of what, in his Scottish contemporary, J. M. Barrie, turned to mawkishness.

Even the *de haut en bas* style of Mahaffy, Oscar Wilde's tutor, Provost of Trinity College, and for many, nowadays, the archetypal Anglo-Irishman, is hardly an Anglo-Irish preserve; it is the style of academic humour. His contemporary, R. L. Tyrrell, Regius Professor of Greek at Trinity, had the same gift, but employed a more throwaway manner, being aided by a beautiful speaking voice. Mahaffy had a lisp and spoke with an almost stage-German gutturalness. The tendency to play on words, which characterised much Irish wit, is partly an antidote to the solemnity from which the Irish are by no means exempt. It can deflate. Jack Yeats, painter–brother of the poet, bored by a conversation in which the name of Cezanne appeared too often for his taste suddenly interjected 'Cezanne, Cezanne, Cezanne. Sez you'. The interpolation conjured up the spirit of that and (oh! how many) similar gatherings—too much intensity, too much reverence. He was letting in air.

When we read of the hideous sufferings of the Irish poor under their landlords, we are not often told how surprised and discouraged those who agitated themselves about the evil were to find the victims so good-humoured and resigned. They were more philosophical in the face of nature than the people whom English rule set over them and whom they tended to imbue with their easy-going attitude. O'Donavan, a great Irish scholar of the last century, who came from the people, said that the result of the Famine was that it put an end to singing in the fields. He implied that happiness had fled; but his picture conjures up Wordsworth's solitary Highland lass, whom the poet supposed sang of

> old, unhappy, far-off things,
> And battles long ago.

What the Irish have—the native as well as the Anglo-Irish—is a keen sense of the ridiculous. This may be of historic origin. Irish chiefs sent their bards to ridicule their rivals to death—the bards were given apparently an immunity against reprisal. Perhaps as a result, Irish sensitivity to ridicule is such that I verily believe an Irishman hates anyone who makes him look silly in public more than one who, in private, plots his death or destruction.

In the Anglo-Irish Parliament in the late eighteenth century there were fierce battles in invective; but Curran was the only notable wit in that assembly. His contemporary, Sheridan, was in London. Wit requires polish; the manner of recruitment for the modern Irish parliament has ensured that it is in short supply; personal abuse is not unknown; it takes, as a rule, an elementary character. But in favourable circumstances it must be admitted that in general the Irish are more amusing than the English or the Scots.

I attribute this characteristic to the ills of the country. A certain fecklessness at worst, a trust in Providence at best. Laughter is one of the antidotes to pain. Mercutio joked after the death blow; he was a very Anglo-Irish type. When we seek a common influence for the Anglo-Irish style of graceful wit, we must pause at Trinity College. Farquhar, Goldsmith, Wilde—I will not go on. All went there. Not that wits in Ireland were ever two a penny; but Trinity has produced one in each generation. It gave style to native genius and kept up a tradition.

It is curious to observe—before we leave the subject—that almost the last practitioner of the high Anglo-Irish style in literature was Welsh with some Irish in him—an unpublicised compound. George Meredith might well have been a descendant of Sheridan, brought up in Germany. There were two kinds of romantic tradition at work on him.

There used to be a fashion for anecdote in Ireland. It was the staple of every public speech, and the lighter side of a tradition at the Irish bar that in cross-examination of witnesses any verbal assault, calculated to confuse and embarrass them, was legitimate.

Meredith understood it very well. 'Irish anecdotes are always popular in England, as promoting, besides the wholesome shake of the sides, a kindly sense of superiority. Anecdotes also are portable, unlike the lightning flash, which will not go into the pocket.'

If reasons of state have identified the Anglo-Irish in English literary criticism, their arrival on the home scene has a different history. The Gaelic revival, which began about a century ago discovered a mythology second only to that of Greece in Europe, it also brought to light poets, unknown to English speakers, whose memory had been kept alive in the hidden Ireland, a culture that went underground when the Gaelic aristocracy left Ireland in two great waves—in 1607, with what was called 'The Flight of the Earls', and after the Williamite wars in 1690—'The Flight of the Wild Geese'.

With the building of the new Irish State went an official policy of the revival of Irish. It was not a new thing. The British Government had acceded to the demand since the beginning of the revival, less than a century after the educational authorities had set about the destruction of the language in the schools.

With new nationhood went an impulse to deprecate the culture of the former colony—the magnificent Georgian architecture of Dublin especially, and the literary tradition which, since Swift, had made Irish writers famous the world over, although the Gaelic revival was in large measure due to the Anglo-Irish themselves, as I hope to demonstrate.

As well as the eighteenth-century writers, who had no national self-consciousness, and the new school of Gaelic revivalists, who regarded English as a trespasser in the cultural domain, there flourished a school who wrote in English on Irish subject matter. Thomas Moore, Byron's friend and biographer, much traduced in modern Ireland, writer of incomparable songs, began the movement. It might be said to have ended with the death of Yeats. To it came contributions from Northern Ireland in the person of Sir Samuel Ferguson and from the Protestant ascendancy, notably from Lady Gregory, Yeats's Egeria, and with him the founder of the Abbey Theatre.

At first Anglo-Irish writing was resented in the new Ireland. This was particularly the case where, as in the books of Somerville and Ross (Edith Somerville and Violet Martin), the peasantry were portrayed. Touchiness was aroused by the writers' approach. An assumption of superiority was detected and resented. More recently wiser counsels have prevailed; and, as with the eighteenth-century architecture which was, and is still, being pulled down, belated recognition has been given to a national asset. Since then Anglo-Irish literature has been made a separate subject, and University College has study centres in Dublin and Galway.

On the assumption that all Irish writers now write in Irish, that would be the end of the story. But they do no such thing. It is, however, noticeable that writing in English used to be largely practised by the class which is called Anglo-Irish, with a different connotation. Since 1921 Irish novels and plays have tended to come from what in Britain would be described as the lower middle class, but in Ireland is more heroically described as 'the risen people'.

In the course of my investigation I give space to several individuals, some rightly famous, others not unreasonably more obscure; and I refer very often to Burke and Sheridan. The reader, when he finds that he is never confronted with any detailed assessment of either of these, may object that they are relegated to the role of Mrs Harris, who was so frequently on the lips of Mrs Gamp.

I refer to them for the same reason that I have avoided dealing with either in detail, because they represent to me the finest of all examples of what it has become the fashion to call the Anglo-Irish. Burke is the serious, Sheridan the ebullient, paragon of the species. Burke, so good, so noble and far-reaching in thought, surrounded by such a seedy pack of relatives and hangers-on: Sheridan with all that brilliant early promise, a youth such as George Meredith might have invented—gifted and gay; but essentially not good, not noble, neglecting his charming wife, perpetually drunk, flagrant not only in money affairs, eventually a wreck. But the wreck of what was once so precious. If I were to deal with them more fully I am afraid they might run away with the book. Burke has been fully written about by pens better qualified. Sheridan is still owed an adequate modern biography.

Burke and Sheridan, I should pray, are looking over my shoulder as I proceed; one to counsel when I trip, the other to grimace when I prose. These, among the Anglo-Irish, I appoint my guardian angels. The loins from which *they* sprung were indeed of no petty people.

I like to think of an Irishman as Jane Austen thought of him, as she tells us in *Persuasion* when Sir Walter Elliot and Lady Dalrymple are conversing:

> 'A well-looking man,' said Sir Walter, 'a very well-looking man.'
>
> 'A very fine young man,' said Lady Dalrymple. 'More than one often sees in Bath. Irish, I dare say.'

Part I

THE CREATION

CHAPTER I

Towards a Definition

IN A HOUSE where I have sometimes dined, the hostess on every occasion, at some time in the course of the evening, refers to one of her acquaintances and says, 'He is Irish, but not what you would call Irish.' I am fascinated when the conversation takes this turn, and I have not yet exhausted the possible nuances of the observation. Why would I not call whomsoever she is referring to Irish? I must guess my hostess to mean that these individuals are unidentifiable from English people and yet have claims to be Irish which I would not concede. Why? I have never had the courage to ask.

Lord Montgomery, the Field-Marshal, could be such a one. He is not a strikingly Irish type although his father's family comes from Donegal. There is something about him that recalls his maternal ancestor, Dean Farrar, author of *Eric, or Little by Little*. Field-Marshal Lord Alexander was another. But these are men who won supreme distinction in the British Army, as did Wellington and Lord Roberts and Lord Kitchener (who was born in Kerry). Kitchener, I believe it was (not Wellington), who said that because he was born in a stable he was not for that reason a horse. The Roberts family was long established in the south-east of Ireland. One of them, Thomas Sautelle Roberts, was quite a good early nineteenth-century landscape painter. Wellington is a test case. Had she been living in the days of his greatness, my enigmatic hostess would certainly have said that he was not what I would call Irish. By that she might only mean that he was out of my social range and that his interests were more extensive than mere Irish concerns. Whenever Wellington distracted himself with Ireland it was as an agent of the British Government. But Shaw in his Preface to *John Bull's Other Island* calls Wellington 'an intensely Irish Irishman' in contrast to Nelson, an 'intensely English Englishman'. This was written when Shaw was at his most Shavian, in those days in the Court Theatre, when the English public—the intelligent members of it—flocked to see with what effect he could stand on his head to laugh at their institutions. Shaw, for those people, became the typical Irishman. And I emphasise *Irishman*. Nobody would have thought for a moment of describing that phenomenon with the carefully cultivated Dublin accent as an *Anglo-Irishman*. That distinction was part of the pedantry of a later age. 'I am,' he said, 'a genuine typical Irishman of the Danish, Norman, Cromwellian, and (of course) Scotch invasion. I am violently and arrogantly Protestant by family tradition . . .'

Shaw may have been pushing paradox to its limit—it was his stock in trade—when he described Wellington 'as intensely Irish', but he would most certainly have regarded Wellington as Irish—as he regarded himself as Irish—with no qualification. In his copious writings about his youth in Dublin he dwells much upon the social peculiarities of Irish life. Because his broken-down, bibulous father was remotely connected with a baronet he looked down on his tailor who had a mansion and a yacht; and Shaw remembered that there were different ways of knocking on doors according to one's social pretensions.

Shaw, who liked to analyse, never bothered his head with this Anglo-Irish puzzle. It would bring a storm about his ears in Ireland now if he were alive and were to publish his views on the Irish revival and Hyde's Gaelic League. 'Only a quaint little offshoot of English pre-Raphaelitism called the Gaelic movement has got a footing by using Nationalism as a stalking-horse, and popularizing itself as an attack on the native language of the Irish people, which is also most fortunately the native language of half the world, including England.' But, at the time, he was not wholly disinterested. *John Bull's Other Island* had been commissioned by Yeats for the Abbey and refused.

Shaw, writing in 1906, prophesied that with the achievement of Home Rule the Irish would sweep the neo-Gaelic movement with 'the garrison hacks together into the dustbin'.

This has not happened because there has been a fixed official attitude towards Irish; a visitor looking at bus signs and sampling native radio and television programmes or attending on public occasions when a Minister says a few words might assume that most people were bilingual. Irish speakers usually wear a *fainne* or gold badge, and by this means invite others to communicate with them in Irish. But if State aid and recognition were withdrawn, Shaw's prophecy would have come true as another is coming true: that in a free Ireland clerical authority would suffer the same fate as in France and Italy.

Shaw was a very persuasive writer because he never troubled himself with qualifications or reservations. Nothing is so helpful to a good prose, such as Swift and Shaw wrote, as a confident dogmatism. They asserted and ridiculed; there was no consideration for an opposing argument.

Shaw attacked Macaulay for annexing Swift 'because he was not an aboriginal Celt' and was worth stealing. It was typical Shavian polemics, ignoring all finer shades. Macaulay had every right to make the claim, and it requires no argument to refute Shaw's gratuitous ridicule in support of his own view, that Macaulay 'might as well have refused the name of Briton to Addison, because he did not stain himself blue and attach scythes to the poles of his sedan chair'. To begin with, I should suppose that Addison would have called himself an Englishman; the use of 'Briton' confuses the issue at once; nobody claimed that Swift was a Celt. Addison had a perfect right to call himself an Englishman. It was what Swift called himself on several occasions. If he was in error, what is Shaw's test of nationality? He refers to those 'hollowest of fictions, the Irish and English races', and declares there is no more an Irish race than there is an English race or a Yankee race. 'There *is* an Irish climate, which will stamp an immigrant more deeply and durably in two years, apparently, than the English climate will in two hundred.' From this he goes on to make his distinction between the Irish and the English character, leaving us with Wellington as the typical Irishman. Anticipating a query, he says that Wellington may, to some, seem more an eighteenth-century aristocratic type than specifically Irish, and goes on to say that Byron and George IV, contrasted with Gladstone, seem Irish 'in respect of a certain humorous blackguardism', and with that to contemplate he takes it away after a few sentences by asserting that faithlessness and the qualities that accompany it produce in all nations a 'gay, sceptical, amusing, blaspheming, witty fashion which suits the flexibility of the Irish mind very well'.

According to Shaw the English had enough of this type at the end of the Restoration and during the Regency, and avoided it by making a merit of stupidity and dullness.

Many Englishmen have stayed longer than two years in Ireland without becoming more fastidiously imaginative, or with a greater capacity for seeing things as they are. Think of all those State and Church grandees who used to govern Ireland during Swift's Dublin sojourn. If Shaw meant anything, he must have meant that Swift's birth and schooldays in Ireland formed his character and his style, and that these are Irish. Nobody in England ever referred to Swift's Irishness. And Shaw himself says that there is nothing in the idea of separate English and Irish races. But he substitutes the theory that the Irish climate works wonders of which the English climate is incapable. If so it destroys the idea of the Anglo-Irish; such a potent climate would have long ago washed away all difference between them and 'the aboriginal Celt'.

He does nothing to help his readers with his theory of climate, and when he gets off English stupidity he rides away on Irish Protestantism, and thereafter uses Protestants and Catholics to demarcate the two elements in Irish society.

I can remember as a child remonstrating with a guide in Westminster Abbey whom I had overheard describing Goldsmith as an English poet. 'He was Irish,' I said. It would not, at the age of eleven, have occurred to me to say 'Anglo-Irish', nor had I heard the expression. Since then it has come into general use. In Ireland, from a desire to push the native product, in England and elsewhere, to define a group that has made a distinctive contribution to English literature. In the time when the Empire flourished, the Irish were thrown into the common pot. The breakdown of Empire, the separation of Ireland, a new awareness of Irish identity, have led to the making of the distinction. And here it is necessary to clear the air for the purpose of the general argument. Abroad, the idea of Anglo-Irish is connected with a certain kind of—may we say?—genius. A very few samples are taken as characteristic of the whole. Those who come in search of them on the home ground will always be disappointed. They were prime samples for export.

When the Irish think of the Anglo-Irish, they have not got a few geniuses in mind. They have in mind loud-voiced, confident people with English accents, wearing tweeds, heading for sales of work in aid of disabled soldiers or parading in the rings at the Horse Show. From that quarter great talent has come. Somerville and Ross and, in our day, Dunsany, Elizabeth Bowen, and others not to be despised. But, on the whole, it is a hearty, horsey, rather than a literary society; and the idea of Yeats as its spokesman (or as spokesman for the Dublin professional class) raises a smile. He was much too great—a world figure—and yet, to their limited specification, not quite the thing. What I mean is illustrated by the case of Shaw. When he married Charlotte Townshend, he was a celebrity, but her cousin, Edith Somerville, was neither pleased with, nor proud of, the match. Listen:

'Charlotte is now Mrs Bernard Shaw and I hope she likes it. He is an advanced socialist (all the same he has kept his weather eye open). They were married at a registrar's office. I have, with much difficulty and anxiety, written to poor Sissy. Of course he is an awfully clever man. He began as an office boy in Townshend French's agency office in Dublin, and now is distinctly somebody in a literary way, but he can't be a gentleman and he is too clever to be in love with Lottie, who is nearly clever, but not quite.'

There is, one observes, no reference to Anglo-Irish community feeling or satisfaction that a cousin has married yet another of what Yeats was to describe as 'no petty people'. Edith Somerville writes, as might one of her own class in the English shires, about a cousin who had married into the purlieus of Fleet Street.

Shaw himself wrote pages about social distinctions in the Dublin of his day and took care to leave no doubt in any reader's mind that Edith Somerville was wrong in her depressing assumption about his social origin.

The emphasis in Ireland a hundred years ago (and until more recently) was not on genes but on gentry. Newman, when he came in the fifties to found what he hoped would be the university of his dreams, was sadly disillusioned by the Irish Catholics, for whom he was making a considerable sacrifice of his time and patience.

He complained that 'you cannot have a University till the gentlemen take it up. I wrote a very strong letter to an Irish layman two years ago; since which time no Irish gentleman has been added, I think, but More O'Ferrall.'

The newly emancipated Catholics were going to Trinity College, and some to Oxford and Cambridge; they had no desire to make common cause with the oppressed peasantry, from whom they were acutely anxious to be distinguished.

They, again, would not have troubled themselves with fine distinctions between Anglo-Irish and Irish; they saw themselves as having religion in common with the people and a better right to social standing than many English settlers who assumed one without any warrant that ran in their country of origin. Young in his *Travels* describes The Mac Dermot ('The' is an Irish clan title) of his day, miserably poor in Roscommon, but still, by courtesy, Prince of Coolavin, in his dilapidated residence, decreeing most severely, who should sit, who should stand, in his presence. The term Anglo-Irish, as it is used in Ireland now, contains an underlying and dishonest assumption that the *real* Irish are a democratic, republican and socialistic people with familiar manners. This has been helped by the destruction and dispersal of the Irish aristocracy. But when I picture, in my mind's eye, any of the present-day representatives of the Mac Dermot or O'Conor families, and contrast their demeanour with, say, that of Mr Cathal Goulding, head of the IRA, I cannot fail to notice that the ancient Irish clansmen are indistinguishable from people of their class in Britain, and the IRA leader bears a name that came to Ireland with Cromwell.

Cathal, Mr Goulding calls himself—the O'Conors are satisfied with the English form—Charles—and if they were to be brought together I surmise that the IRA leader would deem the O'Conors hopelessly Anglo-Irish. Petty, when he compiled the *Political Anatomy of Ireland* in 1672, observed, 'English in Ireland growing poor and discontented, degenerate into Irish; and vice versa; Irish, growing into wealth and favour, reconcile to the English'.

To English and American ears, 'Anglo-Irish' has an encouraging sound. It means wit, elegant writing, Georgian architecture, aristocracy picturesquely decayed—Ireland without priests or patriots—or not, at any rate, the sort of patriots who come to depressing ends. There is, over all, the neigh of horses, and the story unfolds somewhere in a park with a lake and a wood and a poet. The Anglo-Irish say things like, 'Come into the garden, I want my roses to see you.'

Sheridan, having said it once and noted its effect, said it, most probably, on every suitable occasion. When the Anglo-Irish *speak in Irish*, it is an Irish that is like English and quite intelligible if, for practical purposes, somewhat imprecise.

It's lonesome this place having happiness like ours till I'm asking each day, will this day match yesterday, and will tomorrow take a good place beside the same say in the year that's gone, and wondering all times is a game worth playing, living on until you're dried and old, and our joy is gone forever.

Nobody would make a will or order a beefsteak in Synge's language; but it is suitable for a tale of love or sorrow or glory, and pleasant for a change from the colourless norm.

But that last sort of speaking takes place outside those noble Anglo-Irish houses to which Yeats gave a cosmic significance. 'Anglo-Irish' conjures up fine sentiments addressed in silver tones to the senates of the world. Burke—but what Burke said, or Grattan said, or Swift wrote (if it comes to that) is more often taken for granted than read. One has seen Shaw certainly and *The Importance of Being Earnest* and a revival of *The School for Scandal*; read *Gulliver's Travels* in the child's version and ... But then, what makes Swift interesting is Stella and Vanessa, and the doubt who his father was, and all that repulsive language! An odd clergyman, but very Anglo-Irish. The first of them in fact—born of English parents, seeking his career in England, outraged by an Irish deanery when he felt his talents entitled him to an English see. The first of the Anglo-Irish: down the eighteenth century they follow him—Berkeley, Farquhar, Goldsmith, Burke, Grattan, Flood, Charlemont, Tone, Emmet—while the mere Irish from behind their turf stacks watch the splendid entertainment in which they play no part.

It was a fine array of talent, better, I think, than Scotland had to show, but not satisfied with it, other names are being recruited with less excuse—Steele and Sterne and (later) even the Brontës. The literary Anglo-Irish have fled, like the Wild Geese. When Elizabeth Bowen took wing Ireland saw the last of them, the last distinguished name in the line that led from Maria Edgeworth through Lever, Somerville and Ross, and George Moore.

Those who took over—Frank O'Connor, Liam O'Flaherty, Sean O'Faolain, Mary Lavin—nothing 'Anglo' there—never fully realised themselves in the novel form which, I think, is a product of the society Elizabeth Bowen belonged to, in which a certain manner of living gave even to the play of instincts the ritual of a dance. The nearer to the people the closer to the earth, to the tale told at the fireside, and the gossip of the village. Elizabeth Bowen has stated the relation between her section of society and those from whom the later writers came and, one hopes, are coming. 'The Irish landowner', she said, 'leaves his tenants and workpeople to make their own mistakes while he makes his.' She spoke in the present, but now that is past. I was asked to write the history of the Anglo-Irish on the assumption that they are dead, and not the less dead because some ghosts can be met abroad or haunting their former habitations.

CHAPTER II

Yeats as an Anglo-Irishman

GIBBON TOLD, IN a mellifluous passage, how on 15 October 1764, as he sat 'musing amidst the ruins of the Capitol, while the barefooted friars were singing in the Temple of Jupiter, that the idea of writing of the decline and fall of the city first started to my mind'.

I wish that one day as I walked from the former house of the Earls of Kildare in Merrion Square towards the Church of St Stephen in Mount Street and saw, where the intersecting street leads through Fitzwilliam Square towards the distant hills, a monstrous monolith, where used to be a graceful terrace of weathered brick, with fanlights over doors and delicate ironwork on basement and balcony, and tall, small-paned, windows flanked by white revers—I wish I could say that then the idea of writing of the decline and fall of the city first started to *my* mind. If one could only imprison the Anglo-Irish in the lovely city they built and then let fall to ruin; but one cannot. They were spread out, over the country.

And the city is not a vacant tomb as Rome was when Gibbon mused on the Capitol hill. For no great people have ever so thoroughly disappeared as the ancient Romans. Sometimes a water-carrier or a street-sweeper will go past, with a head like an Emperor on an old coin, and make one wonder how many did in fact survive the barbarian raids and creep back from the marshes and start to live again in their historic places.

You might speculate—Gibbon-fashion—some day, preferably at sundown, at Newgrange or one of the other necrophilic mounds in the Boyne valley, and wonder where the people went who built these places and took so much time out of their short lives to bury their dead. Were they driven to the west by the next wave of invaders? And did they make that prodigious fort on

Aran as a last redoubt, defying all the raiders the sea could ever send? Who were they and where did they come from? Did the Gaels drive them out, or live beside them, or enslave them? Is their blood mixed with the blood of the conquerors that were to come? That would make a pleasant book, and a very short one.

But the Anglo-Irish are not to be dreamed about in this manner. To begin with, they have by no means been driven out of Dublin, and, until recently, could be expected to return, in at least two constituencies, parliamentary representatives, who shared their own reluctant acquiescence in the political shape of things. Their children are beginning to be different. As the descendants of the super-Gaels tend to neglect the idols of their parents, so do the grandchildren of the Anglo-Irish pine less for a Prince of Wales or shudder when they see on flagpoles banners that are green and white and orange. A nation that was born of enthusiasm and reared in dissension is being unified by indifference. But, no sooner are these words written, than I wonder what new convulsions await it, spreading from the diseased Northern counties.

There was a time, and it was not long ago—only the day before yesterday—when a glance at a street directory could have directed the stranger to Anglo-Ireland—Trinity College; several clubs; Sir Patrick Dun's and Baggot Street hospitals; a few schools; *The Irish Times*, *The Evening Mail*; Guinness's brewery, Jameson's distillery; all save two banks; Jacob's biscuits; some of the larger stores, and professional offices (local knowledge could identify them by looking at the name). Even certain areas were Anglo-Irish. You could tell going through them. It was in the air as well as on gate posts—'Ferndale', 'Victoria Lodge', 'Richmond', 'Montrose', 'Runnymede'.

Now business instinct, which favours the survival of the fittest, has brought about surface changes. The banks have combined. The distilleries got together and put in control a man of the new age. The State is encroaching on the independence of the hospitals and must eventually neutralise their religious difference. Trinity College has a Catholic Chancellor; and the Government keeps on saying that it will be amalgamated with its Catholic rival.

Catholics are not set against Protestants (in the south, the Church finds the enemy in its own household as much as it has time to cope with). It is from Catholics, not from Protestants, that I hear criticism of, and a rather tiresome jeering at, their own clergy. The most active new social revolutionaries are Catholics—or, at least, come from Catholic families. The young of the Protestants (5 per cent of the population) are usually short-haired, quiet spoken, intent on getting on.

The sober Dublin Protestant who drives in his well-kept car to his office, minding his business, keeping out of controversies, hoping that his children will not form fatal attachments to Catholics (whom he still excludes, if he can, from his tennis clubs)—this quietly dressed, quietly speaking, bourgeois, whose social circle is usually small, has nothing whatever to do with the Anglo-Irish whom fancy depicts—Sheridan and his jests, Yeats and his tower, A.E. (George William Russell) and his fairies. Wilde and his epigrams. Nor are they Protestants with horses. They keep away from the turf, and if horses come into their lives it is because so many better-off children have recently taken to pony clubs. But you may see them at Fairyhouse Races on Easter Monday, a picnic packed in the boot of the Morris. You will meet people just like them in London, Wolverhampton, Nottingham. These are the middle-class. And they differ from members of the same, who happen to be Catholics—a larger group—in their accents, for one thing, and a certain muteness of manner. A few better-off Catholics have always, and do still, send their children to school in England. The ones who go to school in Ireland nowadays speak with brogues and are not always easy to distinguish from prosperous proletarians, neither do they share the Anglo-Irish attitude of the English school-going boys. Boys educated by Irish Jesuits or Benedictines may still regard themselves as a few steps ahead of boys educated by other Orders, and some lengths clear of the large majority whose upbringing has been entrusted to the strap-swinging Christian Brothers.

World changes, especially in the habits of the young, tend in Ireland to have local labels attached to them. It is merely a coincidence that the Protestant ascendancy came to an end in Southern Ireland at the time that the First World War heralded a breaking up of the existing social order. It still, anachronistically, survives in Northern Ireland; but there it is purging itself of its aristocratic element. Major Chichester-Clark followed his cousin, Lord O'Neill of the Maine, into the political shadows, and there emerged, as Protestant leader, a shirt-manufacturer with an ineffably commercial aura about him. He was not less keen than his predecessors to preserve a Protestant ascendancy, if that were possible; but he did not want it to be dominated, or directed, by the social caste which has held power since the separate northern state was set up in 1920. And yet I see that he bought a great house in the country-side and hunts, so that he must in imagination pursue the aristocratic chimera. No Protestant member of the ascendancy has identified himself with the Catholic minority since the Northern State came into being fifty years ago.

Mr Faulkner and his colleagues have nothing to do with anyone's idea of Anglo-Irish. The gentry in Ulster were never thick on the ground—it is the industrial area—but only among them could one hope to find someone answering to the type we are in search of. The vast majority in the North would fit happily into the suburbs or slums of Glasgow, not a region in which people ask their guests to come into the garden so that the roses may see them, not a soil from which would ever spring *The Importance of Being Earnest*.

'Anglo-Irish' on the lips of foreigners suggests distinction; but to Irish ears it means a leftover from the Protestant ascendancy. Deprived of political power it is a social type, and as such appeals to snobbish instincts or raises the hackles of the inverted snob. Snobbery is as much part of the human equipment as vanity (to which it pertains) or any other weakness. It can—and Jack Yeats, artist brother of the poet, used to excuse it on this ground—be romantic. W. B. Yeats was a crashing snob, with every instinct of the classical type of the genus. Molière could have made him the central character of a play on the theme. But Jack—who was proud rather than snobbish and self-confident rather than vain—would have excused his brother as a romantic. And he once told me that W.B. was concerned for the dignity of poets rather than for his own. As he has been in the national shop window as a prize specimen of the Anglo-Irish, Yeats must be discussed at length. He is a key figure if only we could discover the lock.

In the popular imagination W. B. Yeats was the poetical

embodiment of Cathleen ni Houlihan. He expressed agonising doubts that his words might have sent young Irishmen to be shot. But with the new emphasis in politics Yeats is now regarded as the apologist for an aristocratic society.

To contemporary Ireland, the Irish in the saddle now, everything that he stood for is disliked and deemed to be dead. His alleged Fascism, on which the literary-political critics like to dwell, was only a muddled expression of dislike for the change in society he was witnessing, the change that in Britain brought the Harold Wilsons, Jim Callaghans, Barbara Castles, Ted Heaths, etc., into the places of power. Again and again in Yeats's *Autobiographies* the reader will come across sayings that he heard and relished, all of which begin 'A gentleman . . .' From his father he imbibed many of these maxims about what a gentleman should or should not do. Even from John O'Leary—whose relatively humble social origins Yeats noted—he deigned to collect an aphorism pertaining to gentlemanly behaviour. Romance came with Coole and Lady Gregory's circle in Connaught and, later, in England with Lady Dorothy Wellesley. None of this was incompatible with the cultivation of 'the folk' for literary purposes. Yeats went with Lady Gregory to delve into the ancient culture of the people. He stayed outside while she went into their cottages. He saw the people in their proper place in a picture in which swift men on horseback rode against the skyline from great house to great house. He was not inviting the people to revolt against their lot; he inquired into their legends, not their grievances. And in so far as he encouraged the idea of national revolution—he liked to worry over this—it was not a revolution of oppressed people against their lords, but of an ancient civilisation, whose legends had been displaced, against the commercial power that had displaced them. Yeats inherited from his father a certain contempt for the Englishman *per se*.

But Yeats was never regarded by those big houses as one of themselves. There was difficulty in getting him elected to the Kildare Street Club. He liked to stand in the great window, which G. L. Jessop (not Grace) had once broken with a huge swipe from the crease in College Park, and look at the proletariat passing by. When Yeats in the Senate spoke up so vehemently for the

Anglo-Irish, 'we are no petty people', they would not have really understood him. They would not have chosen him for their spokesman. Now he is accepted in literary circles as the Anglo-Irish archetype.

His landowning club-mates were not over-impressed by his poetry, although the Nobel Prize was a sort of passport for him in their circle, a ticket of leave; he was a Senator and there were landed gentlemen in that first Senate—a broad-minded stroke by the Government of W. T. Cosgrave to honour a pledge in Treaty discussions that something would be done for Unionists when Lloyd George was selling them down the river.

Yeats's new friends heartily disliked the ideal of his widely advertised unsuccessful romance—Maud Gonne. A traitor, if ever there was one, to her class, they thought, and bohemian to boot. He had consorted with Fenians before Sinn Féin came into fashion. And the Irish literary renaissance—even if it was sometimes entertaining to go to the Abbey—was *au fond* part of the revolution against the Union. Yeats was a poseur, they thought, who consorted with rebels; and hatred of rebels was all the more sincere because Irish Unionists—as Northern Unionists now—had a vested interest in loyalty. If Ireland left the Union, the Sinn Féiners would take over, the Catholics would take over, the Paddys and Micks would take over—it was not simple loyalty such as the Irish had shown to the miserable James II, by which they lost all—it was a loyalty that under-pinned and guaranteed their position and possessions. Yeats was a Protestant with no social position to speak of, but as such he should not, in their view, have consorted with the people who wanted to uproot the Protestant ascendancy. There was nothing romantic in their attitude. It was precisely the same as that of the majority leaders in the North today, but it was the attitude of a minority which had power so long, and only so long, as it was attached to Britain.

Yeats shared some of their prejudices—it was only in the world of his imagination he was a stranger to them, not when he was writing about 'Casey' to Lady Gregory at the time they rejected the playwright's *The Silver Tassie* for the Abbey. Yeats embarrassed them with his rhetoric when he harangued the Senate in 1925. He was expressing a long-felt contempt for the sort of person that had come to power in Ireland, the Dublin Catholic middle-class in particular, who had opposed Lane's projected gallery on the Liffey—'Paudeens', as he called them then.

I like to imagine him on that June afternoon, in one of those lavender-shaded or french-grey or corn-coloured suits he wore so lovingly in later, prosperous years. Long gone were the days when Moore could compare him to a huge umbrella left behind by a picnic party; his hair, blue-grey, brushed back; his myopic eyes and ever-moving lips, that seemed to be smiling at some mild inner wickedness; a man of weight—his careful waistcoat plumped out—and the whole a living model of a poet come into his kingdom. He had a platform and an opportunity to repeat the performance he gave when the sort of people he was attacking had protested against Synge's *Playboy*. (He would get another opportunity on the first night of *The Plough and the Stars*. 'You have disgraced yourselves again.') He had never any sympathy with that anonymous entity, 'the man in the street', nor had he ever been much impressed by the political friends of Maud Gonne as his poems about 1916 only too clearly reveal. All his admiration had been expended on the old man, John O'Leary, retired from revolution, who had brought them together.

Yeats was speaking on divorce. He thought the new State should make it available for its Protestant citizens. He took the opportunity to range wide, enjoy the hostility he aroused, unaware (most probably) of the perturbation he caused among the former Unionists for whom he purported to speak.

'I think it is tragic that within three years of this country gaining its independence we should be discussing a measure which a minority of this nation considers to be grossly oppressive. I am proud to consider myself a typical man of that minority. We against whom you have done this thing are no petty people. We are one of the great stocks of Europe. We are the people of Burke; we are the people of Grattan; we are the people of Swift, the people of Emmet, the people of Parnell. We have created the most of the modern literature of this country. We have created the best of its political intelligence. Yet I do not altogether regret what has happened. I shall be able to find out, if not I, my children will be able to find out whether we have lost our stamina or not. You have defined our position and given us a popular following. If we have not lost our stamina then your victory will be brief, and your defect final, and when it comes this nation may be transformed.'

The people for whom Yeats was speaking, if we study the examples he gives, were not one by blood—Swift was wholly English; Burke, Norman and Irish—nor, strictly speaking, one by social position, although, had they been contemporaries, they might have sat down in their middle years at the same table. Parnell was a considerable landowner with aristocratic connections, Burke was a solicitor's, Emmet a doctor's son. They were not, that is to say, members of a caste. But they were all Protestants by baptism, whatever vagaries their supernatural beliefs might afterwards take. Yeats was hardly a typical Church of Ireland believer. But he spoke as a Protestant and as if Protestantism were coterminous with a stock and with a people, when it was merely a distinguishing colour in a country of Catholic peasants.

There is further evidence in his diaries, which have only recently been published, of Yeats's condescending views on Catholics. He was never on comfortable terms of friendship with the novelist, George Moore. The older man had tried to patronise him at their first meeting. But they had worked together for the Abbey and they met when Yeats was at Coole under Lady Gregory's catalytic influence. Moore was a mocker, the very type that Shaw complained of as characteristic of the Dublin he fled from; only in Moore's case his spiritual sabotaging was compensated for by a steady devotion to his art. He was probably jealous of Yeats, and he revenged himself by jeering at Yeats's social pretensions. It went so far that, on one occasion, Lady Gregory took a libel action on her own account for some outrage which touched her. With Yeats, Moore was on safer ground. He did not spare him in his mischievous memoirs:

'As soon as the applause died away, Yeats who had lately returned to us from the States with a paunch, a huge stride, and an immense fur overcoat, rose to speak. We were surprised at the change in his appearance, and could hardly believe our ears when, instead of talking to us as he used to do about the old stories come down from generation to generation he began to thunder like

Ben Tillett against the middle classes, stamping his feet, working himself into a great temper and all because the middle classes did not dip their hands into their pockets and give Lane the money he needed for his exhibition. When he spoke the words, "the middle classes", one would have thought that he was speaking against a personal foe, and we looked round asking each other with our eyes where on earth Willie Yeats had picked up the strange belief that none but titled carriage-folk could appreciate pictures. And we asked ourselves why our Willie Yeats should feel himself called upon to denounce his own class; millers and shipowners on one side, and on the other a portrait painter of distinction; and we laughed, remembering A.E.'s story, that one day whilst Yeats was crooning over his fire, Yeats had said that if he had his rights he would be Duke of Ormonde. A.E.'s answer was: "I am afraid, Willie, you are overlooking your father"—a detestable remark to make to a poet in search of an ancestry; and the addition: "We both belong to the same lower-middle class," was in equally bad taste . . .'

Yeats laid himself open to this sort of attack. The Anglo-Irish of Dublin, the large philistine sector at least, regarded him as a poseur, judging him by their own conservative standards. In so far as he posed in his bardic role it was none of their business, but he was invading their territory when he became a social figure, and this tendency increased after he had gone to Sweden to receive the Nobel Prize from the King.

He brooded over Moore's teasing and consoled himself by the reflection, 'I have been told that the crudity common to all the Moores came from the mother's family, Mayo squireens, probably half-peasants in education and occupation, for his father was a man of education and power and old descent. His mother's blood seems to have affected him and his brother as the peasant strain has affected Edward Martyn . . . Both men are examples of the way Irish civilisation is held back by the lack of education of Irish women. An Irish Catholic will not marry a Protestant, and hitherto the women have checked again and again the rise into some world of refinement of Catholic households.'

There spoke what my Catholic grandmother used to describe as 'Protestant impudence'. Yeats had not the temerity to publish those musings to which, if he had, Moore had material available for a shattering riposte in Yeats's rose-tinted accounts of his own family. Merchants and millers in Sligo, outside the County set by the social rules of those days, he wrote of his mother's people as if they were heroes of Arthurian legend. And on his father's side, descent through two generations of clergymen from a Dublin linen merchant was magnified, by marriage in the eighteenth century to Anne Butler and 800 acres in Kildare, to claims to a dukedom.

Yeats might have developed this theme. I am inclined to think that the Anglo-Irish of the eighteenth century were more Irish in accent and manner than in the later period. Burke, for one, had a thick brogue. The explanation could well be—the idea was given to me by Professor Perry Curtis—that Irish landlords tended to marry more with English girls after the Union. The women—as in India—set the tone, and it was an English tone. The men no longer sought comfort with Irish peasant girls, children were not put out to fosterage in the villages, and—with improved transport —the fashion began of going to school in England.

Had Yeats such an ancestor as George Henry Moore, whom he passed over so quickly the world would have had an Odyssey to his memory. Moore's father was the Anglo-Irishman of legend, a good scholar with precocious talents, a gallant horseman, a dashing lover, a benevolent landlord, and the leader of a short-lived national party at Westminster. His origins were not Irish, the family came somehow from England to Mayo and claimed relationship with Sir Thomas More. One had republican notions, and the French, when they landed at Killala in 1798, proclaimed him President of the Irish Republic. Being Catholics they had found wives outside the families of their own caste, although they had intermarried with Protestants, the Marquess of Sligo's family, for one.

The Yeats family had nothing like the social standing of the Moores, but they had never married Catholics. There was little, if any, Irish blood in them for all that the poet and his brother celebrated Ireland in verse and on canvas as she had seldom been celebrated before. Yeats had spoken of the 'stock' and 'people' to which he belonged, prophesying their recall. Would he have included Moore in its ranks?

If not, why should a man of mixed English and Irish blood be less Anglo-Irish than one who has probably no Irish blood in his veins, or very little? (If Yeats had any, it came through the Norman Butlers.) There is, of course, no reason at all. If the expression 'Anglo-Irish' has any claim to accuracy, it fits Moore exactly. If he is to be excluded, it is by Yeats's own assumption that he spoke on behalf of a Protestant people. And it is a coincidence that one of those who interrupted him in the Senate was Colonel Maurice Moore, George's brother. I do not believe that the Anglo-Irishman as he is pictured outside Ireland is necessarily Protestant or Catholic. George Moore would certainly answer, as would Oliver St John Gogarty. But the latter had even less claim than Moore on Yeats's interpretation of the word. He was a Catholic without any county connections. He was nearer in type to Thomas Moore, the darling of Regency drawing-rooms, from whom several generations got their first idea of romance in Irish history.

Yeats liked to remember that his father inherited 800 acres in Kildare, even if it had to be sold and there was no family house on the lands. And he was, on both sides, of Protestant stock. George Moore owned a large estate and a Georgian mansion. His family were among the first in the county. They came to Dublin Castle to the Viceregal entertainments. But they were not Protestants. If we are to be tied to the Protestant definition Moore was not an Anglo-Irishman. But in the upper echelons of the ascendancy the Moores counted for something, the name of Yeats was unknown.

It would serve no purpose to labour this point had Yeats not himself campaigned for freedom for divorce for Protestants on the ground that they were, as such, a separate people and that he represented them.

His was the line that has always been followed in the largely proletarian North. 'A Protestant Parliament for a Protestant people.' It was strictly accurate in the Anglo-Irish golden age to which Yeats was casting back his mind—the eighteenth century, which had seen such oratorical and architectural glories, glories from which every Catholic was excluded. The very few who were aristocratic or well connected—the Fingalls, Kenmares, Gormanstons and their like—toed the line, held their breath, resorted to legal fictions, supported Government, and did everything possible to retain their property as well as their faith. The eccentric Moore, who allowed the French to put him in a republican fool's paradise, was lucky not to get into trouble. He must have had no enemies.

Yeats, as we know from his poetry, was much given to brooding over and to reading—in his aristocratic phase—Swift, Berkeley and Burke. Comparing them with the men he confronted in 1925 he might well be pardoned for thinking that there had been a decline; and when he thought of Shaw, Hyde, Wilde, Lady Gregory, Synge, A.E. and himself, and compared them with the 'paudeens' and contemporary flowerings from peatier soil, he might also be forgiven for thinking that the world, had he appealed to it, would have had little difficulty in deciding which was the fairer crop.

It does not diminish from Yeats's stature as a poet to admit that he was inclined to be portentous, particularly where personal associations of any kind were concerned. Writing in *Responsibilities* of the Butlers, who so heated his genealogical imagination, he soliloquises:

> ... You that did not weigh the cost
> Old Butlers when you took to horse and stood
> Beside the brackish waters of the Boyne
> Till your bad master blenched and all was lost.

And then, on hearing that they had in fact fought for William, gravely changed text while retaining tone.

> A Butler or an Armstrong that withstood
> Beside the brackish waters of the Boyne
> James and the Irish when the Dutchman crossed.

Yeats was overcome by the Swedish court. When the editor of *The Irish Times* rang up to tell him he had won the Nobel Prize his first reaction was 'How much?' But that was the Yeats from the Sligo counting house Pollexfens, not the Tower-dweller or the author of 'Prayer for my Daughter', who was in the ascendant when he wrote:

'The diplomas and medals are to be given us by the King at five in the afternoon of December 10th. The American Ambassador, who is to receive those for an American man of science, unable to be present, and half a dozen men of various nations sit upon the platform. In the body of the Hall every seat is full, and all there are in evening dress, and in the front row are the King, Princess Ingeborg, wife of the King's brother, Prince Wilhelm, Princess Margaretha, and I think another Royalty. The President of the Swedish Academy speaks in English, and I see from the way he stands, from his self-possession, and from his rhythmical utterance, that he is an experienced orator. I study the face of the old King, intelligent and friendly like some country gentleman who can quote Horace and Catullus, and the face of the Princess Margaretha, full of subtle beauty, emotional and precise, and impassive with a still intensity suggesting that final consummate strength which rounds the spiral of a shell. One finds a similar beauty in wooden busts taken from Egyptian tombs of the Eighteenth Dynasty, and not again until Gainsborough paints. Is it very ancient and very modern alone or did painters and sculptors cease to notice it until our day?'

Yeats's description of the Swedish court is in the manner that made George Moore laugh at him. It would not have appealed to Maud Gonne. It shows that by confining this inquiry to genius, with its waywardness, there is a danger of drawing unwarranted conclusions. Nothing, for instance, could be more misleading than to take the career of the poet, Thomas Moore, as an example of the position of grocers' sons at the turn of the eighteenth century. Similarly, we see Yeats coming forward in the Senate as the spokesman for the Protestant ascendancy. He flattered the people he spoke for by admitting them *en bloc* to the company of his fellows; what he had in common with Swift and Burke was genius. This was by no means widely distributed among the Protestant ascendancy. They might well have been astonished on that summer afternoon when they heard how distinguished they were.

CHAPTER III

Back to Swift

AGAIN AND AGAIN I return to Yeats's speech and brood over those names. How can a common case be made for Swift and Burke? Swift's father had come to Ireland when the family was trying to make its fortune. His mother was a Leicestershire woman. Even if one of the Temples was his real father, Swift was only Irish in as much as he was born in Dublin and went to school in Ireland and to Trinity College, Dublin. Thackeray and Kipling were born in India; Winston Churchill's mother was an American; Chesterton's mother was French; in the veins of the present Queen of England runs the blood of Brian Boru. But I have never heard Thackeray described as Anglo-Indian or Churchill as Anglo-American or the Queen as Anglo-Irish. The English Royal family's German ancestry is dominant in their genealogy. But that is only one strain. If we emphasise it, can we say that the Queen is Anglo-German? One would only say so to be offensive.

'We are the people of Swift.' Yeats's boast reminds me that I used quite frequently to be offered introductions to people on the ground that they were 'descendants of Swift'. He left, as we know, no descendants. Swift was a meteor that happened to hit Ireland. His stature as an Irish patriot—and he is accepted as the first of the Anglo-Irish patriots—is accidental. Had he been given a benefice in America he would have been the first American patriot; such was the nature of his cantankerous genius. Injustice and absurdity aroused him, and satire and ridicule were his weapons. In some measure he is archetypal. Mahaffy who personified the anti-Irish, West Briton to a modern generation had a great deal in common with Swift without his genius. Both had a nose for humbug and gave short shrift to solemn fools. Both liked to shock. For clergymen, both were very secular in their manners. Neither had any regard for the remains of Gaelic culture. Swift proposed that 'it would be a noble achievement to abolish the Irish language in this Kingdom, so far at least to oblige all the natives to speak only English on every occasion of business . . . This would, in a great measure, civilise the most barbarous among them, reconcile them to our customs and manners of living, and reduce great numbers to the national religion. I could heartily wish some public thoughts were employed to reduce this uncultivated people from that idle, savage, beastly, thievish manner of life, in which they continue sunk to a degree, that it is almost impossible for a country gentleman to find a servant of human capacity, or the least tincture of natural honesty . . .'

In these lines may be found a precedent for those undertakings in later years which are now cited as major grievances—the efforts of Government to discourage Irish in the schools and the various efforts to proselytise. It may also be noted that Swift says '*our* customs and manner of living'. Who is *us*? The English in Ireland? In his better known writings he has set out the case against English misrule and also harped upon two evils which every candid observer noticed—the amount spent abroad on luxuries and wine and the terrible toll of rents paid to absentees.

Reading Swift one might be in the nineteenth century except for one particular. He speaks of the lack of population, miserably poor though the people be. The problem in later years was the numbers on the land. In the universal condemnation of Irish landlords there is a tendency to over-simplify the agrarian problem. Emigration is counted a great Irish evil. Did every Irish person who escaped from the potato plot think so? Are the Kennedys sorry that they ever left Wexford?

In Swift's writings almost every problem which has vexed Ireland is seen or foreshadowed. He is one of the few in his generation who have recorded conditions in Ulster, the most prosperous of the provinces, where 'some thousands of families are gone, or going, or preparing to go from hence, and settle themselves in America. The poorest sort for want of work, the farmers whose beneficial burdens are become a rack-rent too hard to be borne. And those who have any money . . . because they find their fortunes hourly decaying . . .'

What was the inducement to go? Swift believed that the English who settled in America wanted to entice Irish out there 'to inhabit the tract of ground which lies between them and the wild Indians'.

Some of Swift's satires are savage, one grotesquely so, but he wrote one rather delightful parable in which he likened England to a man who is courting two women, one separated from him by a wall, the other by a river. Swift spoke in the person of the latter. 'This gentleman taking a fancy to my person or fortunes, made his addresses to me.' Undone 'by the common arts of the seducer' she discovered that, once in possession, her lover acted like a conqueror, found fault with her domestic arrangements, sent his steward to govern her house, turned away old servants and tenants, and employed others from his own. These in turn introduced their own friends and acquaintances, and when the lady found herself turned out of house and home her lover started to speak of her as 'an old dependent upon his family', that she cost too much to keep and was under 'vast obligations' for sending her so many people for her own good to teach her manners. All this has rendered her 'so insignificant at home' that the servants to whom she pays the greatest wages and the tenants who have the most beneficial leases have gone over to live with him. His other flirt proved harder to win, so he proposed marriage to her, reducing his distant lady to the role of sempstress for his grooms and footmen.

She might have had advantageous offers from elsewhere, but never entertained any such wicked thought, and now only demanded that she be left quiet and allowed to manage her own affairs. She shared a steward in common, but whatever order he gives for the benefit of his family, she must obey without being consulted or asked for advice . . .

All this was delightful for Grattan and the patriots in the next generation; but the nation for which Swift spoke was a relatively small number of people, and the whole population of Ireland was probably not more than two million.

Swift lived in Ireland when the penal laws were at their most savage, but neither he nor Berkeley ever complained about them. Swift wrote an ingenious memorial, assuming the Catholic position, arguing that they had stood firm in the religion of their original conquerors and remained loyal to the King whom the dissenters murdered, and yet they had to see lands confiscated by the very men who had murdered the King confirmed in their possession after the restoration of Charles II.

'The account therefore stands thus. The Papists aimed at one pernicious act, which was to destroy the Protestant religion, wherein, by God's mercy, and the assistance of our glorious King William, they absolutely failed. The Sectaries attempted the three most infernal actions, that could possibly enter into the hearts of men, forsaken by God; which were the murder of a most pious king, the destruction of the monarchy and the extirpation of the Church; and succeeded in them all.'

Swift is like Scripture in that he can easily be quoted by the Devil for his own purposes. He had the kind of mind that delights in putting a case partly for the intellectual exercise, partly to tease. But I think it is hopeless to argue that he was deeply concerned for the Catholics of Ireland, although he was moved to pity and disgust by their poverty.

'As to Popery in general, which for a thousand years past hath been introducing and multiplying corruption both in doctrine and discipline; I look upon it to be the most absurd system of Christianity professed by any nation. But I cannot apprehend this Kingdom to be in much danger from it. The estates of Papists are very few; crumbling into small parcels and daily diminishing. Their common people are sunk in poverty, ignorance and cowardice; and of as little consequence as women and children. Their nobility and gentry are at least by one half ruined, banished, or converted: they all feel soundly the smart of what they suffered in the late Irish war; some of them are already retired into foreign countries; others, as I am told, intend to follow them; and the rest, I believe to a man, who still possess any lands, are absolutely determined never to hazard them again for the sake of establishing their superstition . . . If it had been thought fit, as some observe, to abate of the law's rigour against popery in this Kingdom, I am confident it was done for very wise reasons, considering the situation of affairs abroad at different times, and the interest of the Protestant religion in general. And, as I do not find the least fault in this proceeding; so I do not conceive why a sunk discarded party, who neither expect nor desire anything more than a quiet life, should, under the name of High-flyers, Jacobites, and many other vile appellations, be charged so often in print, and at common tables, with endeavouring to introduce Popery and the Pretender; while the Papists abhor them above all other men, on account of severities against their priests in her late Majesty's reign; when the now disbanded reprobate party was in power. This I was convinced of some years ago by a long journey into the southern parts; where I had the curiosity to send for many of the priests of the parishes I passed through, and to my great satisfaction found them everywhere abounding in professions of loyalty to the late King George; for which they gave me the reasons above mentioned; at the same time complaining bitterly of the hardships they suffered under the Queen's *last ministry*!'

Before we take leave of Swift, notice that *last ministry* in his italics. Even in Ireland Swift was still the Swift who took a leading part in English politics in Queen Anne's time, and in Ireland was, to a large extent, working off his spleen at his displacement from the centre of that stage.

Dean Swift, writing to Mrs Delany, admits to some advantages in Dublin ('You dare not pretend to say your town equals ours in hospitable evenings'), and Mrs Delany, who was good and kind and intelligent, writes about Dublin in 1731, as a pleasant place to live in. 'I must say the environs of Dublin are delightful. The town is bad enough, narrow streets and dirty-looking houses, but some very good ones scattered about: and as for Stephen's Green, I think it may be preferred justly to any square in London . . .'

Passing through the country by coach she found the roads much better than in England, but the poverty of the people made her 'heart ache'. In Dublin, her letters are taken up with accounts of parties, balls, theatricals, music, opera. She moved in the small circle that surrounded the Viceroy's court—small, that is to say, in proportion to the entire population, but large enough to make overcrowded rooms an outstanding characteristic of Dublin entertainments.

The people about the Court were for the most part officials and placemen who came from England to rule and reside in Ireland, but who were not domiciled there. Their sole occupation being to watch the English interest in Ireland, their policy ran counter to the interest of those who had settled in the country and looked to its prosperity for the safeguarding and increase of their fortunes. All around were the dispossessed and discontented Irish, multiplying with the reckless enthusiasm of the indigent. The colonists would have welcomed a Union with Great Britain, but saw no prospect of it. They looked to England to protect them in the last resort against an attack by the dispossessed natives. They could not afford to throw off the mother country for reasons of security, but they encountered an economic tyranny which could not have been greater had the Irish government been native.

Georgian Ireland, because of the interest aroused in its architecture, tends to get a blanket approval that a calm survey of the age hardly arouses. It began in abject poverty. The Williamite war had devastated the country and left the population so thin that the Irish parliament voted to introduce German refugees from the Marlborough wars. These Palatines, as they were called, came and settled. At first they kept very much to themselves, and Arthur Young, when he observed them towards the end of the century, said that he thought the Irish, given the same assistance, would have done quite as well for themselves. Of their descendants were later to be found only Delmeges, among the Anglo-Irish families. The Switzer family founded Dublin's largest store. As a community they disappeared in the following century. Now were passed the Penal Laws, which in strict application were usually observed rather in the spirit than the letter, but which were efficacious in keeping Catholics out of any sphere of influence. Like Jews in Europe generally, they were able to prosper only in humbler lines of life, and as the better sort had an almost absurd prejudice against trade, many preferred to become outlaws than to submit to social degradation.

These became Tories, giving a name to an English party with somewhat different credentials. They gave leadership to the country people in their running war against an oppressive system, in particular the payment of tithes to an alien church.

In town and country there were people from whose annals we derive a picture of a lively society; but this enjoyed itself against, on the whole, a background of abject poverty. In Lecky's splendid history of the period we read of England's injustice to Ireland, the suppression of Irish manufactures, the restrictions on Irish foreign trade, the destruction of the wool industry—injustices which, with a growing sense of pride in their own achievements and a natural attachment to the place they and their parents were born and bred in, led to a demand for self-government by the colonists (the Anglo-Irish).

But these grievances were exclusive. The great mass of the Irish people were unconcerned by the failure of trades in which they were neither employed nor in any way permitted to share in the profits. And the agitation for Catholic emancipation did not come from the people (until they were worked up). What had they to gain?

The average Irishman was a poor wretch living in an overcrowded hovel. If he had—and he sometimes did have—a good landlord, he was lucky. But he was always poor. It is noticeable that the self-made men of the time—Curran for example—came from Protestant homes. A kindly parson was able to launch them on their course, and Trinity College had sizarships for talented boys of limited means.

Of course there were some Catholics who made the best of it, held land on lease or connived with friendly Protestant neighbours. And in the towns there were some prosperous Catholics. Tom Moore, the poet, a London success, was the son of a Dublin grocer.

The poverty at the beginning of the century was certainly worse than it was towards the close. Swift calculated that the Irish poor would be exterminated before two generations.

Berkeley, if only because he was so much more normal in every way than Swift, is possibly a better example of the Anglo-Irishman of the time. For one thing his family had been longer in the country. The two men were not friends. Vanessa, it may be remembered, when she parted company with Swift, changed her will, and left the residue of her estate to Berkeley for charitable purposes.

Berkeley's *Querist* published in 1735 gives us many clues to the state of the country. It is necessary to distinguish between what he says about the poor and his strictures on his own class; but before we go into that, we are met at the outset by two queries which are strong evidence against the case for the existence, at that time, of such a race as the Anglo-Irish. Berkeley enquires: 'Whether the upper part of this people are not truly English, by blood, language, religion, manners, inclination and interest? Whether we are not as much Englishmen as the children of old Romans, born in Briton, were still Romans?'

From those assumptions he argued that the English in Ireland should not do anything to impede the interests of England and that the English in England should befriend the English in Ireland. Consistent with this was his claim that Ireland should be prepared to forget her wool trade if it inconvenienced British interests at home.

This accommodating spirit was not peculiar to Berkeley; it has persisted even until our day among many with Unionist sympathies. It was later to take the form of pride in the Empire. National interests by this thinking were secondary to the welfare of the larger concern; but very often the concession was made, without demur, simply in England's interest. It was an identification more remarkable than any religious tie.

Berkeley's queries throw light on the conditions of the time. Even then he is aware that the land of Tipperary in the south is better than the land of Armagh in the north; but the latter is much better improved and inhabited.

He inveighs against the habits of the upper class—the large consumption of claret, the importation of women's finery. In this he revealed a certain puritanism. The amount spent by society women on silks and muslins could hardly have disturbed the economy. There was too much of everything imported into Ireland in his opinion. He wanted to found a national bank—this was his pet hobby—and he deplored the lack of artists and craftsmen and the importation of so much corn as well as wine and brandy. Why not native breweries?

As the century progressed some of Berkeley's demands were met. But at first by the immigration of enterprising people from England and abroad. Wilde's ancestors, on both sides, came to Ireland at about this time as builders. Huguenots and Quakers, who fled from persecution, established the linen trade and encouraged lace manufacture. The name La Touche appears in banking.

I find among my own ancestors, on my father's side, a Darley—

the family came with a builder, Moses Darley, in 1680 and later established a brewery. They made some of the good mantelpieces of the time. Many Italians came to do stucco work. And in due course the Irish learnt from them.

Berkeley shared the common view that their religion was the drawback to the Irish character. He was not a bigot. In fact he was far in advance of his time in recommending that Catholics should be admitted to Trinity College, but he took the view that nothing should be left undone to persuade them of the error of their ways.

Under a provision of Henry VIII, every clergyman was obliged to have a school in his parish for the teaching of English and all Catholic education was strictly forbidden. The clergymen neglected their statutory duty, and the Catholics in some cases did contrive to get educated. (Among my Catholic grandmother's relatives, in the records of Leix, I see several hedge schoolmasters, as they were called.) Marsh, Bishop of Clogher, originated and Primate Boulter in 1733 established a system known as Charter Schools. Berkeley, no doubt, approved of them. They were intended 'to rescue the souls of thousands of poor children from the dangers of Popish superstition and idolatry, and their bodies from the miseries of idleness and beggary'. Froude, characteristically, described them as 'the best conceived educational institutions which existed in the world'. There was great enthusiasm for the scheme. George II contributed, and the Irish Parliament put up money. In all £112,200 is said to have gone to the cause. The scheme was the forerunner of 'souperism' in the next century, when zealous evangelists offered that beverage in times of famine in return for a conversion to Protestantism. Proselytising in one form or other survived, and 'they took the soup' was a familiar gibe in Ireland. I remember a rhyme in my youth:

> They sell their souls
> For penny rolls
> And Smyly's
> Hairy bacon.

When Howard, the prison reformer, came to Ireland in 1785 he discovered evils in the Charter schools almost as frightful as any he had discovered in the prisons of England or the continent. The inmates were, for the most part, 'sickly, naked and half-starved'. The children were used as labour gangs in the fields for eight hours a day. After twelve years at school some could neither read nor spell. Dotheboy's Hall had been established in Ireland on an imperial scale.

Berkeley was not alone in sincerely advocating improvements in conditions. It would be unfair to portray Ireland at this time as populated only by claret-drinking tyrants. In Dublin he found kindred spirits, notably Thomas Prior. He was born in Rathdowney, County Leix, in 1682. His grandfather had been an English soldier who settled in Ireland in 1636. Prior was very representative of what I have called 'the colonists'. 'The son of an Englishman' was how he described himself, showing that he regarded himself as differing in this respect from his father—as being, in fact, Irish. His cast of mind was puritan, but he seems to have been free from self-righteous or bigoted opinions. Of his private life we know that he was a schoolfellow of Berkeley at Kilkenny College, and he acted as Berkeley's agent in Dublin. Berkeley's letters to Prior have been preserved and they give us some idea of the recipient. He was very busy and public-spirited, not very efficient in private business, but zealous in public affairs. Too busy, it would seem, to have time to marry: too useful, occupied and constructive to waste time in quarrels. He left behind him no trace of scandal or folly, and such references to him as exist speak only in his praise. His views were radical and he expressed them bravely. His pamphlets ensured him the disfavour of Government because not only did he criticise Irish affairs, but he also questioned conventional beliefs.

His *List of Absentees* gave the names and the incomes of those who lived abroad but who drew money from Ireland. Not content with the amount of unpopularity such a publication was bound to win him, he expressed his radical views in the *Observations* which prefaced the list.

He advocated a change in the laws of inheritance. Instead of giving all to one, who usually went abroad to spend the income, he suggested dividing property between the sons of a family. The idea of an heir, his puritan mind rejected. 'The pride of names and families is despised by all people of sense, and is rarely to be found but in poor countries or persons of reduced fortunes and is generally accompanied with a want of real merit.'

Berkeley, spending his time most virtuously and philanthropically in Rhode Island, was included in Prior's second *List of Absentees*. We do not know if he had already heard of this, or if he did, how he felt about it, but we can hazard a guess as to his feelings when, having waited for some years for news of a legacy from Esther Van Homrigh (Swift's Vanessa) and not having heard from Prior (who was looking after the business) for six months, he at length receives a parcel from Ireland on which he has to pay £4 postage, and inside finds a copy of the *List of Irish Absentees* with his name in it.

Prior turns up everywhere in the history of Ireland at this period. In the last year of his life he was busy promoting the Rotunda Lying-in Hospital for his friend Dr Bartholomew Mosse. He did not fully share with Berkeley, Dobbs, Madden and others of his friends their discouraging view of the native Irish: he described them as being industrious and living 'poor and cheap'. Berkeley in the *Querist* had inquired 'whether our old, native Irish are not the most indolent and supine people in Christendom?'

Prior, without any of Swift's bitterness, has a plainness of speech, a respect for truth, a manliness and independence of spirit, which contrasts very favourably with the respectful and cautious approach of his friends. He did not, as Dobbs (who was a public official), pay court to authority; nor, as Madden, sanctimoniously recommend ale and cider to palates trained to claret; or deplore, as did Dobbs, Berkeley and Madden, the fact that every man, woman, and child in the country were not gainfully employed from morning to night.

Madden, a hen-pecked man, objected to concerts and parties for women, and would only allow them to go if they brought needlework along. He suggested that priests should be compelled by law to have a spinning wheel in their homes.

So much advice is impressive but without action in any form would give point to Berkeley's query 'whether my Countrymen are not readier at finding excuses than remedies?' For his own part, in his diocese in Cloyne, Berkeley worked assiduously for the poor, encouraged local industry, and dispensed 'tar water' as a remedy for all the bodily ills of his parishioners.

Swift gave alms and left his fortune to a madhouse. But the man with a plan and the energy to translate it into action was Prior.

It was he who brought together in 1731 the men who formed the Dublin Society (later known as the Royal Dublin Society). The Reverend Samuel Madden who regarded the granting of premiums as the panacea for all human ills, and who once paid Dr Johnson ten guineas to improve a poem, was a prominent supporter of the RDS in its early days. He spoke of himself 'as a native of Ireland, and have the whole of my fortune settled there, I think myself, though very easy as to my own condition, as much obliged by all the ties of morality and self-interest to labour to relieve the distress of my fellow-countrymen'. A native of Ireland, yet he can write: 'There is no distinction which we are, or indeed ought to be fonder of than that of Englishmen.' He is quite prepared to suffer inconvenience in Ireland for England's benefit. 'If we grow rich and easy, it must not be at the expense of our neighbours but on our own Bottom.' 'And yet', he complained, 'it cannot but seem hard to be us'd and consider'd as aliens by those who . . . persuaded numbers of our people . . . to come over hither and spend their blood in their service to extend their Empire, Commerce and Power . . . and may not the children of those Englishmen who have planted in our colonies in America be as justly reckoned Indians and savages as such familes who are settled here be considered and treated as mere Irishmen and aliens?'

It was not difficult to foresee that in the future men such as Madden would become more nationalistic. In the words of Thomas Prior: 'The love of one's country is seldom found in any remarkable degree but in those who live long in it, agreeable to the intention of nature, which disposes all men and other creatures to a fondness for those places in which they live.'

At this time Ireland had the good fortune to be sent a good Viceroy. Philip Stanhope, Earl of Chesterfield, is one of those characters whom historians have not painted the colour of the rose. He is best remembered by Johnson's damning letter. His mentality was more French than English; his letters to his natural son have won him the title of the English Rochefoucauld. Incorruptible in an age when venality flourished, when every man had his price, Chesterfield, had he been born anywhere else but in England, would have been revered as the Cato of his time. Nature made him ugly, and vanity made him prattle about his amorous adventures. 'As if anyone would believe a woman would like a dwarf baboon', said King George II. Chesterfield's letters to his son which lay so strong an emphasis on the value of appearance added to his reputation as a cold-hearted sinner. In France he would have been understood, but in England people were shocked, not by what Lord Chesterfield did, but by what he said. There was an inherent difficulty in the circumstances of the correspondence: it would require remarkable complacency to play the heavy father in letters to an illegitimate son.

Chesterfield was a man with many conflicting qualities. He was very witty and yet his usual style was sententious. A good example of his wit is his comment when he heard that a young parvenu was marrying the daughter of a lady of too celebrated reputation: 'Nobody's son has married everybody's daughter.' He had a taste for dissipation and complete self-control—a rather inhuman combination. For gambling he had a passion but he could put it aside when he was in office and resume it when he had leisure. He disapproved of drunkenness and inveighed against the claret-drinking propensities of the Irish aristocracy. His definition of fornication is famous: 'The pleasure is momentary; the position ridiculous; the expense prohibitive.' In his old age, crippled with pain, he became increasingly liberal in his political ideas and cheerful about his troubles. 'I consider my present wretched old age as a just compensation for the follies, not to say sins, of my youth', he wrote shortly before his death.

There is as much humbug in the world now as ever there was, and it is a great deal to be able to say of a public man, who did a fair share of good, and declined the honours that were offered to him, that he was absolutely free from canting hypocrisy. Certainly, so far as his Irish career is concerned, Chesterfield was a paragon. To him we owe much of the beauty of Phoenix Park. He took an unfeigned interest in the country and seemed, when he became Lord Lieutenant, to assume a sense of duty towards the people he governed as well as to the Government that appointed him. He was the best Lord Lieutenant that ever came to Ireland.

Chesterfield formed a regard for Prior when he was in Dublin. In a letter to Madden he said, 'The Irish may be a rich and happy people . . . as fit for arts, sciences, industry and labour, as any people in the world, they might, notwithstanding some hard restraints which England, by mistaken policy, has laid them under, push several branches of trade to great perfection and profit; and not only supply themselves with everything they want, but other nations too with many things. But jobs, and claret engross and ruin the people of fashion, and the ordinary people (as is usual in every country) imitate them in little monetary and mistaken views of present profit and whiskey.'

Among landlords, who were to win such an evil name, there were some who deserved a better reputation even then. Lord Molesworth's *Some Considerations for Promoting Agriculture and Employing the Poor*, which appeared in 1723, avoided politics and concentrated on practical difficulties. 'We have always', he wrote, 'a glut or a dearth': and seeking a reason for this, he expressed the conviction 'that the whole Economy of Agriculture is generally mistaken or neglected in this Kingdom'. He was opposed to the English system of parish relief for the poor: 'I know no country where the real poor are worse taken care of.' But he had 'often wondered (when I consider how long it is since this Kingdom of Ireland has been united and annexed to the Crown of England, and the English customs, as to Habit, Language, and Religion, have been encouraged and enjoyed by Laws) how it comes to pass, that we should be so long a time and so universally ignorant of the English manner of managing our tillage and lands as we now are; or if we formerly knew them, how we came to fall off from that knowledge and the practice of it to such a degree, that the English tenants who pay double the rent to their landlords for their acres (which are much shorter than the Irish acres) are able notwithstanding to supply us with corn at a moderate price, over and above the incident charges of freight, porterage, etc.'

The author went on to deal with the answers to this question and to suggest changes in the law both for landlord and tenant. He was alive to the worst features of Irish agriculture—jobbing in land by middlemen who sub-let at a profit to the ruin of farm and farmer alike. He suggested the provision of granaries on the Continental model to combat periodical famine. He deplored the necessity for gentlemen to manage their own lands for lack of stewards and from fear of tenants. 'This forces them in a manner to employ most part of their time in these low employments and mean company . . . thus they lose the best opportunity of reading and improving their natural parts . . . they degenerate by degrees; the best education of most of their sons, reaching no higher, than to know how to make the most of a piece of land. How can the business of Parliament, the duty owing to one's country, and the value of public liberty, be sufficiently understood, under such a cramp'd and low education, help'd by little or no reading? The consequences of which are that they grow narrow spirited, covetous and ungenteel.'

Lord Molesworth recommended the establishment of 'Schools of Husbandry' in every county on a non-sectarian basis, teaching only 'Husbandry and good manners and that the children should daily serve God according to their own religions'. There are many other wise suggestions in his excellent pamphlet, from which later writers (who have received far more attention) were to draw freely and without acknowledgement.

CHAPTER IV

The Lighter Side

BUT THERE WAS a lighter side to Irish life. It was not all politics and pamphlets. At Delville—now destroyed—Mrs Delany offered civilised entertainment. Further out, in Lucan, on Sarsfield's estate, Mrs Vesey had a celebrated blue-stocking circle. A few miles away, the FitzGeralds, Earls of Kildare and later Dukes of Leinster, must have made Carton a pleasant house, especially when the beautiful and fecund Emily was Duchess. And the Conollys at Castletown, as befitted the richest commoners in Ireland, lived in a grand way, and within hail.

If we follow Arthur Young in his conscientious pilgrimage round Ireland, staying in the best houses, we do not hear him remark on any striking differences between the two countries. He does, of course, have plenty to say about the disadvantageous position of the Irish peasantry and he was astonished by the profusion of horses he found, all badly looked after by English standards.

'A landlord in Ireland can scarcely invent an order which a servant, labourer, or cottier dares to refuse to execute. Nothing satisfies him but unlimited submission. Disrespect or anything tending towards sauciness he may punish with his cane or his horsewhip with the most perfect security, a poor man would have his bones broke if he offered to lift his hand in his own defence. Knocking down is spoken of in the country in a manner that makes an Englishman stare. Landlords of consequence have assured me that many of their cottiers would think themselves honoured by having their wives or daughters sent for to the bed of their masters; a mark of slavery that proves the oppression under which such people must live. Nay, I have heard anecdotes of the lives of people being made free with without any apprehension of the justice of a jury. But let it not be imagined that this is common; formerly it happened every day, but law gains ground. It must strike the most careless traveller to see whole strings of cars whipt into a ditch by a gentleman's footman to make way for his carriage; if they are overturned or broken in pieces, no matter, it is taken in patience; were they to complain they would perhaps be horsewhipped. The execution of the law lies very much in the hands of justices of the peace, many of whom are drawn from the most illiberal class in the kingdom. If a poor man lodges a complaint against a gentleman, or any animal that chuses to call himself a gentleman, and the justice issues out a summons for his appearance, it is a fixed affront, and he will infallibly be called out. Where MANNERS are in conspiracy against LAW, to whom are the oppressed people to have recourse? It is a fact that a poor man having a contest with a gentleman must—but I am talking nonsense, they know their situation too well to think of it; they can have no defence but by means of protection from one gentleman against another, who probably protects his vassal as he would the sheep he intends to eat.'

I surmise that Young's course kept him among the more sober and responsible of the landed gentry. He did not, I feel sure, encounter Buck Whaley or spend an evening in the Hell Fire Club or foregather with anyone so notorious as George Robert FitzGerald.

It took three ropes to hang the last named when his time came, and Denis Browne, brother of the Lord Sligo of the day, won the soubriquet 'Soap the Rope' from having suggested that expedient after the second miscarriage. FitzGerald's many enemies included Richard Martin, later known as 'Humanity Dick', the ancestor of Violet Martin of Ross. FitzGerald was tried for various offences in his time; chaining his father to a dray and at other times to a muzzled bear were among his fads. He wore armour as a protection in duelling, and in the course he was able to run in the country, bullying and blackguarding anyone who annoyed him, gives a lurid character to what was to present a more genial face as the stage Irishman.

Jonah Barrington's *Sketches*, in which FitzGerald makes an appearance, stand in good report and are generally considered to be humorous. In fact they paint an almost unrelieved picture of brutality, and the fun, if furious, is not notably mirth-provoking. Through it all runs a strain of violence and blackguardism—it would put me off the Irish if I were not one of them—in some ways, not unlike the rowdier passages in Smollet and Fielding; but Barrington was reticent on sex to the point of squeamishness, and his most daring story is an account of how John Philpot Curran's English mistress threw him out of the house when he proffered only ten pounds in answer to a plea of acute distress.

Donnybrook Fair was then in its heyday, but Barrington gives the impression that all Irish society was conducted on Donnybrook lines. Perhaps I build too much on the anecdotes of an old time-server, hard up, in exile and disgrace, anxious to rake in a little money, writing of a bygone age. Barrington's definition of Irish country society, his 'Gentlemen to the backbone, Gentlemen every inch of them, and Half-mounted gentlemen' has provided a divining rod for all future inquiries in that field. He does not help us to distinguish closely between the two top layers of country society. And Mr Maurice Craig, in his excellent history of Dublin, doesn't help on the general question when he tells us Barrington belonged to the second class. Mr Craig takes the traditional favourable view of Barrington's merits; but I believe that he has fallen into the trap that lies in the path of the devoted antiquarian —an aptitude to delight in anything that his expertise certifies as genuine. It is the same sort of reverence that forbids us to yawn at Shakespeare's clowns or the plays of T. S. Eliot.

The half-mounted gentlemen, according to Barrington, were the yeomanry of Ireland. They were the descendants of smaller Elizabethan, Cromwellian and Williamite settlers, excelling as horsemen, prominent, when there were races, as stewards and at election times. They carried long whips, loaded with lead, to knock the brains out of anyone for whom horse-whipping was insufficient. The last of them in recorded history is Flurry Knox with whom Somerville and Ross adorned the *Irish R.M.* stories. Their sinister side was shown when they practised pitch-capping and other expedients to extort confessions before the outbreak of revolution in 1798. They consumed enormous quantities of claret, and their fortunes in later days may be followed in the novels of Charles Lever. Thackeray had a sharp eye for the genus and portrayed it in his *Barry Lyndon*, a better book than any of Lever's.

They were a detestable type and had no equivalent in England, because an English tenant would not have tolerated their bullying ways. In Ireland they were able to square the law and defy a public opinion that could not dare to be vocal.

Maria Edgeworth may be trusted to describe them exactly:

'In the neighbourhood of Kollpatrickstown, Lady Dashfort said, there were several squireens, or little squires; a race who have succeeded to the buckeens described by Young and Crumpe. Squireens are persons who, with good long leases, or valuable farms, possess incomes from three to eight hundred a year; who keep a pack of hounds; *take out* a commission of the peace, sometimes before they can spell, and almost always before they know anything of law or justice! Busy and loud about small matters; jobbers at assizes; combining with one another, and trying upon every occasion, public or private, to push themselves forward, to the annoyance of their superiors, and the terror of those below them.

'In the usual course of things, these men are not often to be found in the society of gentry; except, perhaps, among those gentlemen or noblemen who like to see hangers-on at their tables; or who find it for their convenience to have underling magistrates, to protect their favourites, or to propose and carry jobs for them on grand juries. At election times, however, these persons rise into sudden importance with all who have views upon the county. Lady Dashfort hinted to Lord Killpatrick, that her private letters from England spoke of an approaching dissolution of Parliament; she knew that, upon this hint, a round of invitations would be sent to the squireens; and she was morally certain that they would be more disagreeable to Lord Colambre, and give him a worse idea of the country, than any other person who could be produced. Day after day some of these personages made their appearance; and Lady Dashfort took care to draw them out upon the subjects on which she knew that they would show the most self-sufficient ignorance, and the most illiberal spirit. This succeeded beyond her most sanguine expectations. "Lord Colambre! how I pity you, for being compelled to these permanent sittings after dinner," said Lady Isabel to him one night, when he came late to the ladies from the dining-room. "Lord Killpatrick insisted upon my staying to help him to push about that never-ending, still-beginning electioneering bottle," said Lord Colambre. "Oh! if that were all, if these gentlemen would only drink—but their conversation! I don't wonder my mother dreads returning to Clonbrony Castle, if my father must have company as this. But, surely, it cannot be necessary."

"'Oh, indispensable! positively indispensable!" cried Lady Dashfort; "no living in Ireland without it. You know in every country in the world, you must live with the people of the country, or be torn to pieces; for my part I should prefer being torn to pieces.'"

Somerville and Ross, a hundred years later, referred to 'buckeens' in County Cork.

A feature of Irish life in the eighteenth century was forcible abduction of heiresses. Froude condemned it as a native practice, but Lecky showed that 'buckeens' of Protestant families were sometimes partial to the sport. John White, an ancestor of mine, disinherited his eldest son Richard for marrying 'beneath him' and left the residue of his estate to his daughter Rebecca. Rebecca was abducted within a few months of her father's death in 1718. One witness described the happening thus: 'that on the 4th instant, between three and four in the afternoon, men to the number of fifteen in all, well armed and mounted, came to Cappagh and there broke open the chamber door of Mrs Rebecca White and Mrs Catherine White and violently forced away Mrs Rebecca White, she crying out "Murther" and calling out for assistance all the while, and they carried her out and put her on horseback behind one John Ryan, son to Teige Ryan of Ballyvistea.'

Another witness deposed that she was sent for and went to a barrack where there was one, James Caffoe, a Popish priest. Rebecca asked him not to marry her to Thomas Fitzgerald, to which he replied that if he refused he would be murdered.

Froude and Lecky both record this incident. A Private Act of Parliament had to be passed to annul the marriage; but there is no record of what happened to the illegal husband. Rebecca White never married anyone else. She lived in Dublin in Fishamble

Street, and the story is told that one day Swift called and was told by the maid that she was not at home. She stuck her head out of the window and shouted after him 'I am at home to you, Mr Dean'. He took occasion to reprove her sharply for having instructed her servant to tell a lie.

Rebecca's property went to her nephew John, of Kilmoylan, who married Catherine Hunt. 'The story goes that he was very favourably received by Mr Hunt and his wife, and was shown into the drawing-room where the young ladies were, with permission to make a choice, and his fancy fell upon Miss Catherine, or "Catty" as she was commonly called. The etiquette of the time, or at least then in use for making proposals of marriage, was that a walk round the garden being agreed upon, the gentleman took the opportunity to make his proposals in due form, it is said, and most probably the story is told by the good lady herself that Mr White on this occasion amongst other speeches said: "I don't think it likely that a young lady like you will fancy a man of my age and appearance" (he was thirty-seven and rather a small man, she about twenty and a fine tall graceful young woman) "but I know that if you refuse me, your father and mother will be very angry with you, and you will get into trouble on my account, now that is what I wish to save you from, so tell me candidly if you cannot like me, and I will break off the match myself on some other account, and you shall have no blame or trouble whatever." This honest and manly speech won her heart. He was accepted, and they were married in the year 1757. They lived together as man and wife for forty-three years, and she survived him about twenty-six years.' So says the family chronicle.

John Fitzgibbon, Earl of Clare, who is usually quoted on the subject of Unionism reported other abductions as late as 1797, writing to his friend Lord Auckland: 'Sir Henry Hayes and Murphy were indicted and tried on the same statute, each with carrying off a woman by force with intent to marry her. Murphy succeeded in ravishing his lady. Sir Henry Hayes attempted to ravish his lady but did not succeed because the cock would not fight, and after standing out all legal process for five years and bidding defiance to two proclamations offering a reward of £500 for apprehending him, he was at last brought to trial, found guilty and respited by Mr Day upon a silly doubt in his mind on a point of law. Poor Murphy had been hanged and Sir Henry Hayes has been pardoned. Another poor wretch of the name of Lupton was hanged almost at the same time upon the same statute. His crime was assisting a friend in carrying off a woman whom he wished to marry. And certainly if ever any crime deserved punishment in a civilised country Mr Murphy's, Sir Henry's and Mr Lupton's did merit it. But it will be difficult to persuade the lower orders of the people that equal justice has been administered to rich and poor.'

All over Ireland there were small pockets of peacefulness and industry where the resident landlord was conscientious—as at Edgeworthstown—or in Huguenot or Quaker communities. These left their traces principally in the midlands where they built neat houses and engaged in lace-making and other crafts. Edmund Burke went to school at Ballitore, run by Shackleton, a Quaker, with whose family he formed a lifelong friendship and correspondence. These were estimable people. The La Touches, Huguenots, settled in Wicklow, ancestors of the girl who caught the eccentric fancy of John Ruskin, were such another family. The La Touches originated a bank which was the parent of the Bank of Ireland, in which a beautiful ceiling from the old bank may be seen. In St Stephen's Green in Dublin there are two splendid La Touche houses. Names like Goodbody and Pim are still prominent; and those that bear them have contributed to the prosperity of Ireland ever since they took refuge here. The linen industry in Northern Ireland is of Huguenot origin.

It would be erroneous to see Irish society in the eighteenth century through Barrington's eyes exclusively. But it would not be unreasonable to say that the craftsmen and merchants who contributed all that was useful, beautiful and permanent served a society that was to a great extent extravagant and irresponsible.

Swift painted a vivid picture of the clergy when he said that:
'Excellent and moral men have been selected on every occasion of vacancy. But it has unfortunately uniformly happened that as these worthy divines cross Hounslow Heath on their way to Ireland to take possession of their bishoprics, they have been

regularly robbed and murdered by highwaymen frequenting that common, who seized upon their robes and patents, come over to Ireland, and are consecrated bishops in their stead.'

Barrington's *Sketches* contain a portrait of one who was possibly more representative of the legendary Anglo-Irish than any I have mentioned. Beauchamp Bagenal of Dunleckney in County Carlow is described as:

'Domesticated in his own mansion at Dunleckney, surrounded by a numerous and devoted tenantry, and possessed of a great and productive territory, Mr Bagenal determined to spend the residue of his days on his native soil according to the usages and customs of country gentlemen, and he was shortly afterwards returned a representative of Parliament for the County Carlow by universal acclamation. He was one of the first country gentlemen who raised a volunteer regiment in the County of Carlow. He commanded several military corps, and was one of the last volunteer colonels in Ireland who could be persuaded upon to discontinue the reviews of their regiments, or to relinquish that noble, patriotic and unprecedented institution.'

It was he who proposed in parliament that Grattan should be awarded £50,000 for his services to the Irish nation. We get another glimpse of him in O'Neill Daunt's *Ireland and Her Agitators*.

'Enthroned at Dunleckney, he gathered around him a host of spirits congenial to his own. He had a tender affection for pistols; a brace of which implements, loaded, were often laid before him on the dinner-table. After dinner the claret was produced in an unbroached cask; Bagenal's practice was to tap the cask with a bullet from one of his pistols, whilst he kept the other pistol *in terrorem* for any of the *convives* who should fail in doing ample justice to the wine.

'Nothing could be more impressive than the bland, fatherly, affectionate air with which the old gentleman used to impart to his junior guests the results of his own experience, and the moral lessons which should regulate their conduct through life.

' "In truth, my young friends, it behoves a youth entering the world to make a character for himself. Respect will only be accorded to character. A young man must show his proofs. I am not a quarrelsome person—I never was—I hate your mere duellist; but experience of the world tells me that there are knotty points of which the only solution is the saw-handle. Rest upon your pistols, my boys. Occasions will arise in which the use of them is absolutely indispensable to character. A man, I repeat, must show his proofs—in this world courage will never be taken upon trust. I protest to heaven, my dear young friends, that I advise you as I should advise my own son."'

Mary Leadbetter, daughter of Burke's Quaker schoolmaster, met him once.

'My father and mother, with others of their families, were by special invitation at the house of their landlord, Clayton Bayley, at Gowran, when Beauchamp Bagenal and a young man of the Butler family, who had dined at Lord Clifden's, came in a state of intoxication to the house. Clayton Bayley was very unwilling to be intruded upon while enjoying the company of his former preceptor; and his wife was greatly distressed, for she was certain that wicked Bagenal would insist that her husband must drink with him all night, or else fight him. It was in vain our host insisted that he was "not at home", which he firmly maintained malgré the lectures of his old mistress; he was at length obliged to appear and as an apology for not receiving them to inform Bagenal that he had Quaker guests in his house. This Bagenal declared was an inducement to him to desire admission, for of all things he loved Quakers. He entered on crutches, having been lately hurt in a duel; and though disfigured by lameness and obscured by intoxication, the grace of his form and the beauty of his countenance were so conspicuous as to excite in no small degree the mingled sensations of admiration, pity and regret . . . It was to my mother that Bagenal addressed his conversation. He repeated his declaration of affection to the Society of Friends, and assured her that he agreed with them in sentiments: and wished to belong to their body, "only that he could not in that case retain his corps of Volunteers".'

CHAPTER V

The Eye of the Stranger

JOHN WESLEY IS not usually consulted as an authority on Ireland in his time, but he came in 1747 and returned on a few occasions, travelling the whole country. His habit of preaching at five o'clock in the morning did not deter his audience although he sometimes expressed doubts about it himself. The explanation is probably this: Wesley's appeal was mainly to the artisan class and they worked from about six o'clock until late in the evening, six days a week.

He records that on arrival he was given 'a genuine account' of the massacre of Protestants in the 1641 rebellion; more than two hundred thousand men, women and children butchered within a few months. 'It is well if God has not a controversy with the nation, on this very account, to this day.' But the most brutal behaviour he himself encountered in Ireland was in Cork, when a local bully, 'a ballad maker', called Butler, organised a terror against Methodists and the authorities showed no great energy in bringing him to heel.

Cork always sounds a 'very Irish' county, but it has played a large part in religious controversy because it was favoured by English settlers. This is Somerville and Ross country. Here Masonry and, for a time, Orangeism were strong. It was the fear—perhaps irrational—of massacre by Orange elements from Cork that drove the people of Wexford into rebellion in 1798 on such a scale and accounts, in part, for their own savagery on that occasion.

But to return to Wesley. Walking about Dublin he discovers that the town has scarcely any public building except the Parliament house, which is at all remarkable. The churches are 'poor and mean'; St Stephen's Green badly kept and surrounded by houses some 'low and bad' and all irregular (but Mrs Delany, in 1731, said the square was to be preferred to any in London). Nor was Wesley much impressed by Trinity College, to which the library had recently been added. A year later he was back again and travelling without molestation round the country. In the country towns he notices frequently soldiers among his hearers. At Easter, in Athlone, he had 'an abundance of Papists', who flocked to hear him. Their priest came in person 'at six' and drove them away 'before him like a flock of sheep'. The Captain of the Dragoons sportingly offered to lay him in irons, and when an egg was thrown in the window, 'about the middle of the sermon', the soldiers were 'full as warm as himself' and the whole congregation were on the point of pulling down the house.

At Clara he competed successfully with the rival attraction of a cock-fight. In Athlone he preached on the Connaught side of the bridge to an audience that included Catholics, the priest, finding they were not to be persuaded to leave, stayed to listen himself.

While he was preaching in Birr, a Carmelite friar interrupted, 'You lie. You lie.' The zealous Protestants cried out 'Knock him down'. And the suggestion was acted upon immediately. In several places he speaks of Papists and Romanists in the congregation, and in Dublin where someone accused him of being a Jesuit, a priest in the audience replied aloud 'No, he is not; I would to God he was.'

At Mardyke in Limerick he addressed an audience of about two thousand people none of whom were observed 'either to laugh, or to look about'. In the afternoon he walked round the walls of the town and remarked that the walls were 'very sufficient to keep out the wild Irish.' A meeting in Cork had to be abandoned for fear of riots organised by Protestants. In the midlands he was favourably received, in Mountmellick, a Quaker settlement, and in Portarlington, 'a town inhabited chiefly by French'.

Indifference was his chief complaint against his audience. 'Oh what a harvest might be in Ireland did not the poor Protestants hate Christianity worse than either Popery or Heathenism.'

In 1773 Wesley returned to Ireland. The Methodists, in the meanwhile, had no easy time of it. Their historian stated that 'a Methodist preacher could not pass through the Protestant town of Enniskillen without endangering his life'.

But in Southern Ireland conditions were milder. In Eyrecourt

Wesley was assured that 'a great awakening had been in the town lately; and many of the most notorious and profligate sinners are entirely changed and are happy witnesses of the gospel salvation.' I hope he was not deceived in this.

In Galway, at that date, he was told there were twenty thousand Papists and five hundred Protestants. The town, of course, was in exclusive Protestant control. Wesley was indifferent to their sects. 'But which of them are Christians, have the mind that was in Christ, and walk as He walked?' The congregation behaved well but 'at the last hymn one of Satan's children came with a great roar, as if he had just come from Hell; but a gentleman laid hold of him and showed him the near way to the door.' He hoped 'he would see some fruit, even in cold, barren Sligo'. But when he crossed the border into Ulster he encountered the fanatical temper which religious differences arouse in the keen northern air. Some masons (stone not free) gave him 'coarse words' on the bridge at Enniskillen; and he had 'an abundance more as he rode through the town'. But soldiers protected the missionary party from the mob. The road was blocked, and a man who attempted to clear the way, was plastered with dirt and mortar. The coach was attacked, but the aim of the stone-throwers was not sufficiently effective, and the coachman escaped unhurt. In Roosky, the next town, the windows of the coach were broken. Wesley was matchlessly brave. One of his preachers had been beaten senseless when dragged out of a house a few months before his own visit. The Grand Jury always threw out all bills against anti-Methodist rioters. 'But where', Wesley asked himself, 'is liberty, civil or religious? Does it exist in Aghalon or Enniskillen?' In Derry he received a hospitable welcome from the Bishop, the splendid Marquis of Bristol, who had lavished money on buildings in the town; and in Armagh he had the good fortune to run into another Englishman who did even better for the Cathedral city. Primate Robinson's judicious patronage of architects, first of Cooley, later of Johnston, can be seen in Armagh—a delightful city—one day, perhaps, the capital of a united Ireland. Its two cathedrals, one Protestant, one Catholic, face one another, a confrontation that embalms the religious history of Ireland.

Robinson told Wesley of his plans to improve the town, and

Wesley confided to his diary that he wondered if the old gentleman would live long enough. He lived, in fact, another twenty years. In the evening the visitor preached to the largest congregation he had met in Ulster; 'and I believed, for the present, all were convinced that nothing will avail without humble, gentle patient love.'

Were Wesley to return, two hundred years having passed in the meanwhile, he might say that again. Before leaving Dublin for ever—Wesley was seventy at this time—he asked leave of the commanding officer to preach in the barracks, 'but he replied he would have no innovations. No: whoredom, drunkenness, cursing and swearing for ever!'

On the voyage back to England Wesley read a history of Ireland (Leland's) and refused to agree with all the author's conclusions.

'I can easily believe that the Irish were originally Tartars or Scythians, though calling at Spain on their way; but not that they were a jot less barbarous than their descendants in Scotland; or that ever they were a civilised nation till they were civilised by the English; much less that Ireland was, in the seventh or eighth century, the grand seat of learning—that it had many famous colleges, in one of which, only, Armagh, there were seven thousand students.'

In more joyful moods, Wesley's journals contain flattering references to the character of the inhabitants.

Wesley, it may be said in passing, was distantly related to the Duke of Wellington's family; and the Wellesleys or Wesleys at Dangan, having no children, had offered to adopt John's brother, Charles as their heir. The offer was refused, and a Colley cousin filled the vacancy and took on the name.

Wesley was not impressed by Dublin, neither was James Gandon when he arrived in 1781 having been commissioned by Beresford to build a new custom house. 'In traversing a city of such large extent, the capital of a kingdom, I was greatly surprised to find but one print-shop. There were two others in which prints were sold, but their trade was that of glaziers. The few houses to which I had access scarcely possessed a picture or print, and those which they had were but indifferent, mostly suspended from the wall, without either frame or glass. Hence, I concluded that the Fine Arts were little attended to, and the profession not much respected. I afterward found this to be the case: there were few painters of eminence, and but two architects, properly so called. The painters were Home, Wheatley, and Hone in portrait; Ashford and Fisher in landscape; but these last two gentlemen depended more for their income on places which they held, than on the result of their professional labours. But it was no wonder that the polite arts should not prosper in a country continually in a political ferment, and where most of the families of distinction seemed wholly employed in converting their political influence into sources of family or personal aggrandisement. The polite arts, or their professors, can obtain little notice and less encouragement amidst such conflicting selfishness. A stranger, indeed, on a visit to Ireland, if his stay be short, will find every possible attention to render his reception agreeable, but should he become a resident he will perceive a cold indifference and neglect, and, like many of its highly-gifted natives, must seek for permanent encouragement and celebrity in England.

'The architects of reputation were Cooley and Ivory. Amongst the public buildings, particularly the churches, few showed anything like an attempt at style, and only two of them had steeples, viz., St Patrick's and Werburgh's. The House of Commons was the chief among the public buildings. The Royal Exchange next, which was then but recently finished. The Blue Coat Hospital was then nearly completed. The Lying-in Hospital had been erected several years previous. There were no halls belonging to public companies; and, with the exception of the Duke of Leinster's, the Marquis of Waterford's, the Earl of Charlemont's and Viscount Powercourt's, there were scarcely any other houses which bore the marks of the residence of the nobility. There were but four collections of pictures of consequence; these were the Duke of Leinster's, the Earl of Farnham's, the Earl of Charlemont's, and Lord Londonderry's. The houses of the gentry were generally inconvenient in their plans, having in most cases but two rooms on a floor, and these adapted for large parties, and as to architectural style, in embellishment, or finish, they were very imperfect. But such must ever be the case where professional architects are not employed, and that was the practice here. The propensity for building was so general, that all professions embarked in it; even the gentry were almost always their own architects; therefore, skill in arrangement or good work was not to be expected. The parties whom they got to contract for the building were generally poor journeymen, who, when left to themselves, were wholly ignorant of the true value of what they undertook to execute; and in the scramble for employment the prices were so low, that they were in many instances more impoverished than benefited by the job; in addition to all which, when the works were completed, instead of receiving cash according to promise, they were constrained to take bills at six or twelve months as a settlement of their accounts. This led to endless petty differences for debts contracted during the work, by those very incompetent contractors, and the poor wretches whom they employed to assist them.'

Gandon was to encounter considerable opposition as well as technical and practical difficulties while the work was in progress. There was a labour shortage for one thing, and when he imported workers from England they had to take an oath of secrecy, subscribe a guinea, and submit to the laws of combination. But in the end the English workers turned out to be even more troublesome, particularly in the article of drinking too much.

Gandon has long since been regarded as the first among the architects who have worked in Ireland; but it is disillusioning to find that good taste in Georgian Ireland was not as general as we should like to believe. Political passions no doubt influenced Grattan to attack Beresford for wasting public money on building the Custom House; but we blush for him when he said that it represented sixth-rate taste in architecture and 'stands a blemish in the eye of the island'.

But Gandon gives a rather jaundiced picture of the Dublin he saw. It had come on a great deal since Wesley last saw it. Gandon was to complete the Custom House and the Four Courts in the next decade, and these, it is generally agreed, are the finest of Dublin's public buildings. He designed the King's Inns, but did not complete the building, retiring from the task, vexed by the importunities of his employers. He made additions to the

Parliament buildings, built by Pearce, an architect of genius who died before the celebrity to which he was entitled came to him.

The history of Dublin's architecture has been told so well by Maurice Craig in his book on the City that I shall not attempt to encroach on territory to which he has staked so authoritative a claim; and I am only concerned with it in so far as it throws light on the Anglo-Irish. The dates of the various buildings show us that trade improved considerably and continued to improve after Swift and Berkeley wrote their Irish tracts. Wesley's visit marked the turn in the middle of the century.

Gandon, as we saw, had little respect for the work of gentlemanly amateurs; but if he were to come back he might admit that an era in which the professional architect is in constant requisition shows a dramatic falling off in taste. The Gardiner family, on the North side of the city, the Fitzwilliams on the south, Lord Charlemont, Primate Robinson in Armagh, Hervey in Derry—these were all men of discernment. The artificers, as a rule, came from abroad; but the Stapletons, Smyths and others showed that there was native talent when it was brought out. The best idea of what was achieved in Dublin is recorded for posterity in Malton's views of Dublin. A set of these is now hard to come by and very expensive if you do; and yet I can remember someone saying of a house in which they were all on display that 'it looked like a dentist's waiting-room'.

Lord Fitzwilliam employed James Ensor to plan Merrion Square in 1762, and that is possibly the date we should choose as the birthday of Georgian Dublin. The squares in the north of the city have been allowed to rot, and St Stephen's Green has suffered appalling depredations in the last decade. Molesworth and Kildare Streets are doomed. Harcourt Street, miraculously, still stands. Merrion Square is spoiled at one corner; when it all goes Dublin will have lost its character and will become another modern city embellished with a more than average number of historic *public* buildings.

If we agree on 1762, then it must be admitted that there were many additions even after the Union: not only three splendid railway stations and Catholic churches which, at last, the law allowed, but most of the work of Francis Johnston. Archbishop

Robinson used Johnston to great purpose in Armagh, but in Dublin his work may be seen in the General Post Office, the Chapel Royal and St George's Church, which recalls London's St Martin-in-the-Fields. All these were built after the Union; and Fitzwilliam Square, long after. The quaint Harcourt Terrace belongs to 1840, and in the Dun Laoghaire area (when it was called Kingstown) there was a large development when people began to live further out of town; it is significant that it was here the first Irish railway was constructed.

Roads with names such as Anglesey, Wellington and Waterloo tell their own story. All of these were built when the heroes and events they commemorate were fresh in memory. Towards the end of the Victorian era taste suffered the same decay as elsewhere. Commerce was in command. Insurance companies have done as much to spoil the appearance of Dublin as any single hostile force. It would not be altogether fair to blame the neglect of the City's architectural heritage or the ugliness of its later buildings to the coming to power of Sinn Féin. The Dublin Victorians allowed the slums to happen. It was not England's fault. It would have happened most likely under any government.

CHAPTER VI

Theobald Wolfe Tone

So far we have seen the Anglo-Irish as loyal to their mother country; but in Ireland, as in America, with increased prosperity and in accordance with a natural reaction against servility, a spirit of independence grew up among the Colonists. It is usual to trace the history of protest through Swift, Lucas, Molyneux, Grattan, and then, in the next century, O'Connell and Parnell. Parnell's successors were never to see the Home Rule they sought actually implemented. It was granted in theory in 1914, but the Act was never made law. Then came the Rising of 1916. Martyrs were made, and after the Act violence became the hallowed course and the patriot's way. Patrick Pearse, who was executed after the suppression of the Rising, has been avoided as a subject for biography by a generation that Freud has informed or corrupted. An early effort by a pious Breton drew freely on the analogy of the Crucifixion, likening the last acts of Pearse to the Stations of the Cross.

The analogy breaks down over one significant detail. Christ ordered Peter to put up his sword when he submitted to his captors.

Pearse's successors sanctioned in his name the methods of guerrilla warfare and terrorism, for which there are no precedents in the Gospels. Lively would be the imagination that could detect any resemblance between the Apostles and the IRA.

One result of the cultivation of violence is to depreciate the patriots who relied on methods of persuasion. O'Connell is not a hero even to Irish Catholic youth. The name of Edmund Burke means nothing in Ireland. And Grattan, to whom every succeeding generation looked up as the architect of Irish freedom, who dominated the life of the Irish parliament for the last and brightest period of its existence—Grattan is forgotten.

All his patriotism counts for nothing because of his double loyalty, and his strict adherence to constitutionalism. The place that he held in the heart of nationalists is now taken by Wolfe Tone. The metamorphosis would have amazed O'Connell. When asked who was the greatest Irishman he answered, 'Why, after me, I suppose old Harry Grattan was.' O'Connell knew Grattan and he was Tone's contemporary; the idea of even comparing them would, to his mind, have been risible or, possibly, offensive. To O'Connell, the overthrow of the parliamentary tradition, and the acceptance of revolution as the only valid mode of national progress would have been simply a vote for public crime. He would have pointed out that the only certain result of the plot in which Wolfe Tone and the United Irishmen were engaged was thirty thousand people dead in the Irish countryside.

O'Connell called off his own greatest demonstration at Clontary in 1843 when he saw Wellington's cannon trained on his followers. Little did he think that if he had given the signal at which hundreds would have fallen, he would be now revered as one who had manured the soil of Ireland with the blood of martyrs.

He did not give the signal, and as a result he has no place in the living Irish imagination.

Meanwhile Theobald Wolfe Tone grows yearly in stature. He is accepted as the John the Baptist—if not the Mahomet—of Irish Republicanism; and so many factions wish to identify themselves with him that it has become the practice to celebrate his birthday on successive Sundays: Government and respectable folk come one day, IRA and their motley following on another. There is a certain licence given to the occasion. The most treasonable utterances have a Hyde Park immunity when uttered at the grave of Wolfe Tone.

In claiming him as the founder of Republicanism, a doctrine which everyone in politics professes—giving the word, in each case, some significance of their own—it is accepted by all that Tone represents Irish rebellion at its most fundamental. In comparison with Tone's philosophy, Anglo-Irish patriotism from Swift to Grattan is merely colonialist capitalist discontent, and essentially self-regarding.

Tone and his principal colleagues were of the same racial origins as Grattan, and none of them as long established in Ireland as the ancestors of Burke. Both these great men saw eye to eye on Irish affairs. The difference between the two sets of patriots in Ireland was not racial; it was the same division as in England. It depended on how one saw the French Revolution. Burke stands in relation to Tone in Ireland as he stood to Fox in England. There was only this difference: Fox lived in a free country. It is not without significance that Fox's first cousin, Lord Edward FitzGerald, was to have led the army of the United Irishmen in 1798. But their ill-kept secrets were all betrayed to the Government well in advance.

Of all the conspirators the most attractive personally was Wolfe Tone. He lacked the solid qualities that made Thomas Addis Emmet, in exile, the leader of the New York bar. He was not a virtuous man as Whitley Stokes was, who resigned from the United Irishmen when he foresaw the bloodshed their activities would inevitably bring about. But he had a frankness and gaiety (manifest in his diaries) which are—and were—irresistible to men (and women). It is a large claim that he is the most attractive of all diarists; but I think it could be made. Certainly a man would prefer to spend an evening in his company than in Boswell's or Pepys'; and to an invitation from all three any woman would give Tone's the preference. His personality has such light and shade. He was, said Barrington (who knew him), too light for the bar. He certainly hated the profession and all that went with it. His dreams were of glory, 'of breaches, ambuscadoes, Spanish blades'.

With no pretensions to taste or learning, he had an instinctive preference for the best, and even his comments on the theatre in London and Paris have an almost startling contemporariness about them.

I choose him of the conspirators because he illustrates the character of the Anglo-Irish in its most attractive form and bears out my contention that Trinity College was a remarkable fosterer of talent.

A coach-maker's son, in uneasy circumstances, he had no pretensions to birth; but he mixed naturally with the aristocrats whom he encountered in his short, brilliant political career. Those were days when one was either an aristocrat or democrat. Your bible was Burke or Paine. Tone was a democrat; the *Rights of Man* was his bible.

In many ways that period is closer to our own than the century that followed it. Fox, too, sounds like a contemporary. We speak the language of Fox and Tone. Reaction set in, and their kind only peeped out again when Victoria began to dodder and Albert was safely dead.

His first love was the wife of Richard Martin of Galway—'Humanity Dick' (the Martins are never out of the picture for long). She was two years older than Tone and they met in lodgings in Dublin. Martin had his family's craze for the theatre and fitted up one in which his wife acted with success. Tone also acquitted himself with credit.

'Mrs Martin, independent of a thousand other attractions, was one of the first actresses I ever saw, and as I lived in the house with her, and being myself somewhat of an actor, was daily thrown into particular situations with her, both in rehearsals and on the stage, and as I had an imagination easily warmed, without one grain of discretion to regulate it, I very soon became in love to a degree almost inconceivable. I have never, never met in history, poetry, or romance a description that comes near what I actually suffered on her account. For two years our acquaintance continued, in which time I made three visits to her house of four or five months each. As I was utterly unable, and indeed unwilling, to conceal my passion from her, she very soon detected me, and as I preserved, as well as felt, the profoundest respect for her, she supposed she might amuse herself innocently in observing the progress of this terrible passion in the mind of an interesting young man of twenty; but this is an experiment no woman ought to make. As Martin neglected her a good deal, and as I was continually on the spot, she could not avoid making daily comparisons between our behaviour towards her, and not at all to the advantage of her husband; in short, without any art on my side, for I was too sincerely in love to be capable of it, I invisibly engaged her affections, so that at length she became at least as much in love with me as I was with her, nor did she attempt to conceal it from me.

'I was the proudest man alive to have engaged the affections of a woman whom even now I recognise to have had extraordinary merit, and who then appeared in my eyes more divine than human. In this intercourse of sentiment which alternately pained and delighted me almost beyond bearing, we continued for about two years, keeping up a regular correspondence by letters in the intervals of my absence, without, however, in a single instance overstepping the bounds of virtue, such was the purity of the extravagant affection I bore her.'

The romance ended over a curious quarrel between husband and lover which had nothing to do with Mrs Martin.

Tone's marriage was in keeping with his first romance. Walking with other college youths in Grafton Street he caught the eye of a pretty girl at a window. Whenever he passed by he looked up and she was always there, looking down. He found out her name, discovered her brother, introduced himself and gained admittance to the house. 'One beautiful morning in the month of July we ran off together and were married.' The bride was only sixteen. She proved, as wife and mother, a woman of incomparable staunchness. And she was very pretty.

Having got him a wife, Tone set about thinking of ways of supporting her. He had never been studious. His chief diversion was to go to Phoenix Park and watch military parades. But he crossed to London to make himself a barrister. There he entered his name at the Middle Temple. His was a nature that liked quick results; it suddenly occurred to him that to take over a South Sea island and found a colony which would 'put a bridle on Spain in time of peace' and 'annoy her grievously' in time of war would be more fun than work in the law library. He drew up a memorial; and left it on Mr Pitt at 10 Downing Street. The Prime Minister sent no acknowledgement: Tone swore revenge. He thought of going to India, but there was no ship. He had to stay at his books. 'At the age of four and twenty, with a tolerable figure and address, in an idle and luxurious Capital, it will not be supposed that I was without adventures with the fair sex. The English neglect their wives exceedingly in many essential circumstances.'

At length he returned, fitted to earn a living at the bar; but the work bored him. Then politics gave him an opening. Grattan, Charlemont and Ponsonby founded the Whig Club, under the remote control of Burke from England. They agreed to let Tone write a pamphlet for them: 'A review of the last session of Parliament'. He won the attention of Sir Lawrence Parsons, afterwards Earl of Rosse—'an old friend' he describes him, and 'one of the very, very few, honest men in the Irish House of Commons'.

But now he began to look with contempt on the 'little politics' of the Whig Club, 'their peddling about petty grievances'. Before he could push his designs further his affairs were interrupted by a falling out with his wife's family, who had been supporting her.

Now followed happy days with congenial friends 'in a little box' at Irishtown, where he lived near the sea, for the sake of his wife's health. It was the last carefree period of his life. His next employment was with the Catholic Committee, newly risen in influence. They had been a very tame body under the eminently safe leadership of Lord Kenmare. Now they began to breathe the atmosphere of revolt and their new leader, John Keogh, was a man of strong personality. Burke managed to secure the secretaryship of the Committee for his darling son; but Richard Burke was a failure. He was paid £2,000 to go away and Tone succeeded him. Tone's next pamphlet had a circulation of 10,000. It recommended him to the Dissenters in Northern Ireland, who were now on fire with the doctrines of the French Revolution.

There, in 1791, he and a group of friends formed the United Irishmen, a brotherhood which at first was almost exclusively Protestant, and operated in Northern Ireland largely through Masonic lodges, causing disruption in that order.

Thomas Emmet, to whom Tone referred always in terms of deep regard, admitted after the revolution that, even after the French expedition to Bantry in 1795, if the Government had given any reasonable hope of reform, he would have persuaded the Committee to send a message to France to say differences between the people and the Government were adjusted. But the proximity of a French invasion stirred up such a ferment in the North and the newly-recruited yeomen acted with such savagery against the Catholics there (who retaliated savagely) that events got out of control. General Lake by butcher tactics suppressed the

United Irishmen in the North, and that province took little part in the eventual rebellion.

In all that followed Tone was out of the country. In 1794 he involved himself with one Jackson, who was discovered with incriminating papers on him—an intrigue with France. At this point Fitzgibbon intervened. The Chancellor was in some way connected with Mrs Tone's family, and that, or a good nature which history does not credit him with, prompted him to intervene for Tone and give him an opportunity to escape. But before they parted company he obtained admissions which, if produced, could hang Tone if he ever came back to Ireland.

Tone nourished no gratitude for Fitzgibbon, but admitted that he preferred his rough honesty to the shilly-shallying of lukewarm friends of liberty.

Tone and his family went to America in an overcrowded ship which was boarded three times en route by British sailors who 'after treating us with the greatest insolence, both officers and sailors, they pressed every one of our hands, save one, and near fifty of my unfortunate fellow-passengers . . .'

But the life of a farmer in Philadelphia did not appeal to Tone.

'For myself I believe I could have borne it, and for my wife it was sufficient to her that I was with her, her incomparable firmness of mind and never-failing equanimity of temper sustaining her and me also, whose happiness depended solely on hers under every difficulty. But when we looked on our little children, we felt both of us our courage fail. Our little boys we could hardly bear to think of rearing in the Boorish ignorance of the peasants about us, and to what purpose give them an education that could only tend to discontent them with the state wherein they were thrown, and wherein learning and talents were useless? But especially our little girl, now eight or nine years old, was our principal uneasiness. How could we bear to see her the wife of a clown without delicacy or refinement, incapable to feel or estimate the value of a mind which had already developed the strongest marks of sensibility and tenderness. For my part the idea tormented me beyond enduring, and I am sure no unfortunate lover, in the paroxysms of jealousy, ever looked forward with horror to the union of his mistress with a rival that I did to the probability of seeing my darling child sacrificed to one of the Boors by whom we were surrounded. I could better bear to see her dead, for with regard to the delicacy and purity of women I entertain notions perhaps extravagant in their refinement.'

We meet him next in France, and there he conducted without assistance negotiations with the Government, with Hoche (who led the expedition to Bantry) and even Napoleon. At that time the future Emperor was twenty-six, a few years younger than his colleagues. Tone describes him at their first meeting:

'He is about five feet six inches high, slender, and well made, but stoops considerably; he looks at least ten years older than he is, owing to the great fatigues he underwent in his immortal campaign of Italy. His face is that of a profound thinker, but bears no marks of that great enthusiasm and unceasing activity by which he has been so much distinguished. It is rather to my mind, the countenance of a mathematician than of a General. He has a fine eye, and a great firmness about his mouth; he speaks low and hollow.'

In France, though lonely, Tone was circumspect. To while away the days of anxious, empty waiting for news from the French authorities, who dallied over plans for invasion, he wrote his autobiography and kept diaries, the length of two average-sized novels. Sometimes he went to the theatre—when he arrived in France he found that his 'music was better than his French'. He avoided all attachments, but he could never entirely avoid romantic occasions. There was one time in a church in Cologne when 'there happened to be no one in the place but myself, and as I was gazing about, I perceived the corner of a green silk curtain behind a thick iron lattice lifted up, and some one behind it. I drew near, in order to discover who it might be, and it proved to be a nun, young I am sure, and I believe handsome, for I saw only her mouth and chin, but a more beautiful mouth I never saw. We continued gazing on one another in this manner for five minutes, when a villainous overgrown friar, entering to say his mass, put her to rout.'

That must be one of the shortest love stories in the world.

The young nun went back to her solitary gloom; very soon Tone was on a French ship of the line. 'During six hours she sustained the fire of a whole fleet, till her masts and rigging were swept away, her scuppers flowed with blood, her wounded filled the cockpit, her shattered ribs yawned at each new stroke and let in five feet of water in the hold.' During the battle Tone commanded one of the batteries—the ship was surrounded—and 'fought with the utmost desperation, and as if he was courting death'.

Recognised on landing by Sir George Hill, who had been at Trinity with him, Tone, in the uniform of a French officer, was put in irons and sent to Dublin. At his trial he disowned all the crimes that had then and have since been committed in his name.

'Under the flag of the French Republic I originally engaged with a view to save and liberate my own country. For that purpose I have encountered the chances of war amongst strangers: for that purpose I have repeatedly braved the terrors of the ocean, covered, as I knew it to be, with the triumphant fleets of that Power which it was my glory and duty to oppose. I have sacrificed all my views in life; I have courted poverty; I have left a beloved wife unprotected, and children whom I adored, fatherless. After such sacrifices, in a cause which I have always conscientiously considered as the cause of justice and freedom—it is no great effort, at this day, to add "the sacrifice of my life".

'But I hear it said that this unfortunate country has been a prey to all sorts of horrors. I sincerely lament it. I beg, however, it may be remembered that I have been absent four years from Ireland. To me these sufferings can never be attributed. I designed by fair and open war to procure the separation of the two countries. For open war I was prepared; but if, instead of that, a system of private assassination has taken place, I repeat, whilst I deplore it, that it is not chargeable on me. Atrocities, it seems, have been committed on both sides. I do not less deplore them; I detest them from my heart; and to those who know my character and sentiments I may safely appeal for the truth of this assertion. With them I need no justification'.

To avoid the ignominy of hanging, he cut his throat in prison.

Nothing illustrates better the conditions of the time than the comment on this by his former Trinity friend, Sir George Hill, to Cooke, the Under-Secretary at Dublin Castle.

'I have received an accurate note of all which passed in King's Bench on Curran's motion *re* Tone. The business has been bitched. The authority of Parliament, the actual existence of Rebellion and Invasion, should have induced a refusal to obey the King's Bench, and execution ought to have taken place. I would have sewn up his neck and finished the business . . .'

Only an abysmal lack of historical perspective can equate the attitude of men like Tone with that of the IRA today. No doubt, in any society, Tone would have been against 'the establishment'. Not least because it stood in the way of his dreams of glory. He dearly loved his country, hated England, wanted independence for Ireland, but for himself and his family he also looked for Dick Whittington's reward. He was not of the type of the social reformer, and would have been closer by instinct to Trotsky than Lenin. A commission in a British Cavalry regiment when he was twenty-one might have seen him leading a charge against the French at Waterloo.

In discussions with members of the French Directory he confessed that he did not want bloodshed, but he was afraid that an inevitable result of invasion would be a massacre of the aristocracy (the French were alarmed at the prospect). He saw an end to the great estates of the absentees; but that was because of their ill-doing. What is anachronistic in the thinking of those who invoke his name is the assumption that he would enjoy what Ferguson was to call 'a plebianising' of society or seek any form of State ownership. He would have been much happier in Drury Lane, in the stalls, with Sheridan—whom he resembled in so many ways—than planning gelignite explosions with proletarian gunmen in Belfast.

CHAPTER VII

The First Unionist

IF WOLFE TONE may stand as the protagonist of Irish Republicanism, there can be no debate about whom we choose to represent the opposing tendency.

There were, at the close of the eighteenth century (if we omit the Presbyterians of Northern Ireland and the mass of the Irish people elsewhere) three political forces. Those attached to the English interest who composed the executive and filled all the great offices of State; the patriots among whom Grattan was pre-eminent; and the revolutionaries: almost as abhorrent to one as to the other constitutional party.

'Castle hacks', was Shaw's name for the successors of the establishment men. But in Shaw's time they had become lackeys. They were not at all like the formidable John Fitzgibbon.

The hero of the present establishment in the six counties of Northern Ireland is Edward Carson, and if we compare his career with that of the chief Irish architect of the Union, John Fitzgibbon, the analogy is not without instruction. It is not a coincidence that Colvin in the third volume of Carson's *Life* writes:

'Such ethnical generalisations are dangerous; but it is possible that the best part of the Irish people are of crossed blood, and it is certain that Carson belonged both by blood and tradition to that class or race among whom we number such great Irishmen as Castlereagh and John Fitzgibbon, who devoted themselves to a British cause believing that there lay the good of Ireland.'

Of the three names Castlereagh's is the most generally execrated in Ireland, as he is not given credit for any Irish feelings, but is seen as an ambitious politician on a larger stage, who came to Dublin as Chief Secretary to put the Union through, by means fair or foul, solely in the interests of England. As the great mass of the Irish population never entered into his consideration at all—

we can be sure of that—he may well have thought that he was also acting in the best interests of the former ruling class in Ireland. If so, it was by the way.

I prefer to take Fitzgibbon as a protagonist. His whole career had been in Dublin. He had been as successful as a lawyer could be in Ireland, as Attorney-General dominating the House of Commons, as Chancellor, of the Lords. His name denotes that he came from Norman stock, later designated 'Old English', and the family were Catholics, living in Clare, reduced, in his grandfather's time, to humble circumstances. Fitzgibbon's father rose to great eminence at the Bar, amassed a very large fortune, having turned Protestant to do so. No Catholic could practise as a barrister at that time. John, his favourite son, was a school-fellow of Grattan, and his contemporary in Trinity College. Both belonged to the generation which had developed, under the stimulus of rising prosperity, a sense of separate nationality, closely parallel to the American colonists, and inspired by the same grievances. Grattan recommended Fitzgibbon's candidature as Attorney-General and ignored the warning of Denis Daly, 'that little fellow will deceive you all'.

Fitzgibbon certainly surprised Grattan. Although continuing to say that the idea of a Union was intolerable, he set himself so completely against concessions to Catholics that he embarrassed his English supporters, and on two significant occasions Pitt's government kept Fitzgibbon out of the secret when their designs favoured Catholics: on the important occasion of the Catholic Relief Bill of 1793 (which gave 'forty shilling' Catholic freeholders the vote) and again, at the time of the Union, when leading Catholics were promised full emancipation after the measure went through.

Fitzgibbon's reasoning was pragmatic and in logic hard to resist. All his speeches may be reduced to one of his more memorable passages.

'The whole power and property of the country has been conferred by successive monarchs of England upon an English colony, composed of three sets of English adventurers, who poured into this country at the termination of three successive rebellions. Confiscation is their common title, and from their first settlement they have been hemmed in on every side by the old inhabitants of the island, brooding over their discontents in sullen indignation.'

Fitzgibbon made no effort to gloss over this set of unpalatable facts or to urge, in the manner of a Gladstone, that it was high time that justice should be done to the discontented; but at least he did not play the hypocrite, and it requires little imagination to picture the sneer with which he would have greeted the following in the fulsome biography of the later champion of the Union: 'and one great reason why he [Carson] opposed Home Rule was because he so clearly understood in what the happiness of the poor peasantry of Ireland consisted. Under the Union they enjoyed their own, they were prosperous, they were helped out of the purse of the big partner. To throw it all away—for what?'

The juxtaposition of 'poor' and 'prosperous' in a paragraph gives a clue to the closeness of the reasoning of the writer, sickening because the general poverty of Ireland, even in my childhood, was so ubiquitous that it seemed incurable—the cabins in the country where tuberculosis ran riot, the bare-foot children, and the foetid slums of the cities.

Fitzgibbon never indulged in nonsense of that kind, nor would it be fair to hold Carson responsible for the eloquence of his biographer. But even the silliest panegyrist could not have penned it on Fitzgibbon's behalf.

His candid expression of bad title, supported only by power, made his case for the Protestants watertight if the Catholics were to be governed by the same unrelenting logic. It is the argument nowadays of Smith in Rhodesia. It had in its time the same appeal. There was nothing to recommend it in spiritual terms; it was the law of the jungle. But it made sense.

Fitzgibbon could have held to it and been genial—as were many robber barons. But not only was his official manner repelling, his political attitude towards the Catholics became a mania. As I have said, it embarrassed Pitt and Fitzgibbon's English supporters. Why was he so unrelenting in this pursuit? His uncle was a priest; his father had been educated in a French seminary—was he plagued by night voices? Was he fighting against atavistic compulsions? He was a strange, haughty, fastidious being; industrious, meticulous, touchy and reticent. When he went to

Jonathan Swift by Charles Jervas

John Philpot Curran by Thomas Lawrence

George Berkeley, Bishop of Cloyne, with his wife and friends

John Fitzgibbon, Earl of Clare, by H. Douglas Hamilton

James Gandon by Tilly Kettle and William Cuming

Gandon's Custom House, Dublin

St. Stephen's Church, Mount Street, Dublin

Ely House, Dublin

Fireplace from Ely House

Plasterwork from the House of Lords, Bank of Ireland, Dublin

Communion, for instance, he took the sacrament outside his own parish, an action that recalls Swift. And if he lacked all the genius of the irascible Dean he resembled him in many other respects, not least in his appetite for power—real power, not merely the show of it. His kindness was done by stealth. I wish I could forget the terribleness of the means by which the '98 rebellion was fomented and put down. It is now common in some quarters to say that it was deliberately brought about so as to give an excuse for extinguishing the parliament, and I am sure that there is plenty of evidence of people in high places saying that it was a blessing in disguise. But in every crisis there is always consolation in a result that solves a dilemma and leaves only one course open. I am sure Fitzgibbon was quite sincere in his early protestations of loyalty to the national parliament, but when he found himself being thwarted on the main question of Catholic emancipation, when England went to war with France, and a large-scale conspiracy began in Ireland to enlist French aid—then, and only then do I suppose that he saw a Union as the one bulwark against the eventual overthrow of the Protestant interest.

Not less swift changes of opinion have taken place in Northern Ireland during the last three years. There the tiny influential aristocratic section has been superseded, and I have heard from some of them that the idea of a united Ireland was preferable to a Northern State ruled by underbred bigots. Similarly Irish republicans have recently advocated the extinction of the Northern parliament and a full return to the United Kingdom; partly to escape from the rule of the clique in power, partly as a step towards renewed agitation for a united Irish republic.

It would be impossible, I should say, to investigate any lengthy correspondence in the eighteenth century which dealt with public affairs in an Irish context without finding reference to the possibility of a Union. The Irish themselves asked for one at the beginning of the century and were turned down. Berkeley advocated it, Burke discussed it. It was not, with the example of Scotland there, a very recondite proposition or one unlikely to occur to any speculative mind. The only inconsistency I could discover in Fitzgibbon is a tart reference, at the beginning of his career, to someone for calling the Irish parliament corrupt; and a full acknowledgment of this conspicuous reality towards the close.

A man's true opinions are most likely to be found in letters to a close friend. Fortunately some of Fitzgibbon's exist, written to his mentor, William Eden, the first Lord Auckland. In these, as early as 1784, Fitzgibbon makes the case to which he held until his death. For example:

'The gentlemen of the country see the necessity of beating down the rabble but are afraid to come forth. The cry is, "Why should we expose ourselves to the fury and indignation of the people? We do not know that the present ministry of England will stand and we can't be certain if there is a change of ministry that we shall not be proscribed for supporting the government." As to parliamentary reform, as it is called in this country, if any alteration is made in the constitution of the House of Commons in Ireland there is an end of any connection with England, unless it can be maintained by the sword. I have very little doubt that French gold is in circulation amongst the lower class of the people in this country. The Puritans of the North are become advocates for religious tolerance, and the catholics profess a strong predilection for republican government. The Puritans tell them, "If you will assist us in reforming the constitution, we will assist you in shaking off every restraint upon you." If the worthy personages succeed in their projects, it does not require any great degree of sagacity to discover that we shall not very long have a protestant government in this country. I am told the King of France is a very popular character in the North of Ireland, that he is considered the great assertor of the liberties of the world. I would to God I could put some of these gentlemen who are so enamoured of French liberty under the government of that great assertor of the rights of Mankind. I think I could effectually tame them in a very short time ... I can truly assure you that nothing but a strong sense of duty would induce me to remain one hour in this country. There is a nasty malignant levelling spirit diffused generally amongst the people that disgusts me beyond the powers of description and unless it is speedily beaten down, most assuredly I will quit Ireland and very probably never return to it.'

The pitch-capping, the house burnings, the floggings, the

hangings, the half-hangings—these horrors hang in the air and poison the reputation of anyone in authority who allowed them to proceed without a protest. For his participation in responsibility Fitzgibbon's reputation must always hang under a black cloud; but Cornwallis said that he was 'by far the most moderate and right-headed man among us' before he and Abercromby, Viceroy and Commander in Chief respectively, returned to England, disgusted with the methods employed by Dublin Castle. Pitt walked out of the House of Lords when he heard Fitzgibbon in later days defend the policy of frightfulness. Sir John Moore, the most efficient British commander in Ireland at the time, expressed his sympathy with the people. Fitzgibbon cannot escape the odium of the policy—and the subsequent purchase of the parliament was of a kind with it.

But having said that, there is much to be said in favour of Fitzgibbon as a man. He was steadfast and brave and candid and—in several instances—humane. His private conduct was much better than his public professions. He let Wolfe Tone escape the consequences of his embroilment with the Jackson conspiracy with France in 1794, and he was entitled to think that Tone had afterwards let him down. He warned the relations of Lord Edward FitzGerald that he was in danger, and left a dinner in his own house to accompany Lady Louisa Conolly to her nephew's deathbed. She had been refused the privilege by the Viceroy. He interviewed the brothers Sheares and advised them to avoid the course which later led to their execution. When the rebellion was put down, he asked for an immediate end to severities at a time when Protestant Dublin was so bloodthirsty that English visitors were astonished at it. He set in motion the treaty with the surviving United Irishmen which enabled them to emigrate. All this can be put to his credit. A letter he is said to have received from one George Nugent Reynolds, whom he had deprived of his magistracy, reflects a less favourable opinion. It was communicated to O'Flanagan, author of *Lord Chancellors of Ireland*, by Chief Baron Palles, and that should warrant its authenticity. Did it emanate from a less creditable source it might be regarded as one of those inspired epistles which are never entrusted to the postman, and are discovered among the papers of the writer, not the addressee.

To the Right Honourable John Earl of Clare, Lord High Chancellor of Ireland.

My Lord,—With surprise and sorrow I received a letter signed 'J. Dwyer,' informing me that your Lordship was pleased to suspend me in the Commission of the Peace for the counties of Leitrim and Roscommon. I say 'with surprise', as I am not conscious of any faults to warrant such a proceeding on the part of your Lordship. I add 'with sorrow', for, low as the appointment is—and low it must be, depending upon the caprice of any individual—yet, as it afforded me the power to protect innocence and counteract tyranny, I part from it with regret, Your Lordship loves not the Constitution with more zeal than I do; it has been the theme of my continued panegyric; nor shall the unkind treatment I experienced at your Lordship's hands tend to democratise my opinions; quite the reverse! It is to me an additional proof of my aristocratic creed, 'that there is in men of mean descent an innate ignobility which no titles of honour can eradicate'. It is not, my Lord in the radiance of the royal sunbeam to give to the mushroom the fragrance of the rose; and when we look to a new man for the bland and golden dignity of manners which mark the genuine noblesse, we too often find a pinchbeck substituted in its stead. When I waited on your Lordship with a letter from the Governor of the county in which my family resides, with an affected hauteur which ill becomes the man of yesterday, you turned on your heels and refused me an opportunity of justifying my conduct. Had your Lordship, like your father, been destined for the Popish priesthood, you would have had the benefit of a St Omer's education, and of consequence, known more decency and more good manners; but probably a giddy head is turned by looking down from a pinnacle to which a fortunate combination of circumstances has raised it. Yet elevated as your Lordship is, it never appeared to me that when I heard your Lordship's voice 'an angel spoke'. Your *tout-ensemble* has rather recalled to my fancy the figure of a sweep, who, climbing through dirt, pops out his sooty-coloured face, and with a shrill tone proclaims his high situation to the world. It has been asserted by your Lordship that I took bail for several persons under the denomination of 'defenders', nothing more being specified in the committal, and your

Lordship is the most competent judge whether that is sufficient to detain his Majesty's subjects. It has been represented that one of the parties houghed a cow and hung a threatening notice on one of her horns; had he houghed your Lordship, and hung a threatening notice on *one of your horns*, under the same committal I would have acted in the same manner. I cannot dismiss this letter without a comment on the impertinence of your Lordship's servant, but that is easily accounted for by recollecting 'that man is an imitative animal'; and perhaps I attributed to impoliteness a conduct which might with more propriety be attributed to fear; but so high is my respect for official situation that though it rained horse-whips, far be it from me to think of laying one of them on the hem of your Lordship's garment.

I am, my Lord, with sincerity to my enemies and respect to myself,

G. N. Reynolds.

The reference to 'one of your horns' seems strangely reckless in a letter to a formidable Chancellor with almost despotic power. Fitzgibbon's private life, like everything about him, is secret. He was said to have loved a girl who passed him over for Henry Sheares, and when Lord Thurlow, Chancellor of England, resisted the idea of an *Irishman* as Chancellor in Ireland, one of the people who pleaded Fitzgibbon's cause was the lovely Duchess of Rutland, widow of a former Viceroy. But all the Viceroys found him their most reliable servant in Ireland; and there is no reason to believe that the Duchess was inspired by any motive other than a sense of her husband's gratitude.

None of Fitzgibbon's pictures suggest a handsome man; he was small with more nose than chin; where, then, did his Adonis of a son come from? Lady Clare, we know, was quite a martinet and tenacious of family rights after her husband died. It may be grossly unfair to her to question her husband's authorship of his heir; his own elder brother had been something of a fop during his short existence.

In any event, Clare's son at Harrow was one of a group including other Irishmen, who attracted Byron's attention. The boy was an orphan, eleven years of age, and Byron was fifteen. 'I never heard the word "Clare",' Byron wrote in his *Detached Thoughts*, 'without a beating of the heart even *now* . . .' One of his fags to whom the poet was also attached was John Wingfield (a son of Lord Powerscourt). Byron was perhaps excessive in his demonstrations—he was a strongly feminine being—a quarrel with Clare sprung from so slight a cause as a letter addressed 'Dear' instead of 'My Dearest'. Byron's affections were jealous. He was outraged and amazed when he met Clare abroad and found that the young man preferred to go shopping with his mother (of whom, perhaps, he was afraid) instead of spending the snatched time with him. They met later in Italy, on the road to Bologna. "This meeting annihilated for a moment all the years between the present time and the days at *Harrow*. It was a new and inexplicable feeling, like rising from the grave, to me. Clare, too, was much agitated . . . We were but five minutes together and in the public road; but I hardly recollect an hour of my existence which could be weighed against them.' He confided in Moore and in Mary Godwin that Clare was dearer to him than any friend. He wrote to Mary, rather tactlessly, it would seem, as men often do who find themselves enormously interesting: 'As to friendship, it is a propensity in which my genius is very limited. I do not know the *male* human being except Lord Clare, the friend of my infancy, for whom I feel anything that deserves the name. All my other are men-of-the-world friendships. I did not even feel it for Shelley, however much I admired and esteemed him; so that you see not even vanity could bribe me into it, for, of all men, Shelley thought highest of my talents—and, perhaps, of my disposition.'

Shelley, as we know, was extremely critical of Byron towards the close, but that is irrelevant here; what is interesting is the presence of young Clare in a charmed circle. A school-friend of Byron said that it gave him confidence to keep in a circle of attractive boys who were fellow peers. Irish peers, had for him the charm they exercised in a later time on the poetic imagination of Sir John Betjeman at Oxford. They may have the appeal of Irish scenery, the aura of picturesque decay. If Byron were so much impressed by Clare, it makes nonsense of the Irish tradition that his father was snubbed in England by the noblemen there as a parvenu. The evidence suggests that Fitzgibbon was almost too fastidious. He refused, for instance, to sit at dinner with some of the informers at the bar on whose services the Government at the time were depending, and whom they were flattering with attentions of that sort.

Fitzgibbon's lifelong opponent was a man who is revered in Ireland as one of its patriots and wits. A glance at John Philpot Curran's face in Lawrence's portrait brings us under what must have been a rare fascination. Delacroix wrote enthusiastically of 'the gleam in the eyes, the parted lips' that Lawrence rendered so skilfully. Curran was given them; but even portraits by less flattering artists reveal that brilliant eye. It was so far as favour went all he had; he was shrunken of figure and simian of face; but genius lit up the unpromising exterior, and it shone in his eyes. When he was speaking his countenance became very animated and he had a flexible voice. 'The most wonderful person I ever met', Byron said. His delight in Curran's company was heightened probably by a gift of mimicry. He wrote one good verse and the catch for a convival society over which he presided, 'The Knights of the Screw'. It was not what modern slang might lead one to suppose—but a dining-club.

Curran shared the mental characteristics of Sheridan. He conjures up our ideal for the Anglo-Irishman—his wit was legendary; but on closer examination the likeness goes. For one thing he was stingy about money; for another there was no streak of recklessness in him. Admittedly he owed his fame to his exertions on the national side; he committed himself wholly in Parliament and his speeches in defence of the United Irishmen won him the reputation of a patriot. And so he was. His services were given wholeheartedly, but in a strictly law-abiding manner. To put it crudely: his clientele was in the nationalist camp with whom his sympathies lay; but his career was much closer to Fitzgibbon's—running in another track—than to the revolutionaries such as Tone, Emmet, and the Sheares brothers, who threw over their professional prospects. Curran spoke eloquently against the Union to the last; but when it came he accepted in due course the Mastership of the Rolls, the second best judicial appointment. By that time, according to his friend Barrington, he had become quite dejected and listless.

His fame is spotted, not by that, but by his harshness to his daughter Sarah when she became involved with Robert Emmet. That dreamy, high-minded revolutionary was not the sort of son-in-law a barrister with an eye to his career would normally encourage. And Curran's indignation is understandable in any terms when the revolution Emmet planned went off at half-cock and led only to a street brawl and the murder of Kilwarden, Curran's friend and one of the most humane judges on the Bench. Emmet might have escaped had he not lingered for a glimpse of Sarah; and Curran, who had been compromised, was at pains to assure the Government that he highly disapproved of the whole proceeding. Many another father might have been exasperated with his daughter in the circumstances; but Curran went further than this—of course we must recall the harsh temper of the times—and treated her with a heartless severity. He was himself a broken man and died not long after—'a mountain of lead on his heart'.

Thomas Moore immortalised Sarah's ill-starred love; and although it is the fashion to despise him, *every* Irish child has responded at some time to 'She is far from the land where her young hero sleeps'. Sarah was, in fact, very far at the time because she married an English officer and went to India. It would be in keeping with that tragic romance to read into her early death a broken heart, but I have a melancholy suspicion that, like other girls, she may have patched her heart up and died, as so many young mothers did, from medical ignorance and surgical *attention*.

Barrington is not always to be trusted, but there is no reason to disbelieve his unattractive account of Curran's failure to respond to his London mistress's demand for assistance; it was a sordid picture. She thumped Curran on the head with a fist as large as a porter's, and called over the bannisters to the maid to 'open the street-door for the gentleman'.

When Curran asked Barrington what she had said after his departure he replied, 'She *only* said that you were the greatest rascal existing and she would next day find you out wherever you were, and expose you all over London as a villain and a seducer!'

Before the ugly subject of money had been raised they had all been happy in the drawing-room where 'Curran was most humorous and enlivening'. He was one of the type of street angels, house devils that Ireland is not unique in producing.

Unlike Sheridan, whose ancestors had been men of mark, Curran was the son of a steward on a property in County Cork. His talents were noticed by the local clergyman who started him on his way to Trinity College. We think of the eighteenth century as a period of very closed society; but there was a place for talent, and in Ireland once a boy got himself into Trinity—where there were sizarships—there was no bar to his promotion. Tone's background—an impoverished carriage-maker's son—never seems to have stood in his way. Moore's father was a grocer. Not only did these men make a mark in public life, there was open house for them in the mansions of the aristocracy. Presumably the class system had not then evolved the secret signs which afterwards complicated entry and are enshrined in that controversy about U and non U language attributed incorrectly to a theory of Miss Nancy Mitford.

That cabbalistic business was a consequence of the Industrial Revolution, a conspiracy to thwart the social aspirations of the successful commercial classes. A Whig aristocrat, secure in his lands, could see a way in which a talented young man might be of use to him; he could also, if he was benevolently inclined, see ways in which he could forward the interests of such a young man; but he could not imagine any situation in which the young man could constitute a danger unless, and only when, he showed politically subversive tendencies.

Curran's feud with Fitzgibbon, he never forgot to point out, cost him money. It was manifestly unwise to employ a barrister in the Chancellor's court who had attacked him in Parliament and been insulted in return. We have one episode which shows the lighter side of their mutual antipathy.

Fitzgibbon, on the bench, while Curran addressed him, spent his time petting a fine dog he had beside him. At last Curran's patience broke and he lapsed into silence. When the Chancellor invited him to continue he apologised. He thought 'Your lordship was in consultation'. But their parliamentary opposition towards each other was less playful. Curran's imputations were that Fitzgibbon had sold his country for office, Fitzgibbon's response was open contempt and undisguised allusion to Curran's unfavourable appearance. He spoke of monkeys and mountebanks and predicted a future for Curran at Sadler's Wells. He referred to *puny* babblers. And on one occasion used a phrase which has been used by others—Sheridan among them—but I cannot find who said it first, in riposte to one of Curran's attacks. 'I am somewhat surprised that he should entertain such a particular asperity against me, as I never did him any favour.'

One could see in Fitzgibbon's expressed contempt for Curran the attitude of one who has lately risen in the world against another man on the make. Curran's connection with the patriot party from whom Fitzgibbon had turned away was not, he was determined, going to allow him any affectation of moral superiority. He might put up with Grattan, whose character he respected, even if they were opposed politically, but he was not going to allow a land steward's son to rebuke him.

He preened himself no doubt on his situation, secure in the highest judicial office, supported by private wealth and well-connected by marriage—he had nothing to envy in Curran's rather dismal domestic situation. Sometimes Fitzgibbon is reminiscent of the first Lord Birkenhead, whose patrician arrogance belied his modest beginnings.

When a duel took place between them in 1789 Curran said that Fitzgibbon took very deliberate aim after his own shot went astray. The story has a sinister ring. If he was anxious to take Curran's life then he must have been more susceptible to the other's attacks than he pretended. I wonder how much justice lay in Plunkett's remark when the duel was reported. 'Curran and Fitzgibbon fought, but unluckily they missed each other.'

Fitzgibbon's detractors, who are legion, like to quote Curran against him; but Grattan, who knew him better and whose testimony is more valuable, never pursued his former school-friend with the same venom, nor did he make little of Fitzgibbon's powers. He was certainly not a coward. When he accompanied a sentence with a calculated insult he was prepared to waive the privilege of office to let the prisoner take a shot at him on his release. A leading case, it could have been, of contempt of court. But the duel did not take place.

It has been hinted that Fitzgibbon's wife had lovers. She was a daughter of Richard Chappel Whaley, who won the soubriquet 'Burn-Chapel-Whaley' because of the enthusiasm which he showed as a magistrate in Wicklow for invoking the Statute enabling a Catholic Chapel to be destroyed if it was used as a centre for conspiracy. Fitzgibbon and his father-in-law had something at least in common. The notorious member of the family was Buck Whaley, one of the Hell Fire Club fraternity, notorious for taking a bet that he would walk from Dublin to Jerusalem and back within two years and, on another occasion, for jumping from a window, over a coach, into the road. He was always in trouble, and there is evidence that his brother-in-law came to his rescue when required. Fitgibbon was faithful to relatives, friends, and servants.

It is one of the nice ironies of history that the Whaley town house in St Stephen's Green was within half a century of Fitzgibbon's death bought for the Catholic University under the Rectorship of John Henry Newman. I cannot look at that decorative mansion without seeing the Chancellor's frown and hearing him thunder, 'I told you so.'

Fitzgibbon's grandfather had been reduced to the condition of a peasant farmer in Clare, but not, one supposes, to the most miserable class of tenant at will, whose condition he perfectly understood. When he was Attorney-General, and still on friendly terms with Grattan and the patriotic Protestants, he gave this eloquent description of the condition of the peasantry.

'I am well acquainted with the province of Munster, and I know that it is impossible for human wretchedness to exceed that of the miserable peasantry of that province. I know that the unhappy tenantry are ground to powder by relentless landlords. I know that far from being able to give the clergy their just dues, they had not food or raiment for themselves; the landlord grasps the whole. And sorry I am to add, that not satisfied with present extortion, some landlords have been so base as to instigate the insurgents to rob the clergy, not in order to alleviate the distresses of the tenantry, but that they might add the clergy's share to the cruel rack rents already paid . . . The poor people of Munster live in a more abject state of poverty than human nature can be supposed to bear; their miseries are intolerable.'

That a man could know that and feel it and yet seem to turn all his talents and energy to the perpetuation of the sytems under which it had come to be is a mystery. But Swift had spoken with equal clarity of the condition of the poor Irish in his day, and had predicted that they would have left the face of the earth within two generations. One must suppose that to Fitzgibbon, not less than Swift, the poor were irrelevant in any discussion of Ireland. The point is worth taking. We read of the destruction of the Irish wool trade and native manufacturers by the greed of the English parliament as a condition against which the Irish—like the American colonists—at length rebelled, but it is probably not an exaggeration to say that the fate of all these undertakings and whether they flourished or failed, affected the poor Irish no more than the Boston tea party affected the Indians of North America.

Beside Stephen's Green is Hume Street, and that leads to Ely Place where Fitzgibbon lived at number six. The upper flights of stone stairs are pierced so that muskets could be fired through them at a mob coming up the stairs. Fitzgibbon had to use his house as a fortress once when he was recognised by an angry crowd. Some of them were to make a row at his funeral and throw a dead cat at his coffin. He was not loved.

Not loved in Ireland or in England—because people are embarrassed by those who do their dirty work—and there was relief when he died, after a fall from a horse, in 1802. I notice in recent writers a tendency to call him old when he was, like Birkenhead, conspicuously young to attain his exalted office.

The dislike in which he was held was not for the activities of his later career but on account of the hopes that were raised when Lord Fitzwilliam came to Ireland in 1795 as Viceroy, and were dashed on his recall. Legend has not been quite fair about this. Fitzwilliam was to a large extent the author of his fate, for which Grattan charged Pitt with broken faith.

The giving of the vote to Catholics in 1793 was followed by a confident belief that all the restrictions of Penal Days would be swept away. It coincided with enthusiasm for republican principles in Northern Ireland, among the dissenters there, who were enthusiastic about the French Revolution.

Anyone who knows Ireland can see the subsequent dilemma.

Those who advocated republicanism on French lines could not have been welcome to Catholic leaders. Had Fitzwilliam been allowed to give Catholics full concessions, their subsequent gratitude would have set them against the leaders of Jacobin conspiracy instead of getting mixed up in the revolution. Edmund Burke exemplified the mental confusion of the time. Nobody had written more forcibly about Catholic grievances, but just then he was the incarnation of reaction against the threat of Jacobinism spreading from France. He confessed himself unable to advise, pulled as he was both ways.

Even Charles James Fox, the apostle of French ideas, announced that Catholic relief in Ireland had gone far enough in 1793, and he was adamant against further concession. Fitzwilliam acted on his own when he raised expectations in Ireland. His conduct, even before he had been officially appointed, was enthusiastic and indiscreet. He was not commissioned to get rid of the ruling junta when he arrived, and he should have acted with more discretion. Beresford, the most influential man in Ireland, was dismissed out of hand. A chancellor was a different proposition. He was virtually irremovable. In any event Fitzgibbon did not wait. He proceeded to get in touch with the King who, as one put it, 'the visitation of Providence had for a time disqualified', and was always likely to disqualify again, and impressed upon that marmoreal mind that his Coronation oath forbade him—it was treason—to tamper with the doctrine of the Supremacy of the Anglican Church. Did Fitzgibbon believe this himself? The answer depends upon one's estimate of his character—was he merely a legal careerist or a man of deep conviction? I cannot see why only rebels should be credited with sincerity. Fitzgibbon's correspondence shows that he held his extreme opinion sincerely. In any event there was no conflict between expediency and conscience on this occasion. The King was impressed, so impressed that he never forgot, and when Pitt made a bargain with Catholic leaders at the time of the Union, refused to allow him to keep it. As Pitt took care not to let Fitzgibbon know about those negotiations he, at least, must have had no doubt in his mind about the Chancellor's inconvenient mania.

Fitzwilliam was recalled. His departure from Dublin was a

scene of national grief. From that time forward Catholic and Republican hopes were identified with revolution. Later the Northerners were to take alarm when they saw that revolution in Wexford—where it was almost successful—took the form of a religious war. But that was in the future. In fact Fitzwilliam would never have been allowed to carry out his happy liberal reforms, but the Chancellor had been the effective means of thwarting him, and to the Chancellor attached all the odium of his recall.

There was never a place for anyone like Fitzgibbon in Ireland under the Union. History had to wait for the emergence of the Ulster crisis to create a situation in which there was any analogy to Ireland in 1800. Then the threat of undoing what had been so unattractively accomplished set in motion similar forces and produced in Edward Carson a successor to Fitzgibbon.

Part II

DECLINE AND FALL

CHAPTER VIII

Thomas Drummond

IRELAND UNDER THE Union may be looked at through the eyes of one of the best men ever to come there. Thomas Drummond, Under-Secretary, from 1835 until 1840, deserves the statue that was erected to his memory in Dublin's City Hall. His short career is unique in that it contains the only sincere effort that was made until Gladstone's to put in practice the promises made at the time of the Union; and it can be studied profitably as a blueprint for the task that would face any administration that took on now control of Northern Ireland from Westminster and Whitehall. Ireland, when Drummond arrived there, was Ulster writ large. Drummond was a Scot. That may explain him. He was something better than an idealist; he was a just man. In the history of Ireland I cannot find his equal among those that came to rule us; and I cannot think of any Irish leader whom it is more difficult to fault. He came as Under-Secretary to work out Melbourne's policy arrived at in a meeting with O'Connell at Lichfield House in London. The Irish demagogue agreed to hold his fire if Melbourne tried to govern Ireland with impartiality. The treaty was faithfully kept. Relations between the two countries had never been so promising; the emancipation of Catholics which had been resisted in practice, was put into operation by a fair distribution of offices, and Ireland started to become peaceful. Then Drummond died; Melbourne was defeated; the Tories came back; and the old policy of coercion—at the behest of Irish landlords and the Orange lodges—was restored. O'Connell returned to the fray. Not far off loomed the Famine and the Rising of 1848.

When Drummond arrived there were three elements of disorder in Ireland; Orange lodges (chiefly in the North), Ribbonmen (the unofficial trades union of the peasantry), and traditional faction fighters. The previous method of government had been to collaborate with the first, coerce the second, and disregard the third—the Donnybrook Fair side of Irish life. It was not interfered with because the authorities were indifferent to any fighting among the Irish which might lead to self-extermination. The chief cause was drink. Drummond put this down, and he was assisted by Father Mathew who conferred a great boon on the people with his remarkable temperance campaign.

To the Ribbonmen Drummond gave impartial justice; but he was the first to see this nuisance in perspective. There was very little crime in Ireland that was not due to bad agricultural conditions.

When Catholic Emancipation was granted in 1829, it was accompanied by a provision disfranchising what were known as 'the forty shilling freeholders'. These had been created by the previous Act of Relief to Catholics in 1793. But then the idea was to create as many Catholic voters as possible to support the candidates of their landlords. Now that Catholics could sit in parliament this large number of voters was a threat to Protestant interests. So their vote was taken away. In the interim the population had very nearly doubled. It had reached eight million by 1840.

Now that the small freeholders were of no use to them their landlords proceeded to consolidate farms and reverse the process of encouraging small holdings. Thousands were made homeless, usually with the assistance of the police or the military. There was nowhere for them to go, not even workhouses before 1838, no plan for emigration even. They became landless beggars or they died in the ditches.

Drummond saw this evil as the cause of rural crime and the explanation of Ribbonmen and other lawless bodies. Evictions were only a part of the trouble; more violent was the war over tithes. The more energetic country folk resisted this impost, having to support a Church to which they did not belong. When they struck against paying, the military were called in.

Another feature of the time was the partial character of the local magistrates. Their decisions reflected their politics. As for jury trials, the practice was to challenge any juryman who was a

Catholic. In Northern districts it was almost impossible to get a conviction against an Orangeman, no matter how blatant the evidence of guilt. A sophisticated or cynical Under-Secretary, even if he found it distasteful, would have submitted to all this as native custom, secure in the knowledge that injustice did not threaten British interests, while reform disaffected the friends of Union.

Drummond's superior officer, Lord Morpeth, gave him a free hand—some of Drummond's more striking letters came officially from Morpeth—and he employed it to clear the Augean stable, unimpressed by interested protests. He created the Royal Irish Constabulary, and insisted that Catholics should serve in it. Hitherto there had been no Catholic policeman in Ireland. He transferred the power of appointing chief constables from the local magistrates to the Viceroy. He refused to allow the forces of the crown to assist in tithe collecting or evicting. He declined to be associated even with a good-natured job, a matter of an appointment, to which the Viceroy was committed by his predecessor. He stood firm and prevented it. He became the chief enemy to reaction—the landlords, the Orangemen, *The Times*. Of course his reforms had to be fought for. Irish peers were usually able to carry the House of Lords with them; and they could always veto Irish concessions made in the House of Commons. What Drummond encountered demonstrates that the chief enemies to good government in Ireland were not the British, but the Protestant ascendancy in Ireland. His career is very relevant to the scene in Northern Ireland in this year, 1972.

He arrived at a traumatic time. The Reform Act of 1832 had been passed in Britain in a near revolutionary atmosphere. This was one of the critical moments of the century; it was the first decisive blow at the landed interest and it rallied that class in every part of the United Kingdom. The Orange Society, which had been suppressed by Canning, was once again a powerful force in opposition. The Grand Master was the King's brother, the Duke of Cumberland, and there was suspicion of a plot to put that sinister individual on the throne if the Reform bill could be overthrown. And in its overthrow some help was expected from the Orange Order which was then 175,000 strong. They were 'staunch to the backbone' and none of them Reformers, Colonel William Blennerhasset Fairman, Grand Secretary and Grand Treasurer of the Society in Britain, informed Sir James Cockburn.

Fairman intrigued—with the knowledge of the Duke of Cumberland—to organise a series of forcible demonstrations against the Reform bill, led by prominent Orangemen. In Ireland —so he informed the Marquis of Londonderry—Lord Longford intimated that 'the brethren were determined to resist all attempts the Liberals might make to put them down'.

The conspiracy never came to anything. Londonderry, for one, advised caution. But a subsequent inquiry in the House of Commons led to the suppression of the Society. The Duke of Cumberland declined to attend. Fairman refused to produce books and avoided the legal efforts to enforce the committee's order for production. However, the Society was suppressed, and King William, who cannot have been grateful to his brother, expressed his 'firm intention to discourage all such societies in my dominions'. It would be difficult for a monarch to express that sentiment now.

Ireland was the exception. The Orange Society was allowed to continue in Ireland as a system of unaffiliated lodges. The Reform Act was not applied to Ireland in its British shape. And yet the bait of Union was the promise of the blessing of equal laws!

Drummond's first activity was the police bill. It was thrown out by the House of Lords. The Irish peers—Roden, Westmeath, Wicklow, Londonderry and Vesey—opposing it. But it passed in the next session.

This gave the Government a police force independent of the local magistrates, and its services were refused when applications came to the Castle from rural clergymen requesting that the police should collect their tithes for them. The tithe war was coming to an end. The impost was soon to be converted into a rent charge; before that it had led to many battles. Barry O'Brien in his *Concessions to Ireland* gives a vivid description of one celebrated affray.

'On the 18th December 1834 a force of horse (4th Royal Irish Dragoons), foot (29th Regiment), and police, under the command of Major Waller (29th Regiment), Lieutenant Tait (dragoons),

Captain Pepper (police), Captain Colles, J.P. and Captain Bagley, R.M., proceeded to collect the tithes of Archdeacon Ryder, J.P., in the parish of Gortroe, County Cork. The dragoons, who marched from Cork City, fell in with a small body of peasants, at a place called Barthelmy's Cross, near the village of Gortroe. The peasants were armed with their usual weapons, sticks and slanes, and some of them were mounted. Archdeacon Ryder, who accompanied the cavalcade in the double capacity of parson and magistrate, suggested to Captain Bagley, on seeing the peasants, that it might be prudent for the dragoons to draw their swords and get ready for action; and at the request of Captain Bagley, Lieutenant Tait ordered his men to do so. The peasants, however, made no effort to obstruct the advance of the dragoons, but retreated steadily before them through the village of Gortroe, falling back on the farmstead of one of the title-defaulters—the widow Ryan by name—whose indebtness to Archdeacon Ryder amounted to the sum of forty shillings. The widow Ryan lived near the hamlet of Rathcormac. Her house (one of a cluster of houses outside the village) stood at some distance from the high road, with which it was connected by the usual boreen entrance. In front of the house was a large yard, and in front of the yard, and on the same side of the boreen, a haggard—both yard and haggard being separated from the boreen by a mud wall about four feet high. To the rear of yard and haggard was a well planted shrubbery ... Bagley addressed the men behind the barricades, requesting them to permit the troops to enter the boreen. The men answered, "No tithes, no parson! You have no right to come." Bagley replied, "We shall force an entrance if you do not give way." The peasants again shouted, "No tithes! no parson! no church!" ...

'Bagley, having read the Riot Act, ordered the police to throw down the barricade; this they quickly did, whereupon the troops entered the boreen, the dragoons leading the way. On approaching the haggard the dragoons halted, and the 29th marched forward. On reaching the haggard wall the 29th halted, and Major Waller sent to Captain Bagley for further instructions.

'Bagley said: "You must dislodge the peasants from the haggard and the yard. If they do not go quietly, you must try the bayonet.

If that is not sufficient, you must fire; but do not fire except in the last resort." . . . Hostilities were commenced by Archdeacon Ryder, who, acting upon his own responsibility succeeded all by himself, in clambering over the wall and entering the haggard. He was seized by the peasants, neck and crop, and literally flung back into the boreen. Alves then mounted the wall, and waving his sword, called on his men to "follow". Seeing Alves on the wall, the leader of the peasants shouted to his comrades, "Don't let him in! Don't let him in! Don't strike him; but don't let him in!" . . . The peasant leader roared to his companions, "Now, boys, at them!" and the peasants (sticks, slanes and pitchforks in hand) made for the soldiers. A fierce fight ensued, the peasants striking furiously at the soldiers with their formidable weapons, and the soldiers vigorously thrusting back with their bayonets. Again and again the soldiers climbed to the top of the wall, maimed and bruised, with their bayonets bent and their firelocks smashed, many of the peasants having been placed *hors de combat* by bayonet wounds. After this struggle had continued for some time, Lieutenant Alves called out to Major Waller, "We cannot, Major, take this place by the bayonet," whereupon Archdeacon Ryder rushed up to Captain Bagley, crying out, "What are we to do? We are so resisted!" . . .

'Shepherd, on hearing Alves' fire, called to Waller, saying, "Major, must I fire?" and Waller answered, "Yes."

'Shepherd turning to the peasants, then said, "Now if you do not give way, I must fire." The leader of the peasants replied, "We are not afraid to die; lives must be lost on either side before ye come in." There was no alternative now left Shepherd but to give the word "fire"; this he promptly did. "I, then," says Major Waller, "looked in the direction of the cart to see the effect. The crowd dispersed after the fire, but quickly closed up, and rushed back to the cart as thick as ever." Such truly had been the case. The peasants, thrown but for a moment into confusion, quickly rallied; and as their leader called out, "Never flinch, my boys! Close up and at them again!" flung themselves once more on the soldiers, who, under the cover of the fire, had jumped into the cart, and clambered over the wall, driving them back with eminent success. But sticks, slanes, and pitchforks, though weapons which in the hands of a martial peasantry could be effectually used against bayonets, were poor instruments of defence against powder and ball. After a struggle—to the gallantry of which Lieutenant Shepherd bore testimony, asserting that he "had never seen such determined bravery as was shown by the people on that day"—the peasantry gave way under the sustained fire of the troops, retreating steadily on the shrubbery . . .

'At this juncture Archdeacon Ryder came up and said, "All right, Major, I have got my tithes." It seems that the Archdeacon —who had performed various strategical movements on his own account during the day (including the escapade in the haggard) had succeeded in taking the widow's house in the rear, while the battle was raging in front, with the result that he saw the widow, and obtained the tithes from her. It was this cheerful fact that he now announced to Waller. The parson being satisfied, all were satisfied, and Major Waller and Lieutenant Tait marched their men back to Cork. The soldiers gone, the peasants emerged from the shrubbery to take up their comrades who had fallen in the fray, and to find that the casualties had been considerable; twelve peasants were killed, and forty-two wounded.

'None of the soldiers had been killed, but many were wounded. An inquest, at which twenty-three jurors were empanelled, was, a few days later, held on the bodies of the peasants who had fallen. The inquiry lasted thirteen days, and resulted in a mixed verdict; thirteen jurors being for a verdict of "wilful murder", two for "manslaughter", and eight for "justifiable homicide".'

Drummond was not prepared to sanction such measures. He insisted that landlords and parsons should have recourse to the courts. The function of the police was to keep the peace not to collect debts. This intrepid Scot faced the force of Orangeism in the North and forbade commemorative processions; when he met resistance he did not hesitate to remove recalcitrant Orangemen from the magistracy. He was unimpressed by rank; when Colonel Verner, Deputy-Lieutenant of the County of Tyrone and an Orange Deputy Grand Master, gave the toast of 'The Battle of the Diamond' at an election dinner, he wrote to inquire if it was the case that 'you were thus a party to the commemoration of a lawless and most disgraceful conflict'.

In his reply from the Carlton Club, the Major avoided the question as one which 'ought not to be proposed to me', and he supposed that 'on cool reflection' Drummond would not expect him to 'condescend to answer it'. Drummond replied through the Chief Secretary at considerable length, ending with the information that 'His Excellency will deem it expedient to recommend to the Lord Chancellor that you should not be included in the new Commission of the Peace about to be issued, and will also direct your name to be omitted from the revised list of Deputy-Lieutenants for the County of Tyrone.'

Verner had the matter raised in the House of Commons, where O'Connell drew the fire. The Government was accused of being in O'Connell's power. In fact he had never asked for a single favour. The Chief Secretary defended Drummond's decision, reading to the House an account of the 'Battle of the Diamond' in 1795 when a group of Protestants killed thirty Catholics in a brawl. The event was the occasion of the founding of the Orange Order.

But Drummond's most celebrated encounter was with the magistrates of Tipperary. His policies were under constant attack; he was encouraging the papists and molesting the loyalists in a wrongheaded gamble to conciliate O'Connell—or so the Tories said. The House of Lords had thrown out three measures attempting to settle tithes and to reform municipal corporations. A modified tithe bill was passed in 1838. In the previous month a Tipperary landlord, Austin Cooper, was shot dead and his companion fatally wounded. The magistrates of the County sent a remonstrance to the Lord Lieutenant, setting out the circumstances of the murder. Neither life nor property was safe in that part of the county, the measures taken so far had not succeeded. They ended by suggesting that the intimidation of juries which was 'terrible' could be prevented 'by again resorting to the old and wholesome practice of challenging'.

Drummond was entrusted by the Viceroy to reply. He addressed his letter to the Earl of Donoughmore, the Lord Lieutenant of the County. It was a short letter deploring the crime, and stating that an inquiry was being made into the allegations in the memorial. Another letter followed, a very long one.

Drummond had sent out letters to the crown Solicitor and stipendiary magistrates for details of failures of juries to convict. Not one instance was reported. And with Scottish thoroughness he adduced much more evidence to show that there was no ground at all for speaking of 'terrible intimidation'. One can see how his detailed precision annoyed men accustomed to broad assertions and impatient of nagging, unhelpful detail.

And then Drummond made what amounted to a case for his Irish policies. Faction fights and riots at fairs, 'heretofore most commonly suffered to pass unchecked and unpunished' had been discouraged. The cause of outrages in Ireland were, to a very great extent, he considered, connected with the tenure and occupation of land and the lamentably destitute condition of the cottier tenantry. 'His Excellency conceives that it may become matter of serious question whether the proprietors of the soil are not in many instances attempting too rapidly to retrace their steps . . . the number of ejectments in 1837 is not less than double the number in 1833.'

At this point Drummond uttered the great heresy with which his name has since been associated. It prevented Lord Donoughmore from publishing the letter, because he and his Tipperary friends decided that it was too dangerous at the time. Drummond wrote: 'Property has its duties as well as its rights.' The words are under his statue in the City Hall in Dublin today; in 1838, they seemed as paradoxical and provocative as Proudhon's 'All property is theft'.

The whole paragraph deserves quotation. Had it been taken to heart even then it might have altered the history of Ireland— 'to the neglect of those duties in times past is mainly to be ascribed that diseased state of society in which such crimes take their rise; and it is not the enactment or enforcement of statutes of extraordinary severity, but chiefly in the faithful performance of those duties, and the more enlightened and humane exercise of those rights, that a permanent remedy for such disorder is to be sought.'

But Drummond was not only engaged on dispute with Orangemen and landlords, he was in Ireland during the sittings of the Royal Commission to consider the establishment of railways in Ireland. He was one of four commissioners, and parts of the report were written by him. These are a major contribution to Irish social history.

The object of the Report was to help the Government to decide whether it would be desirable to build railways in Ireland. The committee of four which included a remarkable man, Sir Richard Griffith, decided that it would be; but recommendation was turned down because it interfered with the freedom of private industry to undertake public works. A Marxist state is not more the slave of iron theorising than Ireland was in the nineteenth century. Food was exported from the country and people left to starve in hundreds of thousands because to retain it would offend the doctrine of *laissez-faire*, and on the same principle no work of a useful nature could be allowed in the eventual schemes of public relief. Nothing has so terrible an effect on human character as belief in an economic theory. Human lives are sacrificed to it with the same cruelty that Aztecs employed in their mode of worship. These pious Victorians, like the Russian Communists in the present century, watched nature defying their preconceived notions and wrote off the subsequent slaughter as a decree of Providence. The Communists used guns, which are quicker than starvation.

The Victorian conscience was aroused, there were good intentions in the air; but the best they had done for Ireland was to recommend the establishment of Workhouses without outdoor relief. And as these Workhouses were a charge on the rates they encouraged landlords to evict tenants at an accelerated tempo in order to make their lands more productive. The rate of eviction increased after the Famine when new owners came into possession under the Incumbered Estates Act and were determined to make their purchases pay. This was the beginning of the mass emigration to America; it was also the beginning of a new style of rebellion against British rule. Dynamite began to make its appearance; and a new class of man took the lead in plans to end the system of government.

But I am anticipating.

Drummond laid the state of the country out so plainly that it amounted to an indictment of British rule. When he wrote the population of Ireland was estimated at eight and a half million, or one third of the population of the United Kingdom. Those in the North were better lodged, clothed and fed than the others; the people in the West were by far the worst off. 'Poverty and misery have deprived them of all energy.'

This book is not a study of the Irish under British rule, and I shall omit what Drummond had to say about the people on the land, who are outside our survey except in so far as their condition throws light on their masters, the Anglo-Irish.

And it does throughout. For instance the report notes that landlords encouraged uneconomic small holdings when they wanted to increase their electoral interest after the Act of 1793 which gave the vote to 'the forty shilling freeholder'. The population had doubled since then. While few at the time saw the evils that would spring from this, while the report exonerated landlords 'from the imputation of culpable design or indifference,' it did not 'exempt them from the necessary consequences of their improvidence, or from the first obligations and duties inseparable from the possession of property'. That sentence betrays its authorship. The representatives of the landlord interest were smouldering under Drummond's doctrine of responsibility. Nobody put the other case so pithily as Lord Palmerston, a considerable proprietor in Ireland. 'Tenant Right is Landlord Wrong'.

Drummond referred in passing to the diet of the majority of the population in the decade before the Famine—'a species of potato called "the lumper" which . . . at its first introduction, was scarcely considered food good enough for swine.' There were signs of improvement in agriculture but 'the poor has not advanced, even in those improved localities. The fair inference to be drawn from this fact is, that the labourer is not allowed a just proportion of the product of his own toil and industry.'

Such were the conditions, something had to be done, it necessarily involved a reduction of the number of those living below subsistence level on the land. During the transition period Drummond and his colleagues proposed that measures should be taken to relieve inevitable hardship.

Reclamation of wasteland was one suggestion; emigration—but this could not be effected on a scale that would 'relieve the pressure of distress'. It was a secondary resort. The measure known as The Irish Poor Law, then passing through parliament, would tax the landed interest, it was therefore desirable that it should be accompanied by 'some works of great magnitude'. To the want of continuous employment and 'adequate remuneration when employed could be attributed the poverty and the bad habits of the Irish people'.

At this stage in the report Drummond let himself go in a sustained tribute to the Irish people. It is too long to quote in full but—to the credit of his memory—I cannot forbear to omit it altogether.

'But the spirit of the Irish peasant is by no means so sunk by adverse circumstances of his lot, as to be insensible to the stimulus which a due measure of encouragement to laborious industry supplies. Where employment is to be obtained without difficulty, and at a fair rate of compensation, his character and habits rise in an incredibly short space of time with the alteration of his circumstances. In a state of destitution no race of people are more patient and resigned. Their uncomplaining endurance seems almost to border on despondency. They make no effort to help themselves, probably because they despair of being able to do so effectually; and it ought to be mentioned to their honour that in such emergencies they have scarcely ever been known to extort by violence that relief which cannot be obtained from their own lawful exertions, or the benevolence of others . . . a populous district on the coast of Donegal was exposed to all the miseries of famine, rendered tenfold more agonising by the knowledge that there was food enough and to spare within a few miles; yet the poor people bore their hard lot with exemplary patience, and throughout the entire period, though numbers were actually without food, and reduced to eat sea-weed, there was no plundering of stores, no theft, nor secret pillage. Such forbearance, almost approaching to insensibility, might be deemed to belong to a character incapable of being roused to exertion in any circumstances; yet the same race, who endure the last extremes of want without a murmur, are no sooner placed in a condition of supporting themselves by independent industry, than they cast aside the torpor which distinguishes them in a depressed state, and become active, diligent and laborious.'

Lord Morpeth, who never failed Drummond, moved in the House of Commons for a preliminary grant of a quarter of a million pounds to begin work on the railways, but the Tories, aided by private speculators, defeated the measure.

In the following year Lord Norbury, son of the Judge who condemned Robert Emmet to the gallows, was shot dead while speaking to a steward on his own property. Drummond's biographer was at a loss to explain the reason (a pencil note on the volume before me says 'he was about to evict half a countryside'). The landlord party now gave vent to their accumulated resentment against Drummond. His letter to the Tipperary magistrates was broadcast; to his incendiary suggestion that 'property had its duties as well as its rights' was attributed the latest crime. *The Times* went into action, referring to 'the insolence displayed by Mr Drummond, Under Secretary, at the Castle, in his treatment on a former occasion of the Tipperary magistrates, when, instead of heartily assisting them to discover and punish the authors of murderous atrocities perpetrated within their county, and to preserve the peace thereof, this Jack-in-office had taken upon himself to lecture the vast body of its landed proprietors in the discharge of their duties as landlords, and to more than insinuate that all the evils they complained of had been caused by their own misconduct.'

The murderers of whom the Tipperary landlords had complained had in fact been caught, two were hanged, the third turned King's evidence. It should have satisfied the Tipperary magistrates; it should have gratified *The Times*. But 'the Thunderer' had it in for Drummond, who had involved himself with their pet aversion—Daniel O'Connell. Drummond's letter, the newspaper said, had held up the landlords 'to the popish multitude as offenders'. His letter to the magistrates 'abetted, encouraged and stimulated' the peasantry. Irish members joined in the abuse of Drummond whom they coupled with O'Connell and the Pope as the enemies of peace in Ireland. Morpeth supported his lieutenant but, as always, it was left to O'Connell to take the defence of the policy of appeasement on himself.

Morpeth gave figures to show that in the previous five years there had been 2,324 evictions, by each of which a family of four, on an average, was made homeless. At a modest computation 46,480 people had been thrown out on the road in that period. O'Connell left statistics to the Chief Secretary and directed his attack against the four gentlemen from Ireland who 'came here for the sole purpose of vilifying their native land'. He got carried away, but how splendidly! 'I rejoice in my native land. I rejoice that I was born in it. I rejoice that I belong to it. Your calumnies cannot diminish my regard for it; your malevolence cannot blacken it in my esteem; and although your vices and crimes have driven its people to outrage and murder. (Order, order.) Yes, I say your vices and crimes. (Order, order, chair, chair.) Well, then, the crimes of men like you have produced these results. (Oh! Oh!).'

It is refreshing to meet O'Connell, someone saying he enjoys Ireland and being Irish, not merely registering despondency and lust for revenge. No wonder he lifted the spirits of the people and won a popularity unknown by any other leader before or since.

CHAPTER IX

Drummond and the Royal Dublin Society

DRUMMOND'S TROUBLES were not confined to the country, although the larger issues of the century were centred there. He found himself at loggerheads with a group who, it is sad to say, had in some instances fallen away from the fine standards of their founders. The Royal Dublin Society, when Drummond came to Dublin, was lodged in the Duke of Leinster's noble mansion in Kildare Street. To join it had become a title to consideration, and many of the newcomers took no interest at all either in science or the improvement of agriculture. They regarded it as a social club, and they were anxious that it should be exclusive, that people of the wrong politics and the wrong religion should not belong. Their attitude reflected a change in the country since the Union.

Ireland, an agricultural country, found itself increasingly under the influence of the town-bred. The member of the College Green parliament, if he were a substantial person, had his house in Dublin, but he was based in his county as were the majority. Mr Perry Curtis identifies them with rural magnates and the decay of the landed interest in Ireland as elsewhere toll'd the knell of their parting day. The type that occupied the cities, apart from the great officials, were not such as set the tone in an age of Whiggery.

The Absentee and *Castle Rackrent* could not be said to paint a rosy picture of Irish life at the time of the Union; and Maria Edgeworth is the only writer I know of who has anything good to say of the conditions that succeeded it.

"'I happened,'" says a character in the first-named novel, "'to be quartered in Dublin soon after the Union took place; and I remember the great but transient change that appeared. From the removal of both Houses of Parliament, most of the nobility, and many of the principal families among the Irish commoners, either hurried in high hopes to London, or retired disgusted and in despair to their houses in the country. Immediately, in Dublin, commerce rose into the vacated seats of rank; wealth rose into the place of birth. New faces and new equipages appeared; people, who had never been heard of before, started into notice, pushed themselves forward, not scrupling to elbow their way even at the Castle; and they were presented to my lord-lieutenant and my lady-lieutenant; for their excellencies, for the time being, might have played their vice-regal parts to empty benches, had they not admitted such persons for the moment to fill their court. Those of former times, of hereditary pretensions and high-bred minds and manners, were scandalised by all this; and they complained with justice that the whole tone of society was altered; that the decorum, elegance, polish and charm of society was gone; and I among the rest (said Sir James) felt and deplored their change. But, now it is all over, we may acknowledge, perhaps, even those things which we felt most disagreeable at the time were productive of eventual benefit.'"

Formerly a few families had set the fashion. From time immemorial everything had, in Dublin, been submitted to their hereditary authority; and conversation, though it had been rendered polite by their example, was, at the same time, limited within narrow bounds. Young people, educated upon a more enlarged plan, in time grew up; and, no authority or fashion forbidding it, necessarily rose to their just place, and enjoyed their due influence in society. The want of manners, joined to the want of knowledge in the new set, created universal disgust: they were compelled, some by ridicule, some by bankruptcies, to fall back into their former places, from which they could never more emerge. In the meantime, some of the Irish nobility and gentry who had been living at an unusual expense in London—an expense beyond their income—were glad to return home to refit; and they brought with them a new stock of ideas, and some taste for science and literature, which, within these latter years, have become fashionable, indeed indispensable, in London. That part of the Irish aristocracy, who, immediately upon the first incursions of the vulgarians, had fled in despair to their fastnesses in the country, hearing of the improvements which had gradually taken place in society, and assured of the final expulsion of the bar-

barians, ventured from their retreats, and returned to their posts in the town. '"So that now," concluded Sir James, "you find a society in Dublin composed of a most agreeable and salutary mixture of birth and education, gentility and knowledge, manner and matter; and you see pervading the whole new life and energy, new talent, new ambition, a desire and determination to improve and be improved—a perception that higher distinction can now be obtained in almost any company, by genius and merit, than by airs and dress. So much for the higher order. Now, among the class of tradesmen and shopkeepers you may amuse yourself, my Lord, with marking the difference between them and persons of the same rank in London."'

The Edgeworths, because they were good themselves, tended to see the best in others. They were not in a narrow sense politically-minded, and their well-bred attitude was quite foreign to the arrogance that was abroad, and which was reflected in the press in Dublin as much as in London—a hectoring tone of intolerable self-sufficiency. The trouble into which Drummond ran with the Royal Dublin Society was ostensibly on the subject of newspapers. The Society was in receipt of a regular grant from public funds and to that extent there was justification for interfering in its affairs. In 1811 O'Connell presented himself for membership and was blackballed. He made no fuss about this, and his exclusion might have been justified on the ground that he was a highly controversial figure whose appearance might conceivably introduce a political element into the atmosphere. But there was no such excuse for refusing to elect Dr Murray. The Catholic Archbishop of Dublin had set a high standard of tact and urbanity and had taken the most scrupulous care not to offend Protestant susceptibilities. Apart from that he was sociable and highly educated. Nevertheless the vote was given against him, and in the Sackville Street Club, one of the three Unionist social clubs in Dublin, a notice was on display in the hall on the day for balloting, reminding members to go to the RDS and 'do their duty'. Dr Murray served on the Board of National Education with Archbishop Whately. His name was seconded by a Senior Fellow of Trinity College.

In the Royal Dublin Society were many members who were

more interested in the inflammatory politics of the day than in Mr Kane's experiments. Mr Davy's lectures, Mr Weld's essays on curious scythes observed in hay fields, or in Mr Griffith's geological surveys. They met in the rooms, read the papers, and probably cursed the Government. There were other members such as Robert Hutton (Thomas Davis was engaged to his daughter), Captain Porlock in charge of the Geological Survey, and Mr C. W. Hamilton, an agricultural expert who deplored the unscientific tendency which had crept into the Society.

That the Society was fully entitled to deny Dr Murray membership, he was the first to admit. When he heard that some members were about to create trouble on his account he wrote a letter to his proposer asking him to convey to the members 'what you know to be my feeling on the subject, together with my earnest solicitation, that, in the future transactions of the Society, I may be wholly lost sight of; that the recent cause of momentary disagreement may be forgotten; and that the whole body may join a cordial union to promote the great objects of national improvement for which the Society was established.'

That would have been a graceful end to a disagreeable incident had the matter been allowed to rest, but the waters were troubled by a stone dropped from another eminence. On the 20 January 1836 Lord Morpeth, the Chief Secretary, wrote to the Society from Dublin Castle . . . 'His Excellency feels that he could not recommend to His Majesty's government, a continuance of the annual vote in the estimates of the ensuing session without certain modifications in the constitution of the Society . . .' and the letter ended with an invitation to a deputation from the Society to discuss these proposals.

A deputation from the Society waited on Drummond, but when they announced on arrival that they had no power to speak for the society, Drummond was annoyed and refused to disclose the government's propositions.

A month later, according to the *Dublin Evening Mail*: 'the insulting and audacious propositions made by Lord Mulgrave' were received by the Society. And their fate is recorded in the issue for 4 March 1836: 'the yearly Stated Meeting of the Society took place yesterday; and, as was to have been expected from any company of Irish Gentlemen, propositions urged by Lord Mulgrave were treated with the contempt and scorn that emanating from such a quarter they must receive in an assembly so constituted.'

At the next meeting of the Society, Mr C. W. Hamilton gave notice of his intention to move a protest against the publication in the *Evening Mail* of a letter written by a member of the Society.

The letter to which Mr Hamilton objected was a curious one, written by a Dr Meyler who had been connected with the Society for some time and had given lectures on chemistry to the members. It was subsequently disclosed that he had written personally to the Lord Lieutenant asking him to attend his chemistry lectures and that Lord Mulgrave had declined the invitation as it had not issued from the Society at large. Dr Meyler's letter is too long to quote in full, but a few passages will convey the temper of the whole:

'In return for his Excellency's certain propositions respecting the future constitution of the Society I would venture to suggest to him the expedience of purchasing Cobbett's grammar for his Under Secretary, as it would be a rather becoming qualification in those who volunteer to reform a scientific institution to convey their directions with precision and correctness.'

The Lord Lieutenant had expressed doubts about the Library and condemned the practice of taking newspapers into the Society. Dr Meyler observed that:

'The Library of the Royal Dublin Society affords a rich treasure of valuable works, well calculated to promote its objects. It has been formed by learned committees and learned librarians and, very fortunately for the country, not by Lords Lieutenants, nor Lords of the Treasury . . .

THERE SHALL BE NO NEWSPAPERS PERMITTED IN THE HOUSE OF THE SOCIETY.

'The autocrat of all the Russian world would scarcely, from his Imperial Palace, have put forth so arbitrary a mandate: verily, my Lord Mulgrave, it has often been said that the Whigs, when in power, out-Tory even the Tories; but a Whig Lord-Lieutenant, under a radical council, out-Herods even Herod...'

It may well be that Drummond's superiors took a more active part in this business than in some of the larger transactions which he conducted in their name.

On St Patrick's Day, 1836, Thomas Drummond wrote a letter deploring the Society's failure to adopt all the proposals and intimating that the withholding of the annual grant would now have to be considered. On this, a memorial was presented by the Society, explaining that its failure to meet the propositions in full arose from the special circumstances of the Society, and its reluctance after a hundred years experience to rush into innovations. It specifically repudiated the charge of religious or political bigotry and pointed out that in thirty-six years eight hundred and eighty-seven members had been elected and only four candidates rejected.

Naper and Hamilton wanted to make the Society more agricultural, and in the end their policies prevailed. They knew the Chief Secretary, Lord Morpeth, and claimed to have his ear. Drummond was probably more concerned about the evidence of religious bias, and his unshakeable opposition to all displays of bigotry is evident here as elsewhere. When Lord Morpeth wrote to the Society, it was clear that a major issue had arisen which would come before Parliament when the estimates were being discussed. Hamilton wanted to enlist William Smith O'Brien on the side of reform and he wrote four long letters to him during the month of March in that year. He explained that he, Naper, and thirty or forty other members had joined the Society to improve its agricultural side.

William Smith O'Brien moved a resolution in the House of Commons on the 24 March 1836 for an inquiry into the affairs of the Society; in the conflict of evidence that followed we get three pictures of the RDS at the time.

Mr Weld in his evidence brought out facts about monthly scientific meetings which had been held recently for the first time in the Society. He drew a picture of one of these: 'Mr Davy had made some discoveries in the laboratory, which he explained tolerably fully; and Dr Kane exhibited some interesting experiments to us on acoustics, of his own invention. We had besides, models of machinery and new implements in optical instruments explained by artisans introduced for the occasion, and who proved to be men of great ingenuity and good address. Mr Nevin gave us the result of some experiments he had made in the Botanic Gardens relative to early grasses; and Mr Mackay of the college Botanic Garden exhibited a rare specimen of a living toad brought from the South of Ireland. We had wherewithal to make even more time pass away very agreeably.'

Mr Hutton, in his evidence before the select committee, complained of the weekly meetings of the Society: 'The effect . . . is to induce persons to join the Society for other objects besides the advancement of Science . . .'

But there were others who were satisfied with the Society as it was—Dr Harty, for example. He, in his evidence, was anxious to prove that so far from the newsroom being used as a political club . . . 'There is no intercourse between the parties; there is no conversation, a more silent and quiet room I never witnessed than the newsroom of the Society.' Dr Meyler, who was in sympathy with Dr Harty, had drawn a more colourful picture. 'Country gentlemen from all parts of Ireland, proprietors of extensive factories, opulent and enlightened merchants, professional men, judges, men of science, all assemble now in this non-interdicted room; they bring to it various knowledge, and various plans of practical improvement; it is a great intellectual treat to enjoy the conversation of such a room . . . every matter pertaining to the object of the society form in it the constant topic of conversation . . . it is, in a most peculiar manner, exempt from all political and religious discussions . . . there is not a matter . . . that is not occasionally discussed in it.'

The Royal Dublin Society created the first art school in Ireland, and the high standard of design in Dublin building in the eighteenth century is partly due to the training given in the Society's classes. Now taken over by Government, it instituted or otherwise encouraged the setting up of the National Museum, National Library and National Gallery, the Botanical Gardens in Glasnevin, the National College of Art and the Veterinary College. No institution in Ireland can hope to put itself so deep into the national debt. And yet there is an undying prejudice against the RDS. It is so Anglo-Irish!

There is a statue to Drummond in the City Hall in Dublin; it stood beside other statues by Hogan, the best regarded Irish sculptor of the time; and these appropriately were of O'Connell and Davis. (Davis's statue has been moved to Mount Jerome, where he is buried.) All three, it must be admitted, are somewhat prosaic as works of art in comparison with the fourth figure in the circular hall. Charles Lucas by Edward Smyth is reminiscent of Bernini, and the best statue in Dublin. It is the proximity to the other great Irishmen whom Hogan carved that is so happy; and anyone who has thought about the history of Ireland must reflect on all three.

O'Connell and Drummond represent an effort to rule Ireland by impartial justice in the given conditions. When it failed O'Connell reverted to his former position and agitated for a repeal of the Union. His relationship with Melbourne's administration, which was effectively represented in Ireland by Drummond, has never been done justice to. O'Connell has been libelled by nationalists as a compromising and weak figure in comparison with the men who resorted to arms. This is one of the great injustices of history; there was nothing weak about O'Connell; and I find something masculine and splendid about the way he took on the House of Commons virtually alone when Drummond's attempts to rule Ireland justly were assailed by English Tories and Irish Unionists alike.

O'Connell is outside this study. There was nothing Anglo-Irish about him; he was out of time, an Irish chieftain born again, a national leader of his people. His jollity and forcefulness, the very description of his walk—umbrella on his shoulders like a gun, kicking his feet out as he marched down the quays to the law courts—brings him to life. Over six feet tall; ruddy faced, with sparkling blue eyes; not a man for treasons, stratagems and spoils; a happy contrast to the conventional picture of Ireland as a weeping woman.

It was impossible to cut this giant out of Irish history—his picture used to be in every country cottage—but in so far as it was possible the attempt has been made. His Christian and civilised determination not to shed blood, in which he persisted though thwarted at every turn by his opponents for a lifetime, is regarded as a sign of imperfect dedication to the cause. It anticipated Gandhi by a century, even if O'Connell's flow of abuse was in startling contrast to the Hindu's low-toned utterance. O'Connell's place in history was challenged immediately after his death by the followers of Thomas Davis.

I will discuss this remarkable man in another chapter; he is mentioned here in relation to Drummond and O'Connell. He wrote, and he was surrounded by clever, ardent young men, some of whom also wrote. One of them—John Mitchel—with a brilliance that will keep his prose alive for ever. Their colleague, Charles Gavan Duffy, who eventually quarrelled bitterly with Mitchel, is the copious historian of the period. He was devoted to Davis and wrote him up at the expense of all his contemporaries. O'Connell had no Boswell, no Macaulay, not even a Gavan Duffy. And the effect of this imbalance has been that a very exaggerated picture of the contemporary significance of Davis and his friends, in comparison with O'Connell's, has been graven for ever on the Irish mind. Since that time Davis's writings have influenced Irish nationalists, and they have been inspired by the purity of his motives.

If the Young Irelanders did little for O'Connell's reputation, they contrived to let Drummond's services pass without any thanks at all. In Mitchel's *Jail Journal* his name does not appear once. The same is true for Gavan Duffy's history of 'Young Ireland'. Over thirty years ago I wrote a *Life* of Isaac Butt, and in preparation for it I soaked myself in contemporary history. On turning up that book now, I find one reference only to Drummond, and I echo, through my protagonist, the contemporary ingratitude to the administration that sent him here. It is interesting to discover for oneself how one can be the victim of propaganda. I am glad to make a little reparation to Drummond here for the neglect of my ungrateful countrymen.

What was his secret? A comparatively simple one: he had not been bred to politics, but came to them, like Larcom, another good friend to Ireland, through the Ordnance Survey. As an officer in the Royal Engineers he had invented a light, based on lime, that brought him such fame he was asked to dine with old King William. His coming to Ireland was in answer to his own wish; he was attracted to it as T. E. Lawrence to Arabia. He brought to his task a strong good character, great practical intelligence, administrative ability, freedom from awe of the mighty, and a love of justice.

Drummond died, not from over-work as he thought, but peritonitis. His last request was that he should be buried in Ireland, 'the country of my adoption—a country which I loved, which I have faithfully served, and for which I believe I have sacrificed my life'.

At his funeral, close to the pall-bearers, followed 'the proud figure of O'Connell . . . Never before, and never since, has an Irish leader, possessing the confidence of the vast majority of his countrymen, followed an English official to the grave,' wrote Drummond's biographer.

That Ireland should produce sons prepared to devote themselves to her service is not remarkable, but I find something almost sublime in the noble service Thomas Drummond gave to Ireland. Had there been such as he even three times in the century, the Union might have worked. As it was, his death coincided with the defeat of Melbourne, and Ireland returned to the familiar rule of coercion and, when reforms accompanied it, increased coercion.

To please the Irish landlords there was placed on the Statute book a law which made it a crime for an ejected person to be found near the site of his former habitation.

So much for a noble Scot; but before I leave him and O'Connell I should like to put on record Gladstone's impression of the latter. It is not generally known, and has an interest, as between them they were active in the Irish cause for most of the century. Gladstone, as a young man, found himself in a coach with O'Connell. He wrote about it, fifty years later. Balzac, in his time, had said that O'Connell was one of the four greatest men in the world. Gladstone 'in a small effort at historical justice acknowledged that in his early years 'he had been blind to his greatness. Almost from the opening of my parliamentary life, I felt that he was the greatest popular leader whom the world had ever seen.' He was vain 'but with an innocuous and sportive vanity . . . Beside him Kossuth and Mazzini were small. He was nearer to the great Cavour . . . If ever he seemed to wander into violence, these were the wanderings of a moment, his boomerang soon came home.' When he died a great man passed 'from the millstream of politics into the domain of history'.

O'Connell had only seven years of life left to him after the failure of the Whig experiment; and when he was challenged at his last monster meeting at Clontarf by Wellington's guns, and declined the opportunity to gain immortality in an Irish Amritsar, his star began to fade. Very soon he was on the verge of senility, and death in 1847 came as a relief. It came during the famine which planted among the Irish in America that hatred of England which was to erupt, first in the abortive Fenian rising of 1867, again, more eventfully, in 1916.

As O'Connell had prophesied, a rebellion took place six months after his death. By that time John Mitchel had been transported to the Antipodes, Gavan Duffy was in prison; but the Young Irelanders were carried on to revolt by the momentum of events. The leader was William Smith O'Brien, descended from King Brian Boru, but more closely connected with Lord Inchiquin. A country gentleman, educated at Harrow, for a time a Conservative in the House of Commons, O'Brien was the most unlikely revolutionist that ever mounted a barricade. His eventual adherence to the extreme wing of nationalist opinion is the best indictment of the method of government.

Travelling across the country he addressed the people from his car, telling them that the hour had struck and calling them to arms. In Mullinahone a great crowd had assembled, armed with pikes and guns. No doubt a very considerable rebellion could have begun, but O'Brien's exhortations to the populace were in most cases nullified by the priests who went among the people begging them to put down their arms. Nor can O'Brien have been a very inspiring leader for so desperate a venture. In Mullinahone, he called on six policemen in the barracks to join him; resistance was hopeless, he gave them time to consider. They refused. Whereupon O'Brien left them alone and made for

Ballingarry. The signal to attack had not yet been given. There seems to have been no one to attack. In a few days it is heard that dragoons are approaching. A barricade is thrown across the road. Captain Longmore in charge of the detachment when confronted with this obstacle, demands the right of passage or he will force it, whereupon he is asked whether he has come to arrest Mr O'Brien. Captain Longmore has not heard of Mr O'Brien. He is on his way to barracks. The barricades are instantly removed and the dragoons go on their way. The best part of a week was spent in this Gilbertian way when a band of constabulary, forty-six strong, marched against the rebels at Ballingarry. The officer in charge, seeing a huge crowd of peasants under arms, declined a contest, and made for a slated house some distance from the road. This was fortified and manned in preparation for the expected attack. As at Mullinahone, O'Brien approached the police and invited them to join him. They, too, declined the offer, then for the first time, and in the language of Her Majesty's Attorney-General, 'fire was opened on the constabulary of the Queen'. The police kept the five children of the widow who owned the house inside with them. When three of the rebels brought up bundles of hay which they meant to put against the house and fire, Smith O'Brien at the entreaty of the mother, prevented them. An hour later, another small party of constabulary arrived on the scene and the crowd scattered.

On hearing that the horse on which he was escaping had been taken from a policeman whom the rebels had captured, O'Brien, a fugitive from justice, almost certain of hanging if he were caught, returned the horse to its owner and proceeded on foot. Shortly afterwards, he was captured and with Thomas Francis Meagher and others, charged with high treason.

O'Brien was duly sentenced to be hanged, drawn and quartered, but the sentence was commuted to transportation for life. However, he was pardoned eventually and returned from the Antipodes and lived until 1864. Characteristically his first comment on being reunited with his family was to deplore the brogue his children had acquired in his absence.

CHAPTER X

Philanthropists

AUBREY DE VERE and his father were among the good landlords to propose emigration as a solution to the problem of the overcrowded countryside. It is not just that those who were prepared to finance this extreme measure as the only alternative to abdication by the landlords—class suicide—should share the reputation of the owners of coffin ships who took emigrants abroad in beastly conditions—and solely for gain—so that many did not survive the passage. Sir Robert Gore-Booth who raised £50,000 on mortgage to feed his tenants also favoured emigration, and so did a saint, who happened to be a landlord in Donegal in those days.

John Hamilton came into his property in 1821 and stayed away from it only for two periods in his long life, never when he took over the management of the estate personally and dispensed with agents. He was fully alive to all the evils of the system—the absenteeism, which meant that £3,000,000 was paid out of Ireland to landlords living in England or abroad. Absenteeism had occupied the attention of reformers for more than a century. Arthur Young in 1780 drew up a list which included the name of Edmund Burke (as Prior's included Berkeley). Young's list contained 195 names, the highest rental £31,000, the lowest £500 a year. Another evil was the uncertainty in which tenants lived as to their rent and possession. Hamilton settled all these matters on his own estate. It was his custom to publish an annual address to his tenants. Before the Famine came he advised the Government that each estate should bear the cost of its own relief, otherwise the landlords who tried to help their tenants would have to pay for those who abandoned them to public assistance. His advice was not taken. On one occasion, during the Famine, he came across a relief officer surrounded by men who had walked barefoot in the snow to get pay for their week's work on a relief scheme. He was explaining to them, without success, that, owing to official red tape, they would have to wait for a week for their wages. Hamilton gave him the money to pay them. As a result the officer was reprimanded and a directive was sent from Dublin that Hamilton was not to be repaid. He recalled that those starving wretches gave him back what he had advanced, at a penny a week, of their own volition.

As it would be unjust to indict him for helping some of his tenants to emigrate—he advanced the fares—he is also exempt from the charge of proselytising as it was commonly practised —bartering souls for soup; but he was a devout evangelist with considerable powers of a mesmeric order. Hundreds of all religions came to his bible classes. When a wind blew the roof off the Catholic chapel he felt in his conscience unable to contribute to its restoration but instead he let all his Catholic tenants off their contributions to the Established Church and paid it himself in future. Later his conscience relaxed—as it does when conscientious young men grow older—and next time the Chapel collapsed he sent five pounds to secure the floor.

He took no part in politics and judged events as he saw them with absolute impartiality. After the passing of the act for Catholic Emancipation in 1829 he noticed that there was at once an ugly Orange reaction. The Catholics lit a tar barrel to express their delight, and were attacked by Orangemen armed with rifles and bayonets. 'On both sides the madness of the people was and is great, but the Orange party have shown among them a cool, deliberate, bloodthirsty spirit which I could not have believed. The same spirit is said to exist on the Roman Catholic side; certainly not to the same degree; indeed, I have not met with it at all.'

He had been brought up with ultra-Tory principles, as a nephew of the Duke of Wellington's wife, a Pakenham. As a boy he doubted the Christianity of the views that prevailed and 'with the increase of years I began to see that the faults and vices which socially presided in Ireland, were those of a conqueror and tyrant race on the one side, and those of a conquered and enslaved, or, at least, trampled and ill-used race on the other and that an end ought to be put to this state of things'. In later meditations he wrote, 'I wonder more at Protestants sticking where they do than at thoughtful pious people becoming Roman Catholics. Roman Catholicism is, at least, very consistent.'

One of the difficulties, as he saw it, towards improvement was the power claimed by the priesthood. It prevented the Catholics from being capable of enjoying freedom in a free society. But he resented the law's attitude towards Catholics and wished them to be as politically equal to Protestants as the law could make them. Living in Ulster, therefore, in 1829, he was more advanced in this matter than the Unionist majority almost a century and a half later.

At the end of his life Home Rule was a practical proposition, but he believed that this movement would burn itself out. He favoured local councils for the four provinces of Ireland, but saw in the complete integration of the United Kingdom the solution of Irish grievances. Irish patriots, lacking judgment, had left behind them 'a legacy of vain aspirations of national glory as a *little* independent nation, instead of the truly glorious position of being an essential part of the United Kingdom . . .'

Hamilton was a child of his time in his deep seriousness about religious matters. He involved himself in the great theological debate; but unlike de Vere, who followed Newman and became a Catholic, Hamilton did not approve of Newman's sermons: his was too evangelistic a temperament. He would have got on splendidly with John Wesley; even in a train or staying overnight in an inn he never lost the opportunity to provoke religious discussion; but always with a complete absence of sectarian bitterness. On his rare visits to London he was shocked by social conditions and, like Gladstone, stopped girls in the street whom he helped to save. He gave them money and called on clergymen to take care of their spiritual needs, not always with the happiest results. The sheer scale of the problem oppressed him and he was glad to return to Donegal where poverty at least was free from the evils of prostitution.

Hamilton gives a pleasanter picture of the Duke of Wellington than is to be found anywhere. He recalled riding on his back as a child when Sir Arthur Wellesley, as he then was, performed prodigies as an improvised horse. Later on he consulted him about his army career and the Duke 'was very kind and gave his opinion and reasons. He opined that I should not go to a military college at all, but carry out Sir Edward's plan of a Cambridge education. "For," said he, "if you are worth your salt, you will learn soldiering when you get your commission and at Cambridge you will get that education both of learning and of habit, which you can never get again. Besides, you will have the advantage which a man must always lose who is brought up to a particular profession, the advantage of a free standing-point untrammelled by the ingrained prejudices that take root in the finest minds which are kept in one circle. You can afford the money and the time for two educations, avail yourself of these advantages, be educated first as if for the pulpit or the bar, and then you will have a double chance of making a first-rate soldier. I would give more than I can mention", added the Duke, "that I had a university education."'

In the Famine years only one person, and that by accident, died on Hamilton's estate; when the land acts came he had anticipated their provisions.

Was he the exception that proved the rule in Ireland? The landlords' evil legend would almost persuade one that it was so. But the truth is that those who abused the system brought all into disrepute. In this particular case there is evidence of the true position in Donegal at least. The local parish priest wrote to the *Derry Journal* in 1880 to exempt Hamilton from a charge of rackrenting which was made by a deputation to Hugh Childers, Gladstone's Chancellor of the Exchequer. Father Doherty thought Hamilton was over-sensitive. 'When bad and oppressive landlords are spoken of, no one intends to include the late Thomas Conolly, the Hamiltons, the Marquis of Conyngham, Mr Brooke of Lough Eske and some others.'

That is not a bad list of exemptions in one area; and it could have been repeated in each county. For instance, what was called Tenant Right, a custom in Ulster but not in other parts of Ireland, which gave the tenant a saleable interest in his holding and which Gladstone made law in 1870, was already in force on the estates of Lord Portsmouth in Wexford, Lord Portarlington, and Lord Devon.

But it was inevitable that a proprietorship of the land of Ireland with such names attached to it was not destined to last for ever. Hamilton welcomed a peasant proprietorship. By the end of the century the landlords themselves saw the writing on the wall.

CHAPTER XI

Thomas Davis and Protestant Nationalists

BUT LET US turn back to consider one who has been more generously recognised than O'Connell or Parnell. To say it in Ireland is a sort of treason because it sounds like a qualification and whatever is disputed, Davis's virtues are agreed on by all. He was one of those active idealists whose purity of motive calls out what is best in others. In religion such men found Orders, and their inspiration sometimes lasts beyond their lifetime. Davis certainly did. He was little more than thirty years old when he died in 1845. He was one of three who founded a newspaper, *The Nation*, to promulgate the views he had formed as a student in Trinity College. These were, in short, the regeneration of pride in Ireland among Irishmen. Davis soon had a group of young men around him; they studied various periods in Irish history, wrote articles, encouraged talent and threw themselves behind O'Connell who, just then, was making his final bid for a restoration of the Irish parliament. When O'Connell's campaign collapsed and he resorted to more desultory methods the young men became disillusioned. By that time they had been joined by a solicitor from Newry, Co. Down, John Mitchel. Mitchel had more genius than Davis, but there was less of the angel about him. Davis, as editor of *The Nation*, became increasingly revolutionary; but the pace was not hot enough for Mitchel; he resigned from the paper after Davis died and the editorship was taken over by Charles Gavan Duffy. Mitchel started his own journal; but its contents were too much for the authorities. He was arrested, tried, and sentenced to be transported to the Antipodes. It must remain a speculation whether Davis would have eventually encouraged a resort to arms. On the whole I believe that with the momentum he had attained, in the appalling state of the country during the Famine, and the ineffectiveness of Government's methods to cope with it—on the whole I think Davis, in despair, would have come out with Smith O'Brien. But, more than likely, by that time his writings would have had put him under lock and key.

This is not a history of Ireland, neither is it a chronology of revolution, therefore I shall omit what can be found in abundance elsewhere—the story of Ireland's decline into famine, fear and revolt in the 1840's.

But the part played by Davis has a peculiar relevance to the Anglo-Irish scene because he introduced a new note. He belonged, not to the revolutionary tradition, but rather to the group that inspired antiquarian interest in the Gaelic past. This began in the eighteenth century and led to the formation of the Royal Irish Academy. General Vallancey, an almost admirable Crichton, was one of the prime movers, and his activities corresponded with the wave of excitement, to which we find many references in Boswell, over Mac Pherson's Ossianic forgeries. Mac Pherson's admirers included Goethe; and he is buried in Westminster Abbey. His work has about as much authenticity as Fitzgerald's *Omar Khayyam*. They were fabrications rather than forgeries proper. He knew a great deal of Gaelic poetry and legend; but success went to his head. Ossian (in Irish *Oisin*), the son of Finn left no poetry behind him. The legends are there—Pearse modelled his boy's school on them—but Mac Pherson had to pretend that he had translated his inventions and, when asked for the originals, could not produce them.

The Ossianic wave hit Ireland. It inspired Speranza, mother of Oscar Wilde. His first two names—Oscar Fingal—tell us what was on his mother's mind when he was born. Speranza was one of those whom Davis inspired; but it was after his death that she began to contribute to *The Nation*.

Davis and his friends aimed to establish Irish culture on its own foundations, to go back, as it were, and take it up at the point where it was left off—when the Gaelic aristocracy fled the country; but their ardour was chiefly spilled out in ballads in the manner of Macaulay's *Lays of Ancient Rome*. Only one of *The Nation's* contributors, James Clarence Mangan, was a poet in any exact use of the word.

Davis began his life work in Trinity College; many of his

followers were his contemporaries there. His father had been a surgeon in the British army who married an Irish woman; and Davis's influence reached a group which, in the ordinary course, would have had nothing to do with national aspirations. At the same time, his newspaper, *The Nation*, gave the people a sort of reading that they had never had before. While he was alive the paper was more creative than destructive, but he died before the horrors of the Famine. After that *The Nation* became frankly revolutionary.

Davis was active in every group which was working for the improvement of the country, and an editor of a paper which encouraged literary effort must always exercise a certain influence. Wilde's mother was eccentric, but her adherence to Davis's successors was a portent. The seeds of nationalism were being sown on what had until then been stony ground. A Fellow of Trinity College, John Kells Ingram, wrote the stirring verses —'Who Fears to Speak of '98?'. Samuel Ferguson, a young barrister from Belfast, was another who felt the influence of Thomas Davis.

Ferguson is one who helps us to an understanding of nineteenth-century Ireland: so often represented as if it were exclusively devoted to politics and agrarian disputes that one is apt to forget people lived at the time who were neither proprietors, politicians, peasants, nor priests.

Ferguson came from a Scottish family that settled at Thrushfield near Antrim. He was not a typical northerner, inasmuch as his people were gentlefolk. Social plainness has ever been a proud boast of the Irish dissenter, and one is seldom given cause to complain that the ideal has been betrayed. Ferguson's father was another rare thing—an extravagant Ulsterman. He died having dissipated his fortune. Young Samuel went to school in Belfast, and then came to Trinity College; which he left without taking a degree. Drifting to London, where he studied for the bar, he made an impression with his first poems, being published by Blackwood's before he was twenty-one. When qualified to practise, he came to Dublin and started his career as a barrister. Law is notoriously a jealous mistress, and Ferguson's literary and archaeological interests may have removed the stimulus a successful barrister requires. He made no great impact at the bar. In 1848 he married one of the Guinness family, and in 1867 resigned from practice for reasons of health and was appointed first Deputy Keeper of the Records of Ireland. In due course he became President of the Royal Irish Academy. He never ceased to publish poetry; based on a genuine passion for the Irish past it is often evocative and sometimes stimulating. Yeats was greatly influenced by Ferguson but came to think of him as overrated. As a poet he suffered from the fault of his age—prolixity.

His widow wrote his biography in two volumes after he died. In the fashion of her time she portrayed him as a plaster saint. The result would have made for dull reading were it not so revealing of an attitude which tempted Lytton Strachey to send up the whole era in *Eminent Victorians*. From the work, because of its copious documentation, we can learn a great deal about the times. It is a pity that in the process Lady Ferguson gives us no picture of what sort of man her husband was. She winds a cocoon of complacency around them both, very representative of the period, and beautifully brought out in the Archbishop of Dublin's funeral oration. His Grace was married to a Guinness, a sister of the Lords Iveagh and Ardilaun. There is a hint that he—while not expressly saying as much—has it from the Almighty himself that Ferguson, as a connection of the Guinnesses, will be looked after in his new abode in the manner to which he has been accustomed. 'All is well', the Archbishop assured his hearers, 'All is well'— It was like a Chairman's statement to the shareholders at the annual general meeting of the company—'His last words—and let us treasure them in our hearts were these, spoken in a whisper which could scarcely be heard—"All is well! All is well!" Oh, what brave words to hear from a dying-bed. Oh, what comforting words to ring again and again within a bereaved and lonely heart!—"All is well!" May every one of us, whether in health or in sickness, in the fullness of life or at the approach of death, be able to say, "All is well!"

'And now, dear brethren, whatsoever is earthly of our dear brother will be taken presently from this Cathedral, and tomorrow will be laid amongst "the graves of Donegore", which he has celebrated in song; and if you ask me, meanwhile, as the prophet's messenger asked of the Shunammite, "Is all well with our brother?" my answer to you is the answer given in our brother's own words, "All is well!"'

And, indeed, it would be curious, after reading the life recorded in these volumes if all had not been well. Even if he had some failings, in common with the rest of humanity, Ferguson's contribution to his time was more than considerable. It is interesting to see how, in the various groups he joins, he links up with people who are heard of again in other connections. For instance, he was drawn into the scheme of an Ordnance Survey Memoir. This was under the direction of Thomas Larcom, like Drummond an officer in the Royal Engineers. The plan embraced a detailed survey of every county, and it is tragic that the Government suddenly decided to drop the scheme. The original manuscript of the County survey, carried out by John O'Donavan, is in the Royal Irish Academy. I know of nothing that gives such a lively and immediate sense of the Irish past as these unpublished volumes.

Larcom described what happened: 'When I first came to Ireland, and found that my life would be chiefly spent there, I thought it desirable that I should learn Irish. Soon after my arrival I was walking down Sackville Street, and read over the door of a large house, The Irish Society. It was open, and I walked in. I mounted the stair without meeting any one, and seeing before me a baize-covered door, pushed it open, and found myself in presence of a group of gentlemen seated round a table. I apologised for my intrusion, and explained my object. I heard in return that the Committee of the Irish Society, whom I had interrupted, desired to convert the people to Protestantism by giving them the scriptures in their native tongue. One of the gentlemen told me he could recommend a thoroughly qualified Irish teacher, but added that he was imperfectly acquainted with English. He wrote on a sheet of paper the name and address of John O'Donavan. I sent my servant to the address with a request that O'Donavan would call on me next day. I was at breakfast when my note was put into my hand, and I was told that the bearer was in the hall. "Show him up", I said, and O'Donavan, in peasant garb, entered the room. I asked him to sit down and share my breakfast, and proposed that he should do so two or three times a week and undertake to teach me Irish without requiring me to write exercises, as I had no leisure for study. He consented. I found him a very able man, a thorough master of the language. Under his instructions I made considerable progress. But it soon occurred to me that if I should teach him English it would be a better arrangement. Accordingly our positions were reversed. As we took our tea and toast I instructed him, and in due time placed him on the staff of the Ordnance Survey, where he did such valuable work for the country.'

Among others employed by Larcom was George Petrie, an artist and antiquarian and the leading authority on Irish Round Towers. Ferguson was drawn into the circle by Petrie who aroused his enthusiasm for Irish antiquarianism, and met there not only Larcom's team, which included, as well as O'Donavan, Curry, the best Irish scholar of his generation, James Clarence Mangan, the poet, and the group which ran the only literary journal in Ireland, *The University Magazine*—Butt, Staneford, the O'Sullivans, Le Fanu. William Wilde was a slightly later addition to the circle. Oscar's father was five years senior to Ferguson. Another friend was William Stokes, a Dublin doctor of international reputation. Stokes was the son of the United Irishman, the friend of Tone, who retired from the revolutionary body when he saw the direction in which it was heading. William Stokes shared the antiquarian enthusiasm of his friend, and his daughter, Margaret, became distinguished in the same field. Inevitably the group came in contact with Thomas Davis. But none of them was involved in the revolutionary plans of 1848.

O'Donavan wrote to a friend about John Mitchel's *United Irishman*. 'The proprietor is in Newgate and will probably be transported—to where? If he is a Government spy I can understand him, if not he is a monomaniac for he has no party in the country and is suspected by many.'

Nobody ever said anything of that kind about Davis, or asked for his credentials.

When Davis died, Ferguson wrote an ode to his memory; the last verse goes as follows:

> Oh, brave young men, my love, my pride, my promise,
> 'Tis on you my hopes are set,
> In manliness, in kindliness, in virtue,
> To make Erin a nation yet;
> Self-respecting, self-relying, self-advancing,
> In union or in severance, free and strong;
> And if God grant this, then, under God, to Thomas Davis,
> Let the greater praise belong!

The sentiments cannot have been wholly pleasing to his Guinness connections.

'Mr Davis was by birth a gentleman, and both in feeling and judgment opposed to all designs for destroying the legitimate powers of the gentry.' This extract from an appreciation of the young patriot by his colleague, Gavan Duffy, helps to explain how people who had been put off by O'Connell's vituperative style and who were later to withdraw completely when nationalism became associated with agrarian conflict and such deeds as the Phoenix murders, were impressed by Davis. The leader of the revolution when it came, Smith O'Brien, was a brother of Lord Inchiquin, and a former Conservative.

There was always a stonewall Unionist party. It was the stumbling block in Drummond's career; and when Ferguson at length declared himself publicly as in favour of a repeal of the Union, he sacrificed, for a time, some of his friendships. The Guinness family has always been Unionist and a contributor to Conservative funds. The circumstances under which Ferguson took his step was not as a disciple of Davis or Smith O'Brien, and it in part explains why there was, twenty years later, a Dublin Protestant and Conservative group ready to support Butt's Home Rule campaign.

The famine years were traumatic in Ireland, and the national disaster led to a situation not unlike that which exists in Northern Ireland, as I write. As well as revolution in the air, there were persistent rumours that the system of Government in Ireland was going to be changed, the office of Viceroy abolished, the administration and even the Courts of Law moved to London. It was at this stage that Ferguson was persuaded to come out in public with his views. They were not at all subversive. He used the threat to the Law Courts as his motive for speaking out, and he shared with every Irishman of any proper pride a sense of outrage at the tone of contempt with which Ireland was referred to in the English press.

> The weakling infants' moans,
> The mother's sobs, the maddened father's groans,
> The evicted cottier's shrieks; the thousand cries
> That swell the ruined nation's obsequies;
> And, 'mid the hubbub of our woes and crimes,
> The daily prate complacent of the 'Times'.

In the manner of Juvenal he rehearsed all the grievances of the time, and showed that he shared the indignation which was driving more reckless spirits into armed revolt. In all Ferguson's writings at this period one gets a complete sense of national feeling. He says of Irish Unionists that while 'becoming every day more sensible of the advantages of connection with Britain they are also *pari passu* becoming more attached to their own country'. And he goes on to say:

'With strong temptations to the gratification of selfish ambitions by assuming their natural place as leaders of the Irish masses, they adhere devotedly to that connection on which they feel the general welfare of the empire to depend; and—which is perhaps as creditable to them as anything else—they have, with little or no Government aid, and without even the encouragement of one generous notice from the capital, laid the foundations in their own county for schools of science, of letters, and of arts, which bid fair to replace Ireland in her old eminence among the homes of learning in the West of Europe'.

Ferguson's wife said in her memoir that he valued the Union because he believed without it there would be Civil War in Ireland between 'Protestant and progressive Ulster and Catholic and Celtic Ireland'. It was the same sort of fear that made many who knew India dread a like tragedy if Britain withdrew. India won her independence, but the prophets of doom were not mistaken. Many thousands paid for that liberty with their lives, not only in Pakistan. Neither is the Civil War in Ireland, which Ferguson feared, beyond the limits of possibility even yet.

But within a few months Ferguson publicly abandoned his adherence to Unionism. He was still preoccupied with the centralising designs attributed to Lord Clarendon, the Viceroy in office. And these objections were fortified by the acute misery in the country and the failure of the Government to deal with the situation. The chief enemy on this occasion was not the Tory party —Peel had shown an understanding of the Irish predicament— but the Whigs under Lord John Russell, grandfather of the philosopher. Their economic theories were maintained in the face of the starvation of thousands. It was a scientific inhumanity less pardonable than natural ferocity. Cromwell was at least more honest and, in a way, more merciful. He slew on sight.

In Dublin there was a closing of the ranks and the formation of an Irish Council, Ferguson was appointed one of the honorary secretaries. In May 1848 he spoke at a meeting of the Protestant Repeal Association, a body he organised which is seldom mentioned in Irish history, because the history of this period was taken over by Gavan Duffy, and nothing gets into it which was not accomplished by the Young Irelanders.

Ferguson began his speech: 'Mr Chairman and gentlemen, I am a Protestant and an inhabitant of Dublin, and I desire the restoration of a domestic legislature.' At this meeting he formally proposed a motion that 'National prosperity is based on social confidence, and that social confidence in Ireland cannot be expected to exist while the Government is conducted and the laws made by strangers to the Irish people.' What Ferguson was inspired by was the same feeling that animated those who fought against the Union in the former Irish parliament. In future Irish claims would be made on behalf of the people as a whole, but Ferguson saw the numerous poor as a responsibility of Government and could hardly have visualised anyone claiming the right of government on their behalf.

In view of the case that is made against Irish landlords—of whom as a class, Butt, their most influential critic, acknowledged that not by any means all were responsible for the outrages against humanity that were perpetrated by some—it should be noted that Ferguson was protesting on their behalf. The tax for relief of the poor had been put on them, he said, as part of a plan 'to eradicate out of Ireland all classes of gentry, to make the country what is vulgarly called a draw-farm for England, and to centralise in London all the wealth, refinement, and social attractions of the empire'.

In the prosecution of their 'plebeianising policy' they had planned to move the law courts to London and to extinguish 'whatever a gentleman of education, spirit, or honourable ambition would deem best worth living for'. And he went on to make a point which had not eluded Swift's attention, which has sometimes been observable in Northern Ireland—the Irish 'are only repaid by the meanest offices, while all offices of dignity and trust are conferred on Englishmen'. He went on to demand, within the boundary of Ireland, the right of 'taxing ourselves and of regulating and administering our own affairs'.

The centralisation of which Ferguson spoke never came to pass. In any event, he was probably pulled up short by the fate of Smith O'Brien and the others who put their convictions to the proof and suffered banishment.

In later years he was taxed with decline in patriotic ardour, and his self-justification is quite consistent with the views he expressed in 1847 and 1848. Times had changed. The attack was now against the land system, and the outcome of Home Rule was bound to be what he had described as 'plebeianising'. In 1885, before Gladstone introduced his first measure for a limited Home Rule, Ferguson wrote:

'I sympathised with the Young Ireland poets and patriots while their aims were directed to a restoration of Grattan's Parliament in which all the estates of the realm should have their old places. But I have quite ceased to sympathise with their successors who have converted their high aspirations to a sordid war of classes carried on by the vilest methods. I was comrade in that sense of Davis, and possibly, but with far less sympathy, of some of his companions. But it was in sympathy only. I never wrote in *The Nation*. To say that I have upborne their banner, therefore, is more than I would like to vouch.'

A growing plebeian tendency may have damped Ferguson's patriotic ardour, but what opened his eyes to new and terrible possibilities was the murder in broad daylight of Lord Frederick Cavendish and Thomas Henry Burke. They were walking together in Phoenix Park on the way to the Chief Secretary's Lodge, Cavendish having arrived to take up that office. Burke was the Under-Secretary; and we know from studying Drummond's career that the practical business of government in Ireland was done by the Under-Secretary.

The murder was done by knives, which gave it a special horror; and Parnell debated whether he should retire from politics, so great was the embarrassment to the Irish cause. It is now definitely linked with savagery. Nowadays 'The Invincibles', as the conspirators were called, have their apologists. Everyone who fought for the Irish cause is hallowed, even the knife is preferable to the tongue as more conducive to effective results.

The Phoenix Park murders made a horrible impression on Ferguson's mind; he wrote interminable verses in the Browning manner to relieve his feelings. As he was a representative figure among those who were awakened to consciousness of Ireland as a nation by the discovery of the existence of an Irish civilisation, it may be assumed that others who were being led sympathetically along the same path became alarmed at the prospect of violence as symbolised by this calculated savage act.

CHAPTER XII

Isaac Butt

THE TRIALS IN 1867 introduced to the nationalist scene the enigmatic figure of Isaac Butt. Beginning life as a Tory, he attained such renown for his abilities and the narrowness of his views that he was pitted, as a very young man, against O'Connell in a public debate on the repeal of the Union, which aroused great interest at the time. He was the hired advocate to oppose the admission of Catholics to the corporations, one of Drummond's schemes. It was a lucky inspiration that prompted his selection as the defender of all the principal conspirators of 1848, and he emerged from that ordeal as a national hero, and a national leader, if he was prepared to take on the role.

From his speeches in defence of O'Brien and others such a vivid picture is painted of the horrors of the Famine—the emotional justification for revolt—that I, having read them, felt that there was nothing more to be said on the subject and wondered when I heard that Mrs Woodham-Smith was devoting years to the task of mastering the history of that catastrophe. Her book, *The Great Hunger*, by its enormous and deserved success, showed how mistaken I was. I had overlooked the fact that the speeches of Isaac Butt are as little read in Ireland as the small print on insurance policies; and elsewhere are not read at all.

Butt was given his chance; and refused it, preferring to go to parliament as Conservative candidate for Harwich. In parliament, I regret to say, he got into trouble over a rather shady business in which he acted for an Indian Ameer. He was always in trouble over money, and his private character was warm but not respectable. He seemed to be ruined as a public man, and then, contrary to what we are taught, he got a second chance.

The Fenian outbreak of 1867, the success of which depended on assistance that was not forthcoming in sufficient strength from soldiers, released from the recent Civil War in America, miscarried hopelessly. There were numerous arrests, and once more Butt's services were called upon.

He was a political economist as well as a lawyer, and he had taken—at the same time as Gladstone—to a study of Irish grievances. In Butt's case the research, prompted by practical experience in the courts and a boyhood spent in the Irish countryside, went much deeper than Gladstone's. He published large pamphlets which are untapped mines of Irish social history on education and land tenure; at the same time he took the lead in a campaign for the release of Fenian prisoners. This time he did seem at last to have donned O'Connell's mantle. These meetings saw thousands of people gathering to hear Butt, as they were wont to flock to listen to O'Connell. And there were the same conflicts with the authorities, who did their best to outlaw the meetings. Here Butt's legal knowledge was of tremendous advantage.

From these amnesty meetings sprang the formation of a new political party. It was intended to be led by Butt and George Henry Moore, father of the novelist.

When Moore contested the Mayo constituency as a nationalist in 1868 he had to sacrifice the friendship of the landlords in his county, notably Lord Sligo, his oldest friend.

The men whom Drummond had attacked were now on the defensive. And Butt's pamphlet on land tenure *The Decline of the Celtic Race*, brought forth long letters of lofty objection from Lords Lifford, Dufferin and Rosse. These were all worthy and self-satisfied men who were conscious of a responsible attitude towards their dependants, and they took umbrage at the strictures of one who shared their religion but not their rank. From such as Butt they expected the under-pinning that a privileged order gets from the next layer in the social pyramid. In their replies there was a measure of dignified rebuke. Butt was not abashed. He answered all three in *The Irish People and the Irish Land*, the best attack, because the most courteous and reasoned, that has ever been delivered at the system which kept the Anglo-Irish in control of the land. In fairness to the three protesting peers it must be said that they regarded themselves as an exemplary contrast to the ruthless new owners who had bought up the bankrupt estates after the Famine. These were 80 per cent Irish, from the towns, who had invested their savings in a business enterprise. So far from wishing to show what models Catholic landlords could be they were ruthless in clearing the lands and sending off the unwanted occupiers by emigrant ship to America.

There is a hideous tale of one of these clearances in Gleveih, in Donegal, where a landlord who, admittedly had suffered considerable harassment, summoned military aid from Dublin, and levelled the cottages of an entire countryside. That was quarter of a century after Drummond had refused the aid of the forces of law to these inhuman exercises.

Lords Rosse, Lifford and Dufferin did not engage in them, and they were offended with Butt for condemning a system which they believed was sacrosanct. He, the most fundamentally conservative of men, had made relatively mild suggestions: the granting of leases for sixty-three years to tenants, compensation for improvements and adjustment of rents upwards only when the circumstances justly warranted it.

But this, according to the landlords, removed from them what they valued most, the power to do what they pleased with their tenants. It converted the latter into fixtures, from being chattels, and they defended the existing system with the same casuistry as the slave trade had been defended by those who wanted to profit by it and have that and Heaven too.

Butt insisted on repeating the lesson of history. He echoed Fitzgibbon's depressing reminder that the tenure of landlords in Ireland was based on three confiscations from the original inhabitants.

'I have been taken to task', he wrote, 'for speaking of the occupiers as constituting the Celtic race. They do so—mingled as they are in blood with the Saxon—the great mass of the Irish population still represent in religion, in feeling, in habits, and in race, the old inhabitants of this island'. (This may be an appropriate place to interpolate another piece of evidence on the vexed subject. Professor Earle Hackett, who did much pioneering work in blood studies in Ireland, immediately after the last World War, took samples from the inhabitants of the Aran islands. *Man of Aran*, O'Flaherty's documentary film, showed the inhabitants of these regions to the world as the last unspoilt, uncontaminated Celts left in the land. Synge had stayed with them to get the feel of genuine Irishry. What a sensation there was when Hackett's findings disclosed English blood in the whole population! Two of Cromwell's troopers had settled there. So much for theories of race.)

To return to Butt; he made the most complete *exposé* that exists of the pretensions of the landlords, but he admitted in the course of doing so, that as a class they had been unfairly damned for the inhumanity of some of their number. There were and always had been some good landlords in Ireland; and the way in which the Gore-Booths—to take an example—despoiled themselves to aid the victims of the Famine was as exemplary as it was unacknowledged. But terrible things could happen on estates when landlords insisted, as did Lords Dufferin, Lifford and Rosse, on absolute power. Butt gave one example. It will suffice.

'On the estate of the Marquis of Lansdowne there lived, a few months ago, a man and his wife, Michael and Judith Donoghue; they lived in the house of one Casey. An order has gone forth on the estate (a common order in Ireland) that no tenant is to admit any lodger into his house. This was a general order. It appears, however, that sometimes special orders are given, having regard to particular individuals. The Donoghues had a nephew, one Denis Shea. This boy had no father living. He had lived with a grandmother who had been turned out of her holding for harbouring him. Denis Shea was twelve years old—a child of decidedly dishonest habits. Orders were given by the driver of this estate that this child should not be harboured upon it. This young Cain, thus branded and prosecuted, being a thief—he had stolen a shilling, a hen, and done many other such crimes as a neglected twelve-year-old famishing child will do—wandered about. One night he came to his aunt Donoghue, who lodged with Casey. He had the hen with him.

'Casey told his lodgers not to "allow him in the house," as the agent's drivers had given orders about it. The woman, the child's aunt, took up a pike, or pitchfork, and struck him down with it; the child was crying at the time. The man, Donoghue, his uncle, with a cord tied the child's hands behind his back. The poor child after a while crawls or staggers to the door of one Sullivan, and tried to get in there. The maid of Sullivan called to Donoghue to take him away. This he did; but he afterwards returned with his hands still tied behind his back. Donoghue had already beaten him severely. The child seeks refuge in other cabins, but is pursued by his character—he was so bad a boy, the fear of the agent and the driver—all were forbidden to shelter him. He is brought back by some neighbours, in the middle of night, to Casey's, where his uncle and aunt lived. The said neighbours tried to force the sinking child in upon his relations. There is a struggle at the door. The child was heard asking somone to put him upright. In the morning there is blood upon the threshold. The child is stiff dead—a corpse with its arms tied; around it every mark of a last fearful struggle for shelter—food—the common rights of humanity.

'The Donoghues were tried at the late Kerry assizes. It was, morally, a clear case of murder; but it was said, or believed, that these Donoghues acted not in malice to the child, but under a sort of sense of self-preservation; that they felt to admit him was to become wanderers themselves. They were indicted for manslaughter and found guilty.

'Those who know the superstitious charity with which the Irish people entertain strangers, the warm and tender affection with which they cherish the feelings of kindred, will understand the terrible coercion under which the poor boy was driven from the doors.

'Yet the estates of the Marquis of Lansdowne are considered among the best managed in Ireland. It suggests very strange reflections to observe that several times during the examination of witnesses before the committee of 1864, those who cross-examined the 'tenant right' witnesses repeatedly put questions as to this very estate, as if it were one with regard to which no one would dare to suggest the necessity of legislative interference.

'I believe that if the whole truth were known, the "best managed" properties are often those upon which the serfdom of the tenant is the most abject and complete. Similar edicts are at this moment enforced upon hundreds of Irish estates.'

These publications, and his campaign for prisoners, put Butt into the popular camp and one would have supposed that as a former militant bigot in the Protestant cause—the equivalent of the most fiery in Northern Ireland today—Butt would have been a pariah in his surroundings. But nothing in Ireland ever takes a simple logical course. Butt found himself at once with an influential body of support among Irish Protestants.

Moore died before the movement got under way, leaving Butt in indisputed control of the new body which called itself the Home Rule Association. Its aim was to win from parliament a measure of self-government in domestic affairs while remaining inside the Empire, of which Butt, in common with his contemporaries, was unashamedly proud.

His adherents—apart from a popular following—were a group consisting of Trinity professors, some landed gentlemen, and even a new resident proprietor from Manchester, Mitchell Henry, who had built a Gothic palace at Kylemore in Galway. What drew this heterogeneous group together was the Gladstone campaign of Irish reform. In 1869 he disestablished the Church of Ireland; now he was going on to make sweeping changes in higher education and in the vexed question of land tenures. In his campaign he had the almost unanimous support of the Catholic hierarchy and the newly emancipated Catholic middle-class who had no affection whatever for revolutionary doctrines.

Butt's colleagues looked with misgiving on an Ireland run by Gladstone in conjunction with the Roman Catholic clergy. This was never said, but it hardly required elaboration. Why, then, did they get a popular following from the masses, all of whom were Catholics? Chiefly because Butt had struck a sympathetic chord, and to the popular mind 'Home Rule' sounded more attractive than even enlightened Whig government. Moreover Gladstone did not trust the Irish as Drummond did; he accompanied his measures of relief with disciplinary enactments. The idea of Home Rule had not entered his own impressionable imagination. When it did, Butt had long vanished from the scene.

For all his writings (which are unjustly neglected) and his speeches at mass meetings, in parliament Butt was ineffective. He lacked the fighting spirit of O'Connell; so that when a leader presented himself who had no respect for House of Commons

The Casino, Dublin

The Irish Volunteers, in College Green, parading round the statue of William III, by Wheatley

Thomas Drummond by Henry William Pickersgill

Isaac Butt by John Butler Yeats

Sarah Purser by Lilian M. Davidson

Augusta Gregory by William Orpen

George Moore by John Butler Yeats

William Butler Yeats by Albert Power

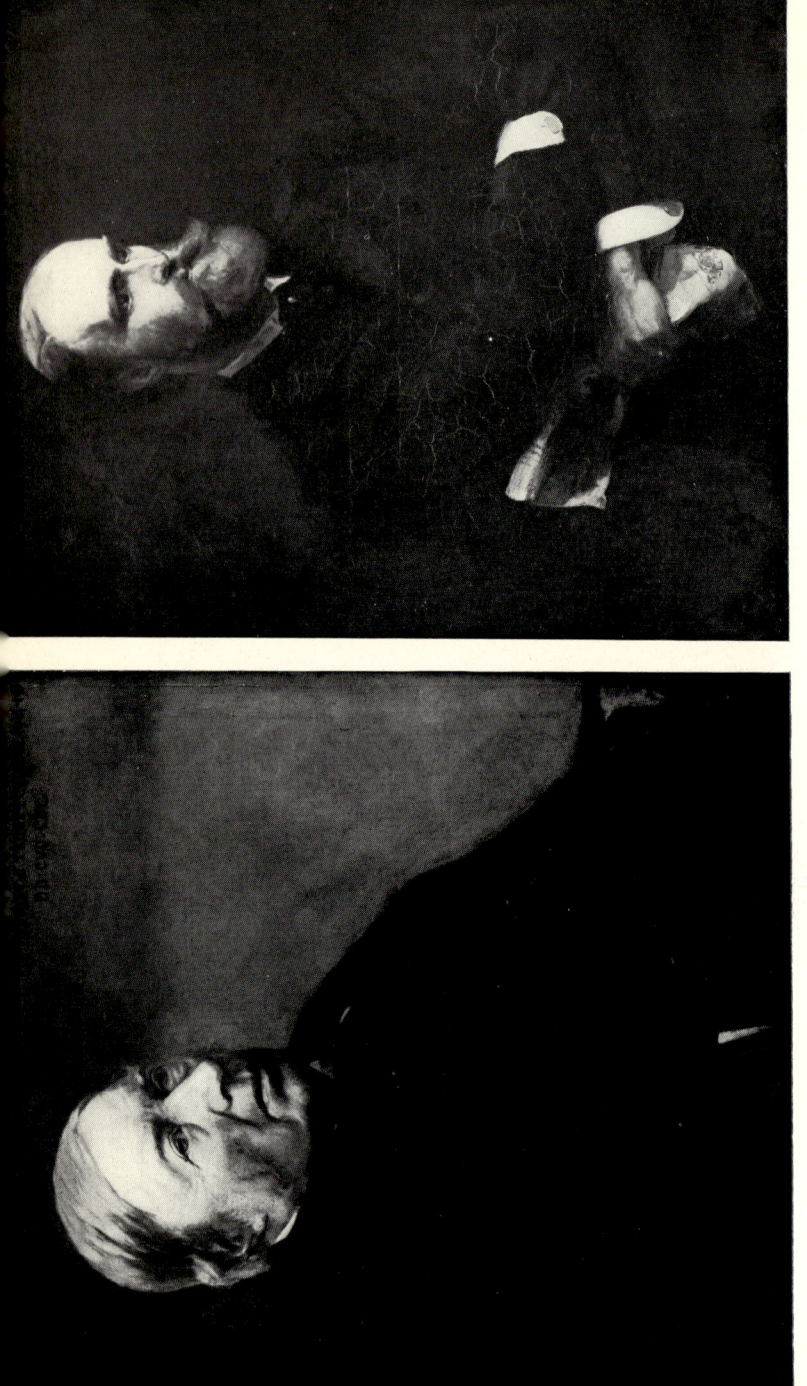

Sir J. P. Mahaffy by S. C. Harrison

Charles Stewart Parnell by Sydney Prior Hall

Grafton Street, Dublin, at the turn of the century

Daisy, Countess of Fingall

tradition and a singular dislike of the English, considering he was himself of English extraction, Butt was hustled off the stage. This new portent was Parnell. The last of the Anglo-Irish to attempt to win back the rule that was filched from his class by the Act of Union.

CHAPTER XIII

Parnell

PARNELL IS ENORMOUSLY significant in any account of the Anglo-Irish. He was the last to lead the country. This assertion will be disputed because his faithful lieutenant, John Redmond, was in fact leader of the Irish party for nearly twenty years. He died in 1917 and was succeeded by John Dillon, whose melancholy task was to lead it to extinction in the 'khaki election' of 1918.

Redmond was a gentleman—as people used confidently to say and save themselves from a great deal of unnecessary analysis—and a landed proprietor in the next county, but he was a Roman Catholic and, when it comes to the crunch, we are forced into the position of identifying the Anglo-Irish with the Protestant ascendancy. The Redmonds were in Ireland long before the Parnells arrived and, oddly enough, the only Irish blood in the great patriot came through his American mother.

She was the daughter of Charles Stewart, an American sailor who had done great damage to British prestige in the Anglo-American war. The Stewarts—related presumably to the family that produced Viscount Castlereagh, the demon of Union—left Northern Ireland in the middle of the eighteenth century. Another family called James, which left at the same time, produced America's greatest novelist. Henry James was an Anglophile, but his sister was a passionate admirer of Parnell, until the details of the O'Shea divorce lost him her approval.

The Stewarts, presumably Scots by origin, were Parnell's closest link with Irishry; but, waiving considerations of blood and race, what Mrs Parnell infused into her son and some of his sisters, was an abiding hatred of England. She was a spoiled beauty and, from all accounts, a tiresome woman. A book could be written on the subject of the effect on Irish history of tiresome

American women—in this case the influence on Parnell was considerable, but, probably, not decisive.

On his father's side there was an intimate connection with home rule. Sir John Parnell, a direct ancestor, had been Chancellor of the Exchequer in Grattan's parliament, a stalwart opponent of the Union and a friend to Catholic emancipation. The family were descended from a silk mercer, Thomas Parnell, Mayor of Congleton in Cheshire, who came to Ireland in the time of James I and bought an estate in Northern Ireland. One of his two sons was Thomas, the poet, a friend of Swift.

The family was prominent in Ireland from its arrival, John was a judge, his son, Sir John, was the Chancellor of the Exchequer. They intermarried with Howards, the family name of the Earls of Wicklow, the Carysforts, and Brookes and Wingfields (Powerscourt). Irish writers usually describe Charles Stewart Parnell as an aristocrat. He certainly conforms to all the requisites for the Anglo-Irish type—Protestant, well-connected, land-owning, and with several horses. In manner he was probably more like an Englishman of his own class. He was aloof and passionate rather than flirtatious. There was nothing gay about him, nothing literary. His intellect had a scientific bent. He had a genius for command, a stubbornness. He rarely gave vent to his feelings—his wife gave a lurid description of his holding her one day on Brighton pier over the sea, and she thought, for a moment, he would throw her in (that was before the divorce scandal). There is a somewhat similar story told of Charles Dickens, another intense, and emotionally overwrought man.

O'Connell, in the House of Commons, stood like a great dog surrounded by a wolf pack, baying defiance. Parnell, more like one of themselves, showed icy contempt for the members. Irish MPs were too often inclined to be overawed by the House of Commons or seduced by London life. Parnell was immune to both. There is an amusing account in the reminiscences of T. P. O'Connor, a nationalist with a notorious weakness for fleshpots, staying for a visit with Parnell at Avondale. The host suggested that they should take lunch out with them. O'Connor's imagination summoned up a vision of a basket, linen napery, chicken or pheasant, cake, champagne. When it was time to set out Parnell went to the side table in the dining room, took some cold meat off it and wrapped it in newspaper, advising O'Connor to do the same. He never attempted to charm. That element in the idealised Anglo-Irishman was absent from this concentrated, masterful being. He disappointed O'Connor on that occasion. But he made an enemy of a much more formidable man when he took no trouble at all to soothe the vanity of T. M. Healy. Healy, a poor boy from West Cork, self-made, a journalist and then a barrister, with an excoriating wit of the type that used to be cultivated at the Irish bar and employed in the intimidation of witnesses, was himself—as is often the case with men who have a talent for wounding—highly sensitive. He was probably sincerely devoted to his leader and needed only recognition. Parnell accepted service and gave no thanks. Healy came of a family with a moral code—in the realms of sex—in comparison with which John Knox was frivolous. When Healy discovered Parnell's secret, he was genuinely shocked; but for the sake of parliamentary unity he had to hold his peace. When, eventually, the revelations of the divorce case produced a national crisis, Healy's resentment of years of slighting added venom to reasonable disapproval. Parnell had compromised his party by consorting with a married woman. Apart from any disapproval on moral grounds, his behaviour was—in party terms, in national terms—reckless to say the least. And then Healy uttered the gibe at the moment when it seemed unchivalrous. (Parnell asked who was to be the master of the party. Healy asked who was to be the 'mistress'.) It was unworthy and Parnellites will never forgive it. Without defending the gibe one can see that Parnell's aloofness and arrogance were going to be out of place in the sort of Ireland that would emerge when Home Rule was achieved. He had gone along with the agrarian revolution led by his colleague, Michael Davitt. Davitt wanted to socialise the land of Ireland; Parnell showed no disposition whatever to part with his patrimony. Nor had his mother, though fulminating against England, refused invitations to Dublin Castle. Being in this like Oscar Wilde's mother, whose finest hour was when her Majesty's representative gave her husband the accolade, 'Sir William' figured much in Speranza's letters to her friends.

Even if Parnell had been successful in obtaining Home Rule, he could not have staged the destruction of the Protestant ascendancy. There had to be a revolution against landed proprietorship. The system had been abused in the nineteenth century as never before.

Another dominating trait in Parnell which was quite at variance with accepted ideas of the Irish character was his apparent contempt for popularity. He preferred to gain his point rather than to be liked. Irishmen usually endeavour to achieve both. Brooke, who played cricket with him, connected with Parnell through marriage, recalled that his father and uncles—long before Parnell went into politics—found he 'always had a grievance of some sort and was inclined to be sulky. He spoiled the enjoyment of the parties and so was gradually allowed to drop out.'

But he was not an unfeeling man. Davitt, when he discovered that a girl Parnell had slept with in some lonely moment was writing to him for support of the child (the letter was opened in a search for Parnell's whereabouts), called him 'a cold sensualist'. But that was, like Healy's bitterness, an expression of Irish Catholic puritanism, a deep regard for chastity, which is historically a dominating feature of the Celtic tradition. Side by side with hearty bawdry ran the monastic impulse.

Parnell was crossed in love as a young man. That embittered him. It is possible that the conventional American girl who refused him found him strange. Eccentricity was in evidence in the family certainly. Some of Parnell's magnetism came from the red flicker in his inward-looking eyes. His flame burned inwardly: his exterior was frigid. A woman, if he was in love with her, or desired her, would have seen a wholly different person from the enigmatic leader of men. He was one of those men who need women because they cannot relax with other men; and he was probably supremely egotistical. Tales in childhood of the horrible deeds perpetrated by the yeomanry in Wicklow in 1798 are said to have coloured his mind as a child. But he said himself that the Fenian trials brought him into contact with the nationalist cause. Fenianism—or their reactions to it—conscripted Gladstone, Butt and Parnell for the cause of Home Rule for Ireland.

He was a compassionate man. To his insistence the Army owes

its relief from the savage tradition of flogging. Pious gentlemen were maintaining it as absolutely essential to the maintenance of discipline. Parnell was the first to insist that they look at the sort of whips which their complacency was licensing annually for flagellation. It was a dramatic and effective way to carry his point. They had preferred not to look.

Parnell was hated in England. It is said that people were seen to dance in the streets of London when the stop-press announcement of his death was displayed. But he was cheered in the House of Commons when he entered, after a Commission of Enquiry published its findings that an attempt to link his name with crime in Ireland was a fabrication based on a forgery. *The Times*, ever active, had published the letters without doing as much as it should to check their authenticity. But the newspaper was influenced by the assumed probity of the group of Irish Unionists who subscribed to purchase the letters.

Parnell's most virulent enemies were among his fellow-countrymen. The base deed recalls O'Connell's outburst when Drummond was attacked in the House of Commons by an earlier generation of Irish Unionists. It does not make proud reading.

The generation that tried to ruin Parnell by foul means was the same that committed the worst act of vandalism in Dublin. In the teeth of the protests of the Corporation of Dublin, they built the suspension bridge across the Liffey, ruining the view of the Custom House.

Progress, they said, must not be impeded by merely aesthetic considerations. I make the point here because it is too often supposed that the present generation was the first to lay waste what used to be a beautiful city.

Dublin merchants in the nineteenth century maintained the doctrine of Protestant ascendancy, but contributed nothing to the country to compare with the Anglo-Irish of the previous century. In this they were children of their age, the heirs of the Industrial Revolution. Except in certain restricted areas, Protestant Dublin in Victoria's reign was a philistine city.

CHAPTER XIV

Social Life in Victorian Ireland

BOOKS ABOUT IRELAND in the nineteenth century are almost invariably depressing. There is the inevitable 'tour of Ireland' promising all the grimmest features of a royal progress, a parliamentary report and a geography lesson, but even worse is the historical survey with its inevitable chapter headings: 'Famine', 'Fenians', 'Felony'. Worst of all are 'humours of Irish life'. These abound and presumably were the contemporary equivalent of *The Wit of Prince Philip* and the like.

If we disregard all these and look for letters and diaries in the not unreasonable hope that our grandfathers did not spend all their time in political discussions or retailing old jokes, the results are rather meagre. There may be several reasons for this; but I think the principal one is that familiar bugbear, the Act of Union.

The visitors to any country mansion in Ireland which still boasts a library will notice that there are very few additions of any significance after approximately 1800. Formidable-looking tomes that nobody would think to pull down to while away a wet afternoon rub shoulders with Agatha Christie or C. P. Snow. There is very little in between; a Rider Haggard, perhaps, and a book on roses by a retired clergyman, and there will certainly be bound copies of *Punch*. That sort of thing—odd volumes—but no sign of laying down of books, or, if it comes to that, of cellars. To do such a thing requires settled belief in continuity. That had gone. For that reason private diaries tend to bear a resemblance to General Gordon's when he was waiting for the Mahdi at Khartoum. Those who were so fortunate as to own properties in England tended to have their chief interests and their fun and games in England. Except for the hunting they afforded, Irish properties came to be regarded by their owners as if they were estates in Basutoland.

Few families lived with more grandeur than the Hamiltons in their heyday. 'The old Marquis', his grandson tells us, insisted that the house-maids wore kid gloves when making the beds, and the footmen had to dip their hands in a bowl of rose-water before handling a dish; but the first Duke of Abercorn could not be persuaded to acknowledge his 'real home in Ulster' until 1878, when Barons Court became the chief family residence. The family found it then, Lord Ernest Hamilton records, severely bare of all but the very necessities of life.

Most books of reminiscences by Irishmen who went out to govern New South Wales, or otherwise achieved eminence, begin with a short Irish chapter containing a joke; the next deals with a school in England; then Oxford or Cambridge. The bulk of the book is composed of chapters on London and life abroad, such as *Mentone Interlude*. Ireland is left like the shell of the egg out of which the chicken emerged.

Politics and periodic agrarian disturbances aside, high life in Ireland in the accepted sense was rare because of physical factors. Outside Dublin there was no city to attract prolonged residence —no Bath, no Harrogate, no Cheltenham. Even if the family were resident in Ireland, sons went away. There was always a shortage of men. All the records testify to this.

The Moores in Mayo were different only from others of their kind in being more gifted, as they were certainly more articulate. Neighbours were few. The most important were the Brownes, Lord Sligo's family, in Westport, with whom for centuries Moores had friendships, quarrels or marriages. It is indicative of how things were ordered in Ireland that for generations every heir to the Sligo title had been born out of Ireland; and, after the family's three hundred years of territorial possession, even the present Lord Sligo was not born an Irish citizen within the meaning of the Act. Moore has described the parties of his youth, principally in *Muslin*, where the heroine 'with epicene bosom and long thighs' is said to have been based on Daisy, Countess of Fingall.

Samples, taken at random, convey the atmosphere: the dinner party in Galway where all the pleasure 'had been spoiled by that horrible Land League discussion': and when the blame for it was fixed upon a Mr Adair, 'Lady Sarah, who, notwithstanding her thirty-five years, had not entirely given up hope' stuck up for him. '"A most superior man," she declared. "He took honours at Trinity."'

And then the ball, superficially not unlike the one in *Pride and Prejudice*, but with a markedly rougher tone. Wild Sports of the West were never wholly kept under at these gatherings, however strenuous the efforts to emulate fashionable society elsewhere. Moore records:

> '"And tell me what do you think of my legs?" she said, advancing a pair of stately calves. "Violet says they are too large."
>
> "They seem to be all right; but, May, dear, you haven't got a petticoat on."
>
> "You can't wear petticoats with these tight dresses; one can't move one's legs as it is."
>
> "But don't you think you'll feel cold—catch cold?"
>
> "Not a bit of it; no danger of cold when you have shammy-leather drawers."'

Moore was in his time a somewhat haunch-haunted witness; but his findings are borne out by more respectable testimony; the rather formidable E. O'E. Somerville, for instance, and her *alter ego*, the delicately satirical Violet Martin.

In *The Real Charlotte*, absolutely authentic we may be sure is the picture of the first tennis-party given by Lady Dysart of Bruff on 15 June, sometime in the eighties. 'The steamer was plying on the lake, the militia was under canvas . . . Lady Dysart had cast her nets over a wide expanse and the result was not encouraging. She stood, tall, dark and majestic, on the terrace, surveying the impracticable row of women that stretched, forlorn of men, along one side of the tennis grounds, much as Cassandra might have scanned the beleaguering hosts from the ramparts of Troy . . . [Lady Dysart] was aware that many of the ladies on her visiting list were vulgar, but it was their subjects of conversation and their opinions that chiefly brought the fact home to her.'

Shortage of men—that was the perennial problem; and it meant that garrison towns had an enormous, if fleeting, advantage over districts which had to rely on the indigenous product.

Lady Dysart was not the first or last Irish hostess who had to remark that she never knew the country so bereft of men or so peopled with girls! '"Even the little Barrington boys are off with the militia, and everyone about has conspired to fill their houses with women, and not only women but dummies."' Awe-inspiring in this state of affairs were the power and importance of the army, that one infallible source of supply of the article most in demand. And the social importance of the military is brought home by advertisements for races at the Curragh in the 'sixties; apart from members of a very few clubs, army officers only were eligible to enter horses. It is impossible to have pleasant social life where people regard their homes as forts from which to go on forays abroad. Ireland was far too much a place which people *used* rather than lived in. This was true not only of visitors or soldiers garrisoned there but of members of families who saw their Irish estates as shaky investments and who regarded their house in England as home. Nor was it much different with Irish families whose sons had to make their careers abroad. What Englishman would write of his own country as, to take an example, Major-General Sir Hugh McCalmont, in his memoirs, wrote of Ireland? His father had preferred the life of a country gentleman to the profitable family business, and married one of the Martins of Ross. She, when she was a young widow, remarried a Barton. The McCalmont literary style is inimitable; how much may be attributed to Martin blood is hardly worth the research it would require to establish. 'We were a nice pair of pickles, Jimmy and I, in those nipper days'—Sir Hugh is referring to himself and his brother. He purchased a cornetcy in the 9th Lancers in 1865; and his reminiscences tell how enjoyable soldiering was in Ireland in those days: excellent sport, 'goodwill displayed by the peasantry' and hospitality to be met with in country-houses. At one of these he met his future wife, when she 'bucketed along in great style on a pony'.

A process-server who had the temerity to call with a writ was made short work of—'on my rushing on the fellow to fire him out, he closed with me'. A servant, Mines, had to be called to bundle the dun out after some effective pummelling. And strong-minded perjury by this invaluable servant successfully scouted the subsequent summons for assault. To prevent things from stagnating McCalmont and others in the mess put night-shirts over their uniforms and careered about the streets on their chargers. Another time they picked 'a brat' out of his pram and McCalmont got in 'to the uproarious delight of everyone' (except the nursemaid, who didn't matter).

'Incidents of that kind, which in the more sober atmosphere of England or Scotland would give rise to remark and even possibly to irritation amongst the community, were taken as quite a matter of course on the banks of the Liffey.'

It would have been difficult, McCalmont thought, '. . . to find a more cheery gang than were the 9th Queen's Royal Lancers in those days, and certainly not the least light-hearted of the party was Bill (Lord William) Beresford, who had joined as a cornet. He made it a practice to tear about the county in a dog-cart, generally driving tandem and always carrying a sack full of potatoes on the foot-board; these vegetables he employed as missiles to hurl at anyone who he passed on the road . . .'

Ireland could boast no monopoly of good fun. In London wrenching knockers off hall-doors had rather died out, but it was still practised by the *jeunesse dorée* in the early seventies and it was fun, even if the knocker resisted, to give a 'thundering rat-tat with it and thereby cause annoyance and possibly alarm to the householder'.

After the Afghan War, McCalmont saw more service in Ireland. Times had changed. The peasantry were no longer pleasant, but '. . . we got on well with the local gentry, so much so that we decided to give a ball . . . all the people, and especially the girls, are already quite cracked. Both the infantry regiments are going to give balls simply not to be caught out. One lady declined on account of domestic affliction, *paper an inch broad of mourning*, but a P.S. informed us that the daughter would with pleasure avail herself of the invitation.'

Lieutenant George H. Lamb, of the 49th Regiment, who was

stationed in Waterford and Buttevant, Co. Cork, in 1852-3 left an unpublished diary, which gives a fair picture of the sort of life a young officer was provided with. One of Lamb's first duties on arriving in Waterford was to hire a field for a cricket pitch at three pounds a year. This whiled away a lot of the time. There was hunting and shooting in winter and, as well as routine festivities of a military life ('I was highly gratified at the kind spirit shown by the men towards me. We all went to the Sergeants' mess and drunk their health in sherry'), there were local entertainments. Frequently going to bed 'screwed', Lieutenant Lamb was always in form next morning for snipe shooting or whatever other rigours of the military life were available.

There were balls and less ambitious dances in the neighbourhood. But he is sparse in recording details, unfortunately.

The fact that the diary is dedicated to his sister may have cramped Boswellian propensities.

Here is one entry: 'Very wet morning. Men occupied getting the room ready for the hop. An escort of the 31st arrived in with ammunition under Bates. Practised pistol shooting in the afternoon. Bates dined with us and we adjourned to the Ball at $9\frac{1}{2}$ with Bartlett, etc. Dancing was kept up with great spirit until eleven when we had supper laid out, lots of pretty girls, etc. Singing and dancing afterwards which was continued until 4 in the morning. Plenty of lush.* To bed at five.'

The etceteras are unlikely to have covered a multitude of sins. On 7 July 1853 after noting 'War to the knife with Russia and Turkey', he adds 'summoned for assault'. This was the outcome of a 'very pleasant picnic and great fun' which led to an injudicious choice of the barrack square for pigeon shooting. 'Broke four panes of glass', for which he was fined six shillings by the Resident Magistrate.

Buttevant is not far from Bowen's Court, of which Elizabeth Bowen writes. Visitors were a great feature. 'The guest-rooms were seldom empty. Not only did relations make protracted stays, but friends (such as the Aldworths) touring the neighbourhood, would come for some days, then move on to the next house.' Luncheon parties and church-going were the staple of the

* Drink.

entertainment; but there were horses for ladies who wanted to ride.

Horses were the backbone of Irish society. Trollope's novel *The Kellys and the O'Kellys*, first published in 1848, gives a picture of Irish country-life, consistent with the accepted pattern. He was a close observer. Thus: 'Lord Ballandine had not rested in his paternal halls the second night, before he had commenced making arrangements for a hunt breakfast, by way of letting all his friends know that he was again among them. And so missives, in Gus and Sophy's hand-writing, were sent round by a bare-legged little boy to all the Mounts, Towers and Castles, belonging to the Dillons, Blakes, Bourkes and Browns of the neighbourhood to tell them that the dogs would draw the Kelly's covers at eleven o'clock on the following Tuesday morning, and that the preparatory breakfast would be on the table at ten.'

Amateur theatricals provided one of the ways in which the winter evenings were disposed of where there was sufficient local talent to draw on. Officers were, of course, in great demand. And the standard of performance was probably uneven.

Robert Martin, brother of Violet, who wrote as 'Ross', was much given to this type of entertainment. But he carried his talents further, and arranged more ambitious entertainments in Dublin, where amateur theatricals, in which officers took part, were a feature of the season. Acting on and off stage has always been a facet of the Irish character, and there is a great deal of amateur activity even now in the county towns.

The most elaborate amateur of his time was Luke Plunkett of Portmarnock House, only eight miles from Dublin. He used to hire the Theatre Royal, together with its stock company, and act the great Shakespearean parts. Richard III was an especial favourite; and he used to die with such thoroughness in the scene of Bosworth Field that he won the nickname 'Die again Plunkett'. It stuck to him after the night when an admirer (or a leg-puller) called for an encore and Mr Plunkett, obligingly, died all over again.

I don't know whether the story is true that encores were thereafter called for on all occasions. One night he appeared in the name-part of *Coriolanus*, an exacting role, as he found by the time that he reached the second act and could not remember any more of his lines. When he told the audience of his difficulty, they took it in good part, calling for a song. Whereupon, he threw his toga over his shoulder, and gave them *Scots Wha' Hae Wi' Wallace Bled*! 'Several glees and a variegated programme supplied by the stock company followed.'

The country knew nothing of such exhibitions as these, ambitions were more modest and the motive social rather than artistic. But there was rarely in nineteenth-century Ireland the equivalent of the English house party which, by the end of the century, had developed into the 'week-end'. Irish country-houses put up travellers, the host showing, Thackeray said, more hospitable manners than he was accustomed to find in England. And then there were the gatherings of neighbours, sometimes ill-assorted; but the difficulties of travel restricted country visiting, and, when trains came in, the tendency was for those who looked for entertainment other than field sports to come to Dublin. There were a few county magnates with intellectual tastes—Lord Rosse with his telescope at Birr, Lord Dunraven interested in archaeology at Adare. At houses such as these scholars came to stay and the noble amateurs took part in some of the discussions at learned societies in Dublin.

Cricket, although it never really caught on in Ireland, had its devotees in various parts of the country; and some landlords enlisted and trained members of their staff for matches or kept open house for cricket weeks. Violet Martin tells of the efforts by her brother Robert to get up a cricket team at Ross. He 'harangued' his eleven on the laws of the game, but they could not disentangle them from the rules of a game of their own called burnt ball, a variety of rounders played with a large soft ball. A match was progressing slowly until at length a batsman managed to hit a ball and run. This excited a fielder, who shied the ball at his head shouting 'Go out! You're burnt!'

The batsman was temporarily disabled: 'and neither then nor subsequently did cricket prosper at Ross'.

As befitted his character, the cricket side led by Charles Stewart Parnell from Avondale in County Wicklow was grimly competitive. Parnell, always indifferent to popularity, had the unsporting habit of timing visiting batsmen from when a wicket fell until the incomer took up his position at the crease. As nobody ever thought that the rules provided a time limit for this operation, Parnell occasionally took an easy wicket for his side by appealing to the umpire and showing his stop watch. He was born for national politics. His dotty sister, Mrs Dickinson, recalled in her unreliable memoirs a three-day cricket match between the officers of the garrison at Dublin and the Wicklow team. The officers were put up at Avondale, where a Mrs Moore and her 'two lovely daughters were staying'.

After a champagne luncheon on the first day the players found it hard to concentrate on the game in the presence of so many of the fair sex. The batch of visitors on the second day coming down from Dublin by train included a pretty young widow. This proved too much for the officers, who 'threw down their bats, and the whole party paired off into the woods'.

'Now commenced a scene of fun and flirtation which surpasses description, and which had probably never before been equalled in the old haunts of Avondale. In every nook and corner were to be seen an isolated couple engaged in the pleasant pastime of love-making, the young widow, notwithstanding her robes of black, being foremost in the practice of the art.'

Mrs Dickinson, whose reliability as a chronicler has been called in question, records that her husband demanded satisfaction on the lawn from an officer who had been too attentive to her. But Charles exercised his privileges as host, and the matter was there-upon patched up.

There were bedroom confusions later in the best tradition of farce. Finally the widow's solicitor, who had amorous intentions himself, summoned her back to Dublin. (Watteau might have done the occasion justice.)

W. P. Hone in his *History of Cricket in Ireland* mentions county clubs that were founded, some as early as 1831. These depended on the patronage of one local enthusiast, and all are now dead.

'Souperism', the name for making evangelical converts among the Catholic Irish by trading souls for soup, has a bad name in the country, where it is still a legend. Gaelic revivalists complained that a somewhat similar corruption was being attempted by the cricket-lovers, the half barrel being the lure used to involve the faithful in 'foreign games'.

Tennis and croquet came to Ireland but there are no records of parties for these games, nothing equivalent to those tales of Balfour and his friends, 'the Souls', playing tennis in the nude before breakfast. Lawn Tennis was concentrated at the Fitzwilliam Club; and one of the short-lived Dublin fashion magazines, *The Jarvey*, has a paragraph in May 1889 telling how: 'Everyone here is tennis mad. Tennis Teas, Tennis At Homes and Tennis Dances are quite the order of the day; in fact no one has a thought beyond or above them.

'Last Thursday a very successful At Home was given by the members of the Fitzwilliam Lawn Tennis Club at the club grounds in Wilton Place. The sun shone delightfully, while the band of the Seaforth Highlanders was a great addition... Everyone still in Dublin was present, amongst whom I noticed Mrs Armytage Moore in brown, Mrs Power O'Donoghue in a wonderful crimson head gear, and Miss Bayley, looking remarkably handsome in a neat grey tailor-made gown.'

None of these ladies can have been competing, otherwise it would have been worth going some distance to see them.

We may be sure that at the same time as these excitements had Dublin in their grip, the officers stationed in Mullingar, in Mallow and at other strategic points were performing on courts in the country-houses of their neighbourhood.

Mrs Ritchie, Thackeray's charming daughter, gives an account of a visit to Edgworthstown and what it was like to go by train from Broadstone station, an interesting contrast with Trollope's account of travel by canal barge from Portobello House forty years earlier. Then an inn, it is now a nursing home.

But all accounts lead to the conclusion that if life there was uproarious enough, and pleasant for sportsmen, Ireland was never a country for women unless they belonged to that hardy type who, if Moore is to be believed, enjoyed an existence that demanded drawers of 'shammy leather'. The west was probably wilder beneath the surface than the district of the Pale, and this may still be true. Maxwell's account in *Wild Sports of the West* of the husband who couldn't keep up with his wife was published in 1832. But it was certainly true to the life Moore knew fifty years later:

'"Is it a fit he has?" inquired an under-sized gentleman with an efflorescent nose, who had been pointed out to me as a six bottle customer. "Phoo!" replied my loving cousin, "the man has no more bottom than a chicken. Lift him; he has a good heart but a weak head. *He'll never do for Galway!* But come, lads" and Marc hopped over my body as I was being taken up by the servants, "I'll give you that *top-sawyer*, his wife, and long may she wear the breeches!"'

In Dublin such matters were conducted more decorously, as befitted the capital. Helen Faucit, a leading actress in early Victorian days, afterwards wife to Sir Theodore Martin, on whom fell the awesome task of writing the official biography of the Prince Consort, tells in her Recollections of delightful social gatherings with the Stokes family. Carlyle in his splenetic manner describes a disastrous dinner-party in Dr Stokes's house in Merrion Square, when Carlyle insults his hostess.

Lady Ferguson tells us in her long tribute to her husband that:

'Society in Dublin, agreeable at all times, becomes brilliant during winter and early spring, when the hospitalities of the Viceregal Court attract to the city many of the nobility and country gentlemen and their families. A succession of estimable noblemen, courteous and gracious, and liberal in expenditure, have as Lords Lieutenant represented Her Majesty the Queen with dignity and splendour. Receptions, dinners, balls, and concerts promote gaiety and circulate money, and are gratifying to the populace, lessening the drain of absenteeism, which so seriously impairs the prosperity of Ireland.

'After Easter the Synod of the Church of Ireland meets in Dublin. Hotels and private houses are refilled, and a period of clerical sociability ensues, the palace of the Archbishop being a truly hospitable centre of general as well as clerical society.'

The sort of entertainment favoured by Ferguson's friends as an alternative to dinner parties were musical parties, meetings for the study of foreign literature and Shakespearian readings. The cast on one of these occasions is a key to this society, revolving round Trinity College and the Royal Irish Academy.

A SOUVENIR OF TUESDAY EVENING, 19th Jan. 1869
Prologue to last three acts of *Cymbeline* with a list of Readers.

Cymbeline	Dr Stokes
Cloten	Professor (now Sir Robert) Ball
Posthumus	Rev. R. P. Graves, LLD
Belarius	Sir Samuel Ferguson
Guiderius	Mr Palmer, FTCD
Aviragus	Professor Edward Dowden
Iachimo	Mr Thomas Ferguson
Lucius	Rev. Dr Salmon (Provost of TCD)
Senator	Mr A. P. Graves
Captain	Mr John Clarke
Pisanio	Dr Ingram (President RIA)
Cornelius	Rev J. P. Mahaffy, FTCD
Queen	Miss Stokes
Imogen	Miss Laura Darley
Lady	Mrs Mahaffy

That cast is a nucleus of academical society in Dublin at the time. One ponders over notable absentees. O'Donovan and Curry, the Irish scholars, would not have been invited to these entertainments. Sir William Wilde might have been but a patient, introduced by Dr Stokes (cast as Cymbeline), brought a case to court in 1864 in which she accused Wilde of raping her in his consulting-room. He had not defended himself, but the jury only gave her a farthing damages. Nevertheless when Wilde died, Ferguson was ready at once with a dirge, even if Archbishop Plunkett was not prepared, on this occasion, to say, 'All is well.'

Butt is another absentee. He was probably too busy for even intellectual recreations. One notices that his family are never mentioned. He kept them in a miserable state of poverty. A cousin of mine, who lived to be a very old woman, told me that she remembered as a child going to Isaac Butt's house to tell him there was a cab at the back door, which would enable him to escape through the garden without being seen by the sheriff. Another absentee is John Gilbert, historian of Dublin.

He was refused admission to the Academy on his first application, and Wilde seems to acknowledge that it was because he was a Catholic. Gilbert resented Ferguson's appointment to the Records Office, for which he felt he was himself better qualified. And it is to be noted that the little company of 1869 does not include a single Catholic. In more bohemian circles there was less exclusiveness. Thackeray recalled splendid entertainment at Charles Lever's house in Templeogue, where William Wilde was induced to be present. And Wilde's suppers, at which Oscar and Willie were present, included Gilbert and other rejects from Ferguson's more 'gracious' circle.

Lady Wilde's parties were, of course, notorious. She used to invite visiting stage celebrities and anyone with literary pretensions. It was W. B. Yeats's first introduction to a salon. She managed, with tremendous courage, to keep her flag flying after the humiliation of the law case. It speaks well for the magnanimity of Dublin, because Sir William did not come out of the ordeal with credit. But Speranza had flown in the face of convention all her life, and passed on to her celebrated son the art of attracting attention. The Wildes seem to have been accepted in respectable Victorian Dublin as the exception that proved the rule. Besides they owed something to what is now forgotten, the code among people who regarded themselves as well-bred not to gossip.

When I was writing a book about the Wilde parents I asked the grandson of Dr Stokes, then well advanced in his eighties, if he ever heard that Sir William Wilde proposed to Helen Faucit, before she married Sir Theodore Martin. I was reproved. 'The Stokes's never went in for gossip.' Lady Ferguson's two fat volumes are without one breath of scandal, one whisper of gossip. No publisher would take them on today. But I do not believe that this reticence cost her any effort. She belonged to a class that did achieve a quality of life which, even if it seems stuffy and unreal today, represented an heroic effort to lift men closer to the angels.

If the Fergusons set store by social refinement, their contemporary, Aubrey de Vere, brought fastidiousness to the pitch of celibacy. As a landlord in Limerick he was active in Relief schemes, and after the Famine took an interest in the humaner aspects of emigration. Nor did he ever indulge in vilification of the peasantry, although even his saintly disposition did not blind him to the reality of local conditions. In a letter to a friend he described them:

'Whatever else is to be learned in this stormy period, there is one of your favourite virtues which the state of things round us has no direct tendency to teach, and that is straightforward dealing. If I were to mention to one informant what I heard from another, the first would probably be shot before evening, and the second before the next morning; and I should go without information in future. There is one man from whom I have derived much information, and whom I have done all that I can to protect from conspiracies formed against him, who is himself so much of a conspirator that to my certain knowledge he was himself the man who got up a party by which his own house was attacked the other night and his servant boy beaten. This was a stroke of policy, as he considered it, to throw suspicion on a rival. The end of his mining and countermining will probably be that both he and his rival will be killed before the end of the year.'

Aubrey de Vere wrote a book called *English Misrule and Irish Misdeeds* which was criticised by that ever present Unionist faction whose policy was to support English government at any price and treat Irish grievances as mischievous propaganda.

As well as his English literary friends ('Alfred Tennyson is a little restive ... I wonder why he came, and whether he is fond of me. I fear not much so') de Vere had female correspondents, one of whom deplored his Romanist leanings and wrote to him no more when he eventually went over to the Scarlet Woman. 'That gentle shadowy poet', Lady Gregory described him. 'He was the first poet I ever met and spoke with, or rather listened to, for I was but a listener in those early days. I hold a later picture of him in my mind, with the background of a London garden party. I think at Lowther Lodge, where he, with the lovely Lady Somers' hand resting on his arm, seemed the very embodiment of imperishable courtesy as she of beauty. His writings were little known I think in the new Ireland that was beginning to assert itself as he grew old.'

The tone of his conversation, judging by his letters and diaries, was of the theological character that was rampant in England at that time, when Darwin was preparing the first land mine to explode under the attempt to rarify the species. De Vere might well have been an English contemporary of Newman or Gladstone, but even so, there was always a difference and he expressed it on one occasion, 'I sat next Mr Gladstone's sister-in-law, and liked her very much. She is very Irish—warm, natural and engaging—in singular contrast to the English ladies, who were handsome, dignified and simple, but hard, and without chiaroscuro.'

There was always this difference; and it still exists so far as the two people are concerned. Where England and Ireland are more alike now is in the growth of an Irish middle class. In nineteenth century Dublin there were many families living at a little over subsistence level who in point of culture were on a level with the well-to-do. In Dublin most people were hard up. Families like Bernard Shaw's would in London have been submerged in the dense mass of the lower middle class. It hardly exists in Ireland. This may partly explain why Irishmen with brains get on so quickly abroad from—in terms of wealth—humble beginnings. Shaw is one example. Another is George Tyrrell who was later to attain fame as a leader of the Modernist heresy in the Roman Catholic Church. Tyrrell was brought up in Dublin in a Church of Ireland family. His father, a journalist, died young, leaving his family so poor that Mrs Tyrrell had at times to take work as a governess, and yet Tyrrell wrote that he never learned how to be at ease talking familiarly to servants, and when the family went to lodgings in Skerries in the summer—

'There was the tawdry little Roman chapel in the village (my first experience of the Scarlet Lady) which my uncle's friends the Barrys (afterwards Judge Barry) and Judge Waters' family used to attend; and I wondered to see gentlefolk belonging to such a vulgar religion, suited only for servants. That Romanism was the religion of the Helots and of vulgar and uneducated classes in Ireland was one of the strongest, if the least rational, prejudices of my childhood. I mention this as an anti-Roman influence not existent in England. "That a son of mine should go to Mass with the cook" was perhaps the most sensible sting that my mother felt, relative to my subsequent "conversion". And certainly the interior of the Dublin "Chapels", with their dirt and tinsel and flashy gew-gaws, and staring pictures and images, all tended to confirm my belief in the essential "commonness" of Romanism.'

Even so late as 1932 an Irish peer who showed leanings towards Rome was taken by his father to look at the Sunday congregation streaming out of the Catholic church on the estate, and asked how he could ally himself with them. Tyrrell attended a school in Rathmines kept by a splendid character, Dr Benson. Very many of his pupils, including my own relations, paid reduced fees, and sometimes none. One of Tyrrell's contemporaries, the Rev. Charles E. Osborne, whose brother was one of Ireland's most considerable artists, explained:

'There is much in George Tyrrell's earlier period which would be unintelligible to purely English readers, unless these latter realise the existence in Ireland of an educated, and in some cases highly educated, upper middle class, less wealthy than the corresponding social class in England, and sometimes indeed with very small means, but with associations and intellectual interests entirely distinct from those of the very limited mental outlook of the lower middle class of the larger country, as described in Dickens' novels. The truth is that the lower middle, or bourgeois, class, on any large scale, has had but little existence in Ireland, there being no large mass of shop-keeping population between the professional and artisan class.

'Another circumstance to be taken strongly into account, is the fact that, until recently, and even still to a considerable extent, Ireland is living in the sixteenth century, as far as theological and sectarian antagonisms are concerned. There is no neutral zone, and the Oxford Movement has made few, if any, converts from among the children of the Revolution. Everyone is either bluntly a "Protestant" or a "Catholic" (i.e., Roman Catholic). Half shades are practically unknown, and notwithstanding the existence of a broad-minded and learned type of Churchman among the clergy, not of the Puritan school but rather holding sacramental principles, the great body of the laity of the Irish Church are still, as far as they are religious, Puritan to the core in their rejection of "sacerdotalism", i.e., the historic type of religion prevalent in Christendom from the second to the sixteenth century. Still, the Oxford Movement formed for itself some curious little eddies in Dublin intellectual life, especially among some of the undergraduates of Trinity College, or those preparing to enter the University, and not among candidates for the ministry alone.'

Another aspect of this society was the intensity of its Protestantism. English people are constantly astonished by the violence with which the Irish hold opinions. A great-uncle of mine, Newport J. D. White, was a school-friend of George Tyrrell's. When asked to recall him for his biographer he wrote:

'The only biographical value of what I can say about G.T. lies in the fact that we were boys together, and that my impressions of his boyhood had not been transfigured by contact with Tyrrell the man. We never met or exchanged letters after he became a Roman Catholic. Tyrrell's change of religion was to me a far greater severance than his death would have been. Those who know Ireland need not be told that, thirty years ago, the feeling of the average Irish Protestant towards Irish Roman Catholics was a repugnance, instinctive rather than reasoned, based on racial and social as much as on religious antipathies. Today, these antipathies do not, speaking generally, obtrude themselves to the same degree. Sensible people in each community are learning to appreciate what is good and praiseworthy in those from whom they differ; and indifference to all religion, which asserts itself more and more, also makes for toleration. If G.T. had died in 1878, much of him would have been embalmed in affectionate memory; as it was, I hastened to bury him out of my sight.'

This intensity of feeling obtained in England earlier in the century. One recalls Gladstone's virtual bullying of a sister who showed Romish tendencies. Perhaps the toleration of a later time has some of its origin in a decline in enthusiasm, a paling of conviction.

Sir Shane Leslie in *Film of Memory* reflects that 'there was no place for the seething originality of Father Tyrrell in the Church of Pius X', and recalls the impression made by Tyrrell on intellectual Catholics of his generation.

'Tyrrell was Irish enough not only by name but by temperament. He had a malicious love of irritating his superiors or flicking grave Cardinals with his very accurate peashooter. Unclaimed by the Church of his origin or his adoption Father Tyrrell belongs to the legion of Irish free-lances who have played their part in every country but their own.

'There was no religious writer whom we read with more enthusiasm at Cambridge as Anglicans and High Churchmen. He had the same charm that Cardinal Newman's writings exerted on our fathers. It is incredible that Tyrrell's are forgotten to-day. The beauty of his English, the mystery of his thought and his amazing power of pouring the old wine into new bottles were certainly as great as Newman's. But he utterly lacked Newman's sweetness and pathos. He was without the genius or personality which made Newman an evening star, albeit a misty one for his generation. Tyrrell posed for a time as a morning star in the theological skies, but he fell like a bolt which has missed fire. Tyrrell seemed to possess the same battery of gifts and talents, but they broke off short. Something was lacking, theologians would say charity, without which all can be but a tinkling cymbal. Today we should say he lacked personality, the curious mixture between charm and uniqueness of the starlike soul that certain individuals share with none other. In spite of an angel's pen, which he could dip in blood or tears, Father Tyrrell was arid and bitter, almost crude, and he thrust himself into darkness. When he was excommunicated, he received an address of sympathy from the young men at Cambridge, whose souls he had touched with fire. I think the present Dean of Winchester and the Master of Corpus were among them. As to his writings I shall feel to the end of my days what Cardinal Mercier confessed to me his own feelings had been. He gave us to think of Newman ... Abelard ... Lamennais!'

CHAPTER XV

The Irish Revival and Provost Mahaffy

THERE IS SOMETHING rather depressing about the thought of Protestantism in late Victorian Dublin. It is reflected in those early paintings of Walter Osborne, one of the Rathmines School pupils at this time. Poverty is seen in a melancholy rather than a harsh light, and the prevailing attitude towards death—the spirit that inspired the creation of Little Nell—casts a gloom. The poverty in the country was no less acute—there was the added horror of evictions—but, somehow, it is impossible to be wholly miserable, or miserable for long in the Irish countryside. And we turn with a sense of relief from the sectarian grimness of Dublin to contemplate the cheerful if sadly plain features of Douglas Hyde. He was many things, a poet, a sportsman; as a person, a dear. Everybody loved him. Under his enthusiastic banner they flocked to Irish revivals. That was in 1893. Since then, and not in Ireland only, has come the fashion for Irish christian names. Hyde wanted to replace shoddy imported English values with a revived Gaelic culture. The old tongue and its literature, submerged since Stuart times, was untainted with the dross of a Northcliffe or a Woolworth age.

Hyde's idea was splendid, and it should have led to an Irish renascence as it certainly heralded a literary renascence. In the climate he created the Abbey Theatre was born. But he did not foresee, and he wished to avoid, the taking over of his cultural revolution by the politicians and the militants. Such a one as Mahaffy saw at once that with the Irish revival the peasants would forget their place. He poured scorn on it. It was sad to see a scholar adopt a philistine pose, but most of Mahaffy's Trinity contemporaries followed his example and declared that the Irish renascence was the resurrection of a myth for sinister political ends. It was either eccentric or common to take it seriously. One would be ashamed to make a mistake in a classical allusion or a French accent, but it was positively funny to get Irish words wrong. Never has ignorance had such a holiday. And Mahaffy, whom Wilde was to charge with provincialism, was one of the first to declare that he was an example of 'that splendid breed of mongrel, the Anglo-Irishman', when one glance at that upper lip proclaimed him for what he was—as Irish as Carlyle was Scottish.

The Irish renascence should have been helped by such as Mahaffy. It would have been a much happier development than that which took place as a result of rebellion, guerrilla warfare and mutual murder. The element of hate might have been minimised or avoided, the bond of co-operative effort forged, and the new State would have been proud of all its traditions. In such an Ireland the term Anglo-Irish would have been as meaningless as Anglo-Saxon in the context of modern Britain, and the Gaelic revival would have aroused competitiveness instead of reluctant acquiescence, sporadic enthusiasm and downright dislike.

Gaeldom is a closed book to all but the Gaels. They say that the Irish literature we got from the revival is an ersatz product in comparison with the real thing. Reviewing one another they do not hesitate to bring in Homer, Dante, Virgil (not Milton: he was English).

But to those who have to take the matter on trust, it seems that Yeats and Synge created a literature of magical potency. It is, frankly, hard to believe something better lies hidden from only English-reading eyes. Ireland, as opposed to Anglo-Ireland, has gone out to the world from Yeats and Synge—Anglo-Irishmen, by their own profession. Synge had expressed sympathy with the declining landlord class, whom he described as having 'many genuine qualities, but little patriotism in the right sense, few ideas and no seed for future life, so it has gone to the wall'.

Mahaffy and Trinity College fought on the wrong field. They helped to bring class distinction into scholarship. It was an egregious blunder. They helped to manufacture the Anglo-Irish label when, by studying the question instead of ignoring it, they could have led a real Irish revival. Hyde was one of them. He—and Yeats—tried to join the staff of Trinity College. Both were refused. Mrs Hyde told me that he was very unhappy about it, he did not relish the company he had to keep in University College, which gave him a chair.

So long as antiquarian research was a private cult nobody in Trinity circles objected to it. Wilde's parents were prominently identified with it when the Royal Irish Academy and the Ordnance Survey department were unearthing the past. Men like Sir Samuel Ferguson, from the North, were writing in English on Irish folk lore. Rolleston made his beautiful translation that we can read in the *Oxford Book of English Verse*:

> In a quiet water'd land, a land of roses,
> Stands St Kieran's city fair;
> And the warriors of Erin in their famous generations
> Slumber there.

That this sort of lovely thing should have led to political rebellion only seems extraordinary to anyone who did not know what had happened in 1848. Consequently Hyde's movement, half a century later, though demonstrably cultural and not political, contained possibilities which men like Mahaffy recognised. They saw a Gaelic revival as a toe in the door of Protestant ascendancy. Because that, I fear, is what replaced the local patriotism of the eighteenth century. There was no room for romance.

Sir John Pentland Mahaffy, a future provost of Trinity College, was a friend of the Wildes, and Oscar's tutor in Trinity College. It seems to be fairly well established that his origins were purely Irish and his the anglicised form of an old clan name. But he became notorious in his lifetime for his wholehearted enmity to the Gaelic revival, which he expressed with the uninhibited ridicule that characterised his more celebrated utterances.

He knew Shaw as an acquaintance, but Yeats's father painted his portrait, and he met Yeats twice about a literary post in Trinity College. Mahaffy, apparently was unimpressed by Yeats's poetry, but when Dowden's chair of English fell vacant, he energetically supported Yeats's candidature. Yeats, according to Mahaffy's biographers, 'showed his magnanimity' on a controversial occasion.

Mahaffy's designation as the archetypal Unionist snob is in

large part due to his phrase 'a man called Pearse', a phrase that betrayed an arrogance which was Mahaffy's least attractive characteristic and the basis of much of his humour. The occasion for the remark was in connection with a meeting on 20 November 1914 to celebrate the centenary of the birth of Thomas Davis. It was to have been held under the auspices of the Gaelic Society in Trinity College and addressed by W. B. Yeats. Mahaffy, then Vice-Provost, had agreed to preside. Separatists, not all of whom were in the Sinn Féin movement, were then actively opposing recruitment for the British Army; and when Mahaffy heard that Patrick Pearse, whom he took to represent Sinn Féin, was going to speak at the meeting, he wrote to the Auditor:

My dear Sir,
I am informed that a man called Pearse is set down among your speakers at the opening of the Gaelic Society.

I am also informed that he is a declared supporter of the anti-recruitment agitation, as it appeared in the *Irish Volunteer* and other such publications. Unless these assertions, which I have on very good authority, are disproved to me, I cannot permit him to appear as a speaker in any such College meeting.

I cannot be here to meet you at four to-day, as I have to take the chair at the King's Hospital, but would gladly be present at 5.30. Why do you put me to this unpleasant necessity?

I am,
Yours sincerely,
J. P. Mahaffy.

A moderate reply was composed, explaining that a change of plan at that late hour was impossible. To which Mahaffy replied:

Just as the late Provost objected to Captain White addressing a College meeting last year, though the Provost was not in the chair, so I, as Vice-Provost, object to Mr Pearse speaking at your meeting, unless he assures me (through you) that he has said nothing against enlisting in the Imperial Army.

I regret that his name should have been published in your notices, but the information on which I act only reached me two days ago, and I will not allow a speaker with these, to me, traitorous views to address a meeting in College.

Captain White, to whom Mahaffy referred, was the wayward son of Sir George White, South African-war hero. 'Misfit', he called himself in his eccentric autobiography. He trained the Irish Citizen Army, the spearhead of the 1916 Rising.

Use of Trinity College for the meeting was forbidden, and in his final letter to Mahaffy, Charles Power, the Auditor, expressed the regret of his committee 'that the teaching of Thomas Davis which at least represented the gospel of free speech and liberty of conscience, should have borne no fruit in Trinity College'.

Mahaffy's attitude, in the context of the time, was not really surprising; and this is borne out by the fact that for the meeting, which was eventually held in the Antient Concert Rooms, Douglas Hyde, Horace Plunkett and Canon Hannay (the novelist George A. Birmingham) all refused to be persuaded into taking the chair.

Tom Kettle, wearing khaki, spoke at the meeting. A Nationalist MP killed in action in the First World War, he was one of the three friends—Griffith and A.E. were the others—that Gogarty never mocked. Denis Gwynn, the chairman, who later joined the British Army, recalls that some of Pearse's supporters, who largely constituted the audience, attempted to shout Kettle down in disapproval of his recruiting speeches. They had no more respect for the teaching of Thomas Davis than Mahaffy had.

It is convenient now to pretend that Mahaffy represented the views of an arrogant minority. This is the opposite of the truth. From the Volunteer organisation—formed in 1913 as an answer to Carson's Ulster Volunteers—there was a great mass of enlistment in the British Army in 1914. The section to which Pearse belonged that stayed at home and took part in the 1916 Rising was a small minority of the body. John Redmond, the popular Nationalist leader, was to the fore in the War recruiting campaign. This is now counted against him. But it is unhistorical and dishonest to distort the true picture at the time. Shaw was awkwardly involved. Yeats took no interest. But they were quite unrepresentative; and when, eight years later, Yeats as a Senator and a member of the

Kildare Street Club spoke on behalf of the Protestant people, he represented a group the vast majority of whom still shared Mahaffy's views about Pearse (if they ever thought about him). Mahaffy only differed from the average Anglo-Irishman in being more unrestrained in his expression of his opinions in public.

Whatever chance there was of getting the class to which he belonged to take up the Gaelic revival was killed when it became associated with rebellion. Canon Hannay, who achieved fame as George A. Birmingham, was a rare bird among parsons when he took up Hyde's ideas enthusiastically; but in an early novel, a *roman à clef*, he paints an unflattering picture of the circle into which his activities had led him. It included Maud Gonne.

In 1914, despite the advance made by Home Rule, Dublin was a thoroughly provincial city. Power and influence lay in London, not in the back-rooms where the Gaelic League held its classes. Mahaffy's snobbery was partly humorous. He developed some kind of mania about kings and queens, as if he had invented a private card game. His travels in Greece had brought him into touch with that King, and his publications had a wide vogue before Greek travel became an industry. On the strength of this connection and his reputation as a scholar, who was also a sportsman and a wit, he became a social figure. It compensated for rebuffs from colleagues in Trinity, who disliked his flamboyant style. To some extent it was a game, but it was largely a counter-offensive. He had had several setbacks in Trinity, the worst when he was denied the Provostship in 1904; and it was a form of compensation to write and to speak as if he inhabited naturally a more exalted sphere. His taste was not impeccable. A snob is always coarse. He was snubbed by Queen Victoria, in Dublin in her dotage, when he made an unfortunate attempt to pass himself off as a friend of the family. His Cambridge contemporary, Oscar Browning, got into similar scrapes, as when he rushed up to Tennyson and said, 'I am Browning', and the poet replied, 'You are not.'

Only inveterate political prejudice, reinforced by fears of revolution, can explain the philistine attitude Mahaffy adopted towards the Irish language. His authority, a polyglot, Atkinson, was an Englishman, and Mahaffy liked to quote him that anything in ancient Irish literature that wasn't silly was indecent. Atkinson had a detestation of folk-lore, a subject in which the elder Wildes were thoroughly versed and which, of course, was Yeats's original inspiration. It left Mahaffy cold. He had felt instinctively that the Gaelic revival, which he tried to discourage with ridicule, had ominous political possibilities. In 1911 he wrote:

'Even now the recoil from the Penal Laws is being felt; the long oppressed Roman Catholics are rising rapidly in power, wealth and influence, and it will be strange indeed if this recovered influence does not lead to acts of injustice, and even to confiscation in some polite form, even though the days of massacre and armed rapine are over.'

In the same article, with the rising five years off, Mahaffy declared that the clergy, both Protestant and Roman Catholic, were growing more bigoted. Maynooth was a narrower school than St Omer or Douay, while the Protestant clergy were too much controlled by the ignorant and bigoted laity in their disestablished church where only one type of Protestant theology is tolerated. He was not himself, he liked to say, a clergyman in any offensive sense of the word. He accepted a knighthood and disdained the use of a clerical collar. Like Yeats, he regarded himself as one of what he described as 'these splendid mongrels by whom the pure Irish have always been led'. And Stephen Gwynn, when a Nationalist MP, recalled that Mahaffy, while deploring Home Rule, looked not without satisfaction at the prospect of pontificating in a reconstituted House of Lords.

Mahaffy was the originator of the Georgian Society in Ireland. And the Ireland that appealed to him was the one with tangible reminders of ancient glories and great occasions in which he might have expected to find himself cutting a decent figure.

He did not share Pearse's dream of young warriors with white limbs taking a heroic part in unending interprovincial warfare. He could see himself exchanging repartee with a Chesterfield in the Viceregal Lodge. But Mahaffy was a political realist. As Fitzgibbon, a century before, had seen in the emancipation of Catholics the end of Protestant supremacy, Mahaffy was no less convinced that Hyde, the parson's son who inspired the Gaelic revival, had sold the pass with his Irish enthusiasms. Hyde,

Mahaffy would have considered, had made an ass of himself. He should have been well beaten by his father for going into country cottages and learning to speak Irish from the peasants instead of studying his Greek grammar.

The Gaelic enthusiasts were demanding that knowledge of Irish should be a pre-condition for certain appointments. It was made compulsory at entrance to the National University when it was established in 1908. The rescue of the language in the south and west where it still hung on was then, as now, the chief concern of the Gaels, but Mahaffy would have none of this and wrote an article to condemn the forced use of 'a most difficult and useless tongue'.

Like Fitzgibbon, the architect of the Union, the later Earl of Clare, he had a trenchant way of not sparing opponents when he had a home truth to deliver. 'There is no country in which sham excuses, political and religious, for appointing incompetent men to responsible posts flourish more signally than in Ireland.'

There is truth in that, and the language policy since the foundation of the State has enabled the incompetent on many occasions to oust the better-qualified.

I have tried to find out exactly what sort of man Mahaffy was. The result of my endeavour has been to reinforce a conviction that Henry Ford was shrewd in his estimate of history. I cannot get consistent testimony; and if that is the case about someone who is remembered by people still alive, what chance have we of learning the truth about the long dead? Even if we judge them only by their deeds, we may be misled as to their motives. For example, most of the reforms proposed by Liberals were made law by Conservative governments.

I have been hearing about Mahaffy all my life. Gogarty saw the fun in his name-dropping; but here is Gogarty himself on a meeting with the Duke of Connaught. 'To me the gestures of the Duke as he sat at the table bespoke more than even his terse and considered words. He had what beauty seldom companions, and that is grace. Even the movement of his raising his glass seemed more like a dispensation than a personal movement.'

Many years ago I asked a friend of mine, Joshua Watson, about Mahaffy. Watson was his ward, his father having died when he was a child. He described him as very worldly. When he asked Watson what he intended to do for a living, he said he wanted to be a violinist. 'A fiddler,' Mahaffy said, 'is no occupation for a gentleman. Now I still have some influence, and I might be able to pick you up a living in the south of England if you would become a clergyman. There are still some nice livings in the south of England, and you could play your fiddle there as much as you liked.'

A friend, who prefers to be referred to as 'Mrs X', remembers Mahaffy as a frequent diner in her mother's house. He had a rather greedy way of eating. He had also a habit of kissing the girls of the family, not unlike his method of eating soup. This began to get on her nerves, and she told her mother that she wouldn't put up with it any longer. 'You will put up with it,' a brother broke in, 'until we are all through the Divinity School.' (When I told Mrs X I was quoting her she wrote to me: 'But I think of him with gratitude and, perhaps, pride. I would hate to give the wrong impression and, anyhow, I was a very unkissable girl.')

He had to be talking to someone, and Mrs Moorhead, Stephen Gwynn's daughter, remembers her embarrassment as a child when he recognised her on the Howth tram, going into Dublin, and insisted on addressing her in his loud guttural voice, to the edification of the other passengers.

But these are superficialities, what of the man underneath them? Walter Starkie saw a great deal of Mahaffy. His father was a close friend, and they shared a passion for classical scholarship; Starkie being the more precise of the two. Walter was encouraged in his music by Mahaffy who gave him his Stainer when the younger man showed real proficiency on the violin. Mahaffy lunched on Sundays at the Starkies (from all accounts he rarely ate at home). When he came he was 'always kind . . . After lunch he would take us out in the garden and talk to us in the most fascinating way about birds and flowers.' On excursions, while the elders were employed, 'Dr Mahaffy would lead us children into the meadow outside and talk to us by the hour of wild flowers and birds'. He recalls Mahaffy on other occasions—once when he welcomed guests into his study—'Come in, boys: I have a great treat for you this evening—woodcock—shot by lords—Lord Granard sent them to me yesterday.'

There is something ludicrous in this snobbery, as when Mahaffy on hearing that the King of Greece favoured the Germans in the First World War, exclaimed, 'I'm deeply disappointed in him—I'll cut that King.'

It sounds almost as if he was playing a game, indulging a fantasy, which he invited others to watch—King-collecting, as others collected coins or china. It did not give any evidence upon which the whole man could be judged. Wherever Mahaffy discoursed on morals, as when he denounced Wagner's music (because Wagner was a cad who should have been hounded out of decent society) he always came to rest on what was 'gentlemanly'. It was, perhaps, because he accepted Arnold's definition and gave the word a moral connotation. Starkie said his 'snobbery sprang from his Anglo-Irish characteristics and it can be explained by a remark made by W. B. Yeats when he was asked whether Oscar Wilde was a snob. "No, I would not say that; England is a strange country to the Irish. To Wilde the aristocrats of England were like the nobles of Bagdad."'

We might leave Mahaffy there did there not exist the evidence of Walter's sister, Enid. At the beginning of the last World War, Enid Starkie fluttered the Dublin dovecotes with a book of childhood reminiscences called *A Lady's Child*. Written without malice, it was sometimes lacking in tact; she did not expect her relations to be offended by her embarrassing candour and rather lofty pronouncements on their characters and habits. The book gives a vivid picture of childhood in a very typical Anglo-Irish Dublin home. The Starkies were Catholics, but not—in Mahaffy's phrase—'in any offensive sense of the word'. Walter, as had his father before him, went to Shrewsbury after Strangways in Dublin (where I was also at school).

The Starkie girls went to Alexandra School and College. None of these establishments was Catholic. I should think most Irish children with the same background would recognise this picture as valid; but not every child had such easy access to music and scholarship as the little Starkies. Enid confirms Walter's impression that Mahaffy was ubiquitous in their young lives.

'I remember also Professor J. P. Mahaffy, who was a weekly visitor to our house for Sunday lunch, almost to the day of his death. I ought to be able to remember witty and clever things that he said, for I saw him often enough when I was a child, but my mind is a blank on that score. I remember chiefly his never-failing snobbishness, his talk of the kings and queens with whom he had shaken hands, of the noble houses in England and abroad at which he had been a guest. Later, when I began to be able to understand what he was saying, I used to be irritated by his profound and undisguised contempt for Irishmen. He professed to love only the country, but not the people, and it was noticeable that any second-rate European, especially a second-rate Englishman, was always praised by him when he would have little to say about a first-rate Irishman. I suppose he did not consider Irishmen—snobbishly speaking—sufficiently distinguished, and Irishman though he was himself, he found it hard to believe that anything good could come out of Ireland. In Trinity College, Dublin, whenever possible, he always appointed Englishmen.'

Here, when all is said, is only a hostile reaction to foibles which an older and more tolerant person might have not judged quite so harshly.

Enid Starkie is not conspicuously accurate in the rest of her narrative. She was too subjective to be a faithful recorder; and her irritation with Mahaffy may have been the outcome of some disagreeable incident or the impression of one unhappy evening which persisted in memory.

Enid Starkie was an Irishwoman who had a distinguished career at Oxford. She broke away from home and was able to measure herself against English standards. A tendency to overrate them and to think too meanly of home-made things was certainly conspicuous in Dublin, and Mahaffy's attitude to the Irish language was an example of it. Perhaps, he was to be seen at his best in the surroundings he most enjoyed. One of the houses he used to frequent was Sir John Leslie's at Glaslough, Co. Monaghan. Leslie was married to a Jerome, sister of Lady Randolph Churchill. Shane Leslie, their son, in his reminiscences has only happy memories of Mahaffy, as when after the American Minister Lowell expressed delight at his conversation, he said 'Poor man, has he never listened to the conversation of an Irish gentleman before?'

There is an inexplicable tendency to put forward the most distinguished as representative and to elect eccentrics as types; Mahaffy is for many people the typical Anglo-Irishman. It is forgotten that he was not popular with many of his Trinity colleagues, and they laughed at or resented his pretensions. 'Stick-in-the-muds', he called them, but they punished him at various times. He was, for instance, forbidden to preach in the College Chapel.

He was not typical; he was extreme, and bore to the average Anglo-Irishman the likeness that a caricature does to the original —more like than like. And in his prejudices he was not nearly so unshakeable as many of his quieter colleagues. His liberality in religion lost him the Provostship in 1904.

CHAPTER XVI

Oscar Wilde

WHEN YEATS CALLED his roll of honour, he left out the name of Wilde. In 1925 it might have spoiled his effect. But not today, although so far as land and horse-owning is concerned he fails to qualify as an Anglo-Irishman. The Wildes owned a house in Merrion Square, a terrace in Bray, a shooting lodge on an island in Galway, and a larger one at Cong, Co. Mayo. That does not constitute landlordism. The man who described fox-hunting as 'the pursuit of the uneatable by the unspeakable' was not a 'Protestant with a horse'. Wilde was, what Shaw said he much disliked, 'a Merrion Square snob', but so far as genes went a complete mixture of Irish and English.

The Frenchman who kept a statue of the Blessed Virgin in his garden, and when congratulated on his piety, explained that there was a family connection, was regarded as eccentric. An extreme example, perhaps, but there was something about him which reminds me of the Wildes and, in certain moments, Yeats. Shaw protested that he was free of all this, and early in life saw how silly his father's pretensions were; but in the act of telling us this he lets fall that his father was second cousin to a baronet, and he took pleasure in the fantastic idea that the Shaws were descended from the Thane of Fife. When it came to marriage, not only did he connect himself with money, but with a member of an Anglo-Irish family. Nevertheless there is a breeziness about Shaw, a no-nonsense air, that separates him from his distinguished Irish fellow writers.

Wilde inherited snobbery from his father and his mother, but from the latter particularly. Her passion for consequence, her condescension, would have fitted her admirably for a Sheridan comedy. But, again, to be fair to her, her dreams were not merely of rank. While she was inordinately proud of her husband's knighthood and wanted Oscar to get one—as she planned incessantly for suitable matches for her hopeless son, Willie—her imagination soared to loftier peaks. She sought connections that would establish her family on Parnassus as well as in Debrett. She put it about that she was related to Dante—a magnificent start—and she avoided references to humbler associations. She was sarcastic, for instance, about attorneys without mentioning that her father was one of that fraternity and obscurely unsuccessful. As a result of this there has been confusion, and in many books it is stated that she was the daughter of the Archdeacon of Wexford, her grandfather. Her position was complicated by her husband's doubtful reputation—it blew up into a major scandal when a former patient accused him of rape. She had to live with that, a dreadful preparation for the scandal that made her son notorious. And in the background her other son, Willie, was always getting into scrapes (he had a peculiar habit of proposing to almost every girl he met and then pledging her to silence). Added to this was continuous uncertainty about money. Her husband borrowed all she had, and she lived in miserable poverty, putting a brave face on it, in London after he died. When Oscar was flooring competitors with his epigrams he had still to have recourse to Mahaffy and others to get his mother a State pension.

When Oscar described his mother's adoption of nationalism to an American audience, he told them that she had been brought up 'in an atmosphere of alien English thought, among people high in Bench and Senate and far removed from any love or knowledge of those wrongs of the people to which she afterwards gave such passionate expression. And one day in 1845, standing at the window of her lordly house, she saw a great funeral pass in its solemn trappings of sorrow down the street . . .' It was Thomas Davis's funeral; she bought and read his poems and discovered her country.

Who would believe that Miss Elgee, as she then was, looked out in fact from the top window of rented rooms in Leeson Street? She lived with her mother, widow of a solicitor, who had emigrated to India after failure in Dublin and died out there. And it is a further tribute to Wilde's pictorial imagination that the funeral of Thomas Davis did not pass down Leeson Street.

In the same grandiloquent way, in *De Profundis*, he wrote at length of his sorrow and remorse at the disgrace he had brought on the names of his parents. 'What I suffered then, and still suffer, is not for pen to write or paper to record.'

As I look up the books from which these quotations are taken I find Wilde and Yeats, not less than Shaw, speaking of 'the Irish'. The word Anglo-Irish never confused their utterance. Stephen Gwynn, a nationalist in politics and a great lover of the Irish countryside, who was born in an Irish rectory and wrote on Irish topics, expressed his chagrin, his wholly justified chagrin, at this determination to deprive him of his nationality.

'I was brought up to think myself Irish without question or qualification; but the new nationalism prefers to describe me and the like of me as Anglo-Irish. A.E. has even set me down in print as being the Anglo-Irishman *par excellence*—or, to put it more modestly, the typical Anglo-Irishman. So all my life I have been spiritually hyphenated without knowing it.'

Perhaps choice of names is as good a clue as any to social aspirations. Every Yeats had Butler in his name. Wilde was christened Oscar Fingal O'Flahertie Wills Wilde. Oscar and Fingal were pure poetry. Lady Wilde at the time of his birth was taken up with Ossian. The O'Flaherties were connected by marriage with Sir William Wilde. They were a large and formidable clan of ancient Irish. This fitted in with Lady Wilde's revolutionary period. It antedated Oscar's birth by six years. Wills celebrated the Wilde connection with the Mount Sandford family. There is no indication that there was any blood connection, a Wilde had been a land agent on the estate. That was all or, apparently, all. But the names the future Lady Wilde gave her son are more indicative of poetry and patriotism than simple snobbery. And her tendency was to over-rate her literary rather than her social importance. Wilde, however harum-scarum his home, went into the world with immensely more advantages than either Shaw or Yeats. A public school, Trinity and Oxford, a father at the top of his profession, a celebrated mother—the scandal of 1865 might have overcome less buoyant spirits, and after it Wilde *père* seems to have declined. But, on the whole, the family lived it down. Wilde had less need for props to self-esteem than Shaw or Yeats.

Lady Wilde in her youth breathed defiance at the British Government in prose and verse no less voluminous and extravagant than herself; in her latter days she was encouraging Oscar to be civil to the Prince of Wales in order to improve his chance of a royal favour. And she was tireless in pursuit of a pension from the Government she had urged the Irish to rise and destroy.

Nevertheless, she and her husband, to the end, retained their interest in Irish folklore and history, and he, who described himself as English in his first publication, came to call himself Irish. Both of them were delighted when the Queen knighted Sir William; but he was not pleased when the honour was attributed to his work on the census.

Oscar played down his Irishness in London. None of his writing has anything in it to remind readers of his origin. Shaw frequently referred to his Irish past; but it is impossible to imagine Wilde writing *John Bull's Other Island*.

If the Anglo-Irish are regarded as a socially superior race, a good deal of this springs from their own good opinion of themselves. Shaw wrote of the absurdity of his father's pretensions, but would not have liked the way Edith Somerville wrote about his own. Lord Alfred Douglas, Wilde's evil genius, wrote scathingly of his snobbish pride in his mother's ladyship ('Of Papa Wilde we did not hear quite so frequently'). More recently Lord David Cecil has described Wilde as 'a genial, brilliant, spirited Irish buccaneer, with a thirst for self-advertisement, incurably crude taste, and a strong streak of sentimental vulgarity'. A harsh, but not an unsustainable verdict. And in the light of it, it is amusing to cite Yeats's embarrassment when he called on Wilde in London. The older man was then at the height of his short lived success and anxious to help a young compatriot.

'"We Irish are too poetical to be poets; we are a nation of brilliant failures, but we are the greatest talkers since the Greeks." When dinner was over he read to me from the proofs of *The Decay of Lying* and when he came to the sentence, "Schopenhauer has analysed the pessimism that characterises modern thought, but

Hamlet invented it. The world has become sad because a puppet was once melancholy", I said "Why do you change 'sad' to 'melancholy'?" He replied that he wanted a full sound at the close of his sentence, and I thought it no excuse and an example of the vague impressiveness that spoilt his writing for me . . .

'When, however, I called, wearing shoes a little too yellow—unblackened leather had just become fashionable—I realised their extravagance when I saw his eyes fixed upon them; and another day Wilde asked me to tell his little boy a faery story and I got as far as "Once upon a time there was a giant" when the little boy screamed and ran out of the room. Wilde looked grave and I was plunged into the shame of clumsiness that afflicts the young. And when I asked for some literary gossip for some provincial newspaper, that paid me a few shillings a month, I was told that writing literary gossip was no job for a gentleman.'

CHAPTER XVII

Emergence of a Middle Class

AT THE END of the eighteenth century, what may be termed a loose partnership, was formed between Pitt in England and Fitzgibbon in Dublin; towards the close of the Victorian era an even closer relationship was established between Arthur Balfour and Edward Carson.

Balfour's uncle, Lord Salisbury, cannot be counted among the friends of Ireland. As an ardent churchman, he was initially prejudiced against the prevailing religion for one thing. On one occasion he likened the Irish to Hottentots. It was much resented at the time, but nowadays only a 'racist' would be expected to find the parallel invidious. That was in the eighties when in some way the tide turned in Irish affairs. The decade began with the land war at its height, but Gladstone's Land Act of 1881 gave the tenants the things they had been asking for—'the three F's'—fair rents, fixity of tenure and free sale. Gladstone was not the only British statesman to believe that if Ireland's practical needs were met she would become reconciled to the Union. Other than he were to be disappointed.

The decade was not far advanced when it was marred by the horror of the Phoenix Park murders. It speaks volumes for Gladstone's essential goodness that this, involving as it did the loss of a close family connection (Lord Frederick Cavendish), did not embitter him. It enormously embarrassed Parnell and almost drove him out of public life. But he convinced Gladstone that the choice was dealing with him or with more desperate men. The revolutionary sediment at the bottom of Irish society was beginning at last to rise to the top. Gladstone was imaginative enough to grasp this; and his practical effort to anticipate it was the first Home Rule Bill of 1886. When this was emphatically defeated in the House of Commons—winning the first battle in the war which it was eventually to lose—Salisbury came back and made a sensational appointment, his nephew, Arthur Balfour, as Chief Secretary for Ireland.

Balfour's languid pose proved deceptive; he became 'Bloody Balfour' in Irish legend, principally on account of an affray in Mitchelstown where the police took life (incidentally, it was a sign of the times that this attracted such publicity when the death roll was so insignificant in comparison with similar incidents earlier in the century).

Carson was present at Mitchelstown; Balfour met him at a Dublin dinner party and took a liking to him. It was the making of Carson as a political figure. His success as a barrister was already assured, but only in Dublin. Now he was to follow his patron to London having earned in nationalist circles the soubriquet 'Coercion Carson'. It is sometimes urged against this enigmatic personality that his devotion to Ulster in later years was patently fraudulent. The son of a Dublin architect of Italian origin, how could he sincerely feel any bond with the Northern province?

His career is quite consistent if this junction with Balfour is taken as its starting point. He set his course by Balfour and never wandered thenceforth, showing his mettle by taking a lead at once in the prosecutions instituted by the Government in a new policy of toughness. Balfour's policy was to establish control and then to institute thoroughgoing reforms. He had no sympathy with Lord Clanricarde and other despotic absentees who gave their order such a bad name. But he was determined at the same time that they should not be intimidated. It was a pattern of progressive Conservative government, and he enlisted in it, in later years, his brother, Gerald Balfour, who came to Ireland as Chief Secretary.

The century ended with a flood of belated paternalist concern for Ireland, the sort of concern, it is only reasonable to say, that was not much in the air anywhere until then. Balfour was making the last attempt to make the Union work, and those like Sir Horace Plunkett who put forward his schemes for agricultural co-operation at the time were accused of trying to kill Home Rule by kindness. The fearful overcrowding of the land which had been tackled hitherto by wholesale eviction was now subjected to ordered transplantation by the Congested Districts Board. Horace Plunkett's schemes, in which he enlisted the mystic A.E., were taken up by Government and a Department of Agriculture formed. The Royal Dublin Society leased land from Lord Pembroke in Ballsbridge and inaugurated Shows on a scale that was quite impossible in the restricted grounds of Leinster House.

With these progressive tendencies marched the pioneers of Gaelic revival—Douglas Hyde and Eoin Mac Neill, a civil servant from Antrim. The young Yeats was learning about Fenianism from the veteran rebel John O'Leary, who introduced him also to Maud Gonne. Back from Australia, where he had become Prime Minister and was knighted for his services, came Sir Charles Gavan Duffy to revive interest in the cultural side of the Young Ireland programme.

And in Dublin, half a century after emancipation, a Catholic middle-class was growing in self-confidence. It was, in Irish terms, a hopeful time; but the scene on the parliamentary front was squalid. His followers, after Parnell fell, fought over his bones and pulled, until they tore it to tatters, his fallen mantle. A new movement began; it called itself Sinn Féin. Its chief proponent was Arthur Griffith, a Dublin journalist, who had worked for a time in South Africa. Griffith edited a succession of newspapers—they were suppressed as their revolutionary ardour increased to be replaced by others—in which he carried on a war of invective against British Government. *The United Irishman* conducted a bitterly pro-Boer campaign during the South African War. As well as polemics, its pages were opened to literature, and Griffith became the first nurse of talent since the death of Davis.

Various occasions lent themselves to a rallying of the disparate forces of nationalism. The centenary of the 1798 Rebellion was one of them. A Royal visit by the new king Edward VII was another.

In its insistence on palliation as the cure, Balfour's Government went further than ever Gladstone had done. A scheme of land purchase was put through in 1903, and the idea of a Catholic University was tackled again. A Commission was set up at which Mahaffy enjoyed himself, mocking at the idea of Gaelic as a subject for scholarship. But Mahaffy sensed a change in the political climate. He was apparently favourably inclined to the idea of a

Catholic college in Dublin University. This cost him the Provostship in 1904, when Balfour appointed Traill, the nominee of the Ulster Unionist faction.

Sir Anthony McDonnell, an Irishman, gave up a splendid prospect in India, to return to Ireland as under-secretary. George Wyndham, the Chief Secretary—a fine flower of a select culture doomed to extinction in a decade—was inclined not to read official letters when they were long. He was pushed by McDonnell further than he had intended to go. Lord Dunraven, Sir Hutchinson Poë, and other landlords co-operated in these schemes. Not only in the sales to tenants but in a new solution to Home Rule. They called it Devolution; and when Wyndham discovered that this was propounded in a letter which he had read with insufficient care he had to resign.

Balfour was not the first reformer to discover that his policy, so far from giving satisfaction, only increased appetite. And Plunkett, among those who most actively worked for amelioration of conditions, was to find himself, as he said, in the position of a dog on a tennis-court, a nuisance to both sides. The momentum of the demand for independence was increasing and entrenched Unionism was digging itself in. Inevitably it found its last redoubt in north-east Ulster. There the battle of Unionism was to be fought out, and is being fought out still. When Carson accepted the leadership of the Unionist Party, the Liberal Government, kept in office by the Irish Nationalists, was committed to Home Rule. Carson went to Ulster to raise resistance there, in his role as leader of the Unionists, not as an Ulster leader. He organised the Ulster Volunteers that resisted Home Rule; his policy undermined discipline in the British Army and encouraged German hopes on the eve of war; he effectually showed the way to Sinn Féin, who copied him by raising a rival corps of Volunteers, organised gunrunning, and eventually (in 1916) broke out in open rebellion. Such were the consequences of Edward Carson. But he has never been a hated figure in Ireland generally, as Fitzgibbon or Castlereagh were. He lent a sense of adventure to what was always a severely prosaic cause.

The Anglo-Irishman is a Protestant because only Protestants were allowed to enjoy the Constitution in the eighteenth century, their heyday. But in the century that followed, in which the outstanding political Irishmen were O'Connell and Parnell, there emerged a type of Irishman, which has embarrassed both parties, since his Irish culture came from Thomas Moore, his political stance from Daniel O'Connell. He was the Irishman of the enfranchisement, a threat to Government because he had a vote, a brake on revolution because he was in the majority. He had, for one thing, a traditional respect for the clergy, based on their services to the people in the Penal Days, not only the fruit of superstition. He was the Irishman that Yeats hoped to see defeated. He is seen at his shoddy worst in the Synge rows in 1907.

After the rows about *The Playboy*, Synge wrote to Stephen Mac Kenna, translator of Plotinus, 'I sometimes wish I had never left my garret in the rue D'Assas—it seems funny to write the words again—the scurrility, and ignorance and treachery of some of the attacks on me have rather disgruntled me with the middle class Irish Catholic. As you know I have the wildest admiration for the Irish peasants, and for Irishmen of known or unknown genius —do you bow?—but between the two there's an ungodly ruck of fat faced, sweaty headed swine. They are in Dublin and in Kingstown, and also in all the country towns.'

Among Synge's attackers were Arthur Griffith and Patrick Pearse; but it would give a false picture of Dublin at the time to think that only Catholics disapproved of literary realism. *The Irish Times* in 1907 might be taken as very representative of Dublin Protestant middle-class opinion, and it thought the dialogue in *The Playboy* contained 'indiscretions'. The Rathmines and Kingstown Protestant was not less squeamish than his Catholic neighbour; but his raised eyebrow at 'indiscretions' was mild because he did not take the nationalist line that Synge libelled the Irish people. Griffith and Pearse announced the death of the Anglo-Irish theatre and the need for a truly Irish one. Pearse would not have had Mayo women in their shifts, but young white-limbed warriors, companions of Finn, dedicated to heroism—not far from the Arthurian romanticism of Tennyson, but somewhat lacking his mellifluousness. Griffith, who had taken exception to Synge's work before the riots, asserted that Irish women were the most virtuous on earth. James Connolly, the signatory to the Proclamation of 1916 and the only Marxist prominent among the leaders of the Rising, agreed with Griffith. He too wanted some other instead of the Abbey as a national theatre. Maud Gonne took his side.

Of the Irish who obtained later celebrity the youthful James Joyce stands out as one of the few who backed Synge against small town puritanism and national monomania.

But Synge, under pressure, as it were, responded by reference to atavistic prejudices. When the Irish-Ireland mob howled down *The Playboy of the Western World* he accused the Gaelic League of being formed on 'ignorance, fraud and hypocrisy' and was astringent about the 'senile and slobbering' elements in its doctrine. Synge, I might add, was descended from an ancestor who had wielded great power in Ireland at the time of Swift. And when this Anglo-Irish talk began A.E., who was gentle and wise and usually right, wrote to Yeats about the Gaelic League in a tone that might have surprised an Irish audience, 'the Anglo-Irish were the best Irish, but I can see very little future for them as the present belongs to that half-crazy Gaeldom which is growing dominant about us'.

Let us pause at A.E. and take stock. Divergent though their paths became in middle life, A.E. was one of Yeats's boyhood friends; and they worked together in late middle-age on the *Irish Statesman*, the best journal ever to appear in Ireland. Although he was generous and indefatigable in the promotion of talent, the *Statesman* was, to a large extent, the handiwork of A.E. Under several pseudonyms he contributed an endless flow of articles and reviews. Politics, economics, philosophy, literature, art—nothing was outside his interest or incapable of setting in motion that ready pen. What Lady Gregory was to Yeats, Horace Plunkett was to A.E., or George Russell, to give him his everyday name. A.E. (which he sometimes wrote as a diphthong) owed its origin to a printer's error. Russell signed an article AEON, the compositor left out the last two letters, and Russell accepted the result as a pseudonymic christening. Thereafter he was A.E. or AE or Æ.

It is surprising that nobody has attempted a full biography; but his essence is beautifully caught in a memoir, written by John Eglinton. We are concerned with him here only in so far as he can be related to the Anglo-Irish. By every definition that I have employed he was not one of them. He was born in Lurgan, County Armagh, in 1867, that is to say in Northern Ireland, which I put outside the pale. Then, again, his social origins were relatively humble and nothing could be further from the idea of Protestants with horses than the sober and serious upbringing of this cottage child. His father was a book-keeper, his mother had worked in a store; but they were people of superior mind, and young Russell grew up in a more intellectual atmosphere than would have been his lot had he been born a Catholic in the same circumstances in a small town in the South of Ireland. His father's fortunes improved when he moved to Dublin to work for Craig and Gardiner, a leading firm of accountants. Now A.E. was sent for a time to Dr Benson's remarkable academy in Rathmines, where boys learnt what they liked and parents paid what they could.

It was in Art School that A.E. met Yeats. They were drawn into the theosophy of Madame Blavatsky and Annie Besant; they were attracted by mysticism and the religions of the East; but in the case of Yeats it seemed that every experience was essentially food and exercise for his poetry; of the two Russell was the genuine mystic. He chose to be poor and began his working life in Pims, a large Dublin shop. His circumstances altered when Horace Plunkett founded the Irish Agricultural Organisation Society and at Yeats's suggestion, employed Russell to act as a travelling demonstrator of the theory of co-operative farming. As a missionary among Irish farmers, founding the creameries which exist to this day, Russell spent his middle years. Plunkett influenced the course of his life again when he put up the money to establish the *Irish Statesman* in 1923. Russell at the time was editing the *Irish Homestead*, as a supplement to his agricultural pioneering. The new journal was more ambitious and wider in its scope. In its pages were discussed the questions—including censorship—which agitated the intellectuals in the newly formed Irish Free State as well as the matters to be found in the back pages of its contemporary, *The New Statesman and Nation*.

Long before he became an editor, A.E. had established himself as a poet, a painter, and an occasional commentator on public affairs. His letter to the employers of Dublin during the lock-out and labour troubles of 1913 is still remembered. Less well known

EMERGENCE OF A MIDDLE CLASS

is a similar appeal during the Civil War to Republicans to cease their efforts to strangle the new state in its cradle. All these activities must have interfered with his growth as a poet and an artist. He liked to describe himself as a painter, and for periods in his life, he took himself for some months in the summer to Donegal—his paradise—where he painted the scenery, decorated frequently with fairy figures—his visions. Russell is unique in that he emerged from George Moore's autobiographical trilogy unwounded. After Edward Martyn and Yeats, he is the principal figure in those mischievous recollections. There is an account of a bicycle tour to New Grange. Russell came to Moore's assistance when he explained that the loops of tape at the top of men's drawers were intended for securing them to the trouser braces. He was practical as well as mystical. He was also good. Moore recalled 'the sweetness of his long grey eyes'. To say 'good' has a flat sound, but Russell's goodness enriched the lives of many. It was positive and creative, if its expression in his verse, as in his painting, is somewhat woolly. He composed his poems, as he painted his pictures, out of doors. They came too readily, and his vocabulary was limited. But his pride in his poetry was absolute. If he had human weakness, it was jealousy of Yeats's reputation.

Russell's love poems, like all his art, lack precision. He was not created for conventional social or domestic life. His marriage surprised everyone; Mrs Russell kept in the background, and brought up their two sons. As a young man he had received with an incredulous smile John Eglinton's plea of family obligation when Russell called him out for his usual walk on Christmas day. And he never changed. His eyes were set on eternity and his visions were never translated into a form that allowed the outsider to share their clarity. Consequently he was at his best when he was physically present; and his verses when they were occasional had a vigour which was missing when they were merely reflective.

Possibly the most important friendship—or love—of his life was with his secretary, Susan Mitchell. She resented George Moore's belittling manner and her acid little book on Moore was probably prompted by a womanly feeling that he got more from A.E. than he gave. It was after this that Moore began to call A.E. 'The Donegal Dauber'; and Russell, to whom hatred was wholly alien, and whose anger was brief, occasional, and immediately regretted, revealed a pent-up aversion to Moore in the last book of his life. *The Avatars* was not a success; through its clouds Moore may be perceived in a picture of spiritual evil. 'That thing has worms slinking through its veins not blood. It would pollute earth to bury him in it.' Such an outburst was unique. The essential Russell is to be found in such a remark as this, culled from a letter to a friend: 'There are two points in our lives never to be spoken of: the highest, which is sacred, and to speak of it would turn earthwards the soaring meditative spirit; and there is the depth in us which we never speak of for pity's sake. It must never, never, be sung.'

Gradually he became disillusioned. Susan Mitchell died and this affected him greatly. Kevin O'Higgins, Minister for Justice, to whom A.E. as well as Yeats looked upon as the chief moral force in the Government, was murdered in 1927. A year afterwards, one of the new men whom Yeats expected the Anglo-Irish to be called back to replace, brought down the *Irish Statesman*. Offended by a harsh review of a sloppy book, he took a libel action, and lost it. But legal costs had to be paid. A subscription was collected in America. If A.E. had wished it, he might have carried on, but Dublin had lost its charm. Old friends were dying off. Yeats had been taken up by English admirers, Lady Dorothy Wellesley for one. The younger men were less patient with his monologues. In America and from Americans he received the warm recognition that Ireland denied. To America he went on a prolonged tour; and when he returned, he settled in London, not Dublin. Donegal was still Paradise. But he died in Bournemouth.

When it was known that he was ill, Gogarty and other friends came from Ireland to be with him. Before the end—and not without prompting—arrived what he seemed most anxiously to watch for—a letter from Yeats.

Dunsany, nephew of Horace Plunkett, wrote Russell's epitaph.

> A lovely radiance of a passing star
> Upon a sudden journey through the gloaming,
> Lighting low Irish hills, and then afar
> To its own regions homing.

CHAPTER XVIII

Edward Martyn and the Kildare Street Club

A.E. HAS LED us on too far. The narrative must go back to let us glance at some of the other characters who decorated Dublin at the turn of the century. Edward Martyn, to many readers, is a character in fiction. George Moore made him his favourite butt in his autobiographical trilogy, revelling in detailed descriptions of his uncouth appearance.

'His churchwarden was drawing famously, and I noticed his great square hands with strong fingers and square nails pared closely away, and as heretofore I admired the curve of the great belly, the thickness of the thighs, the length and breadth of his foot hanging over the edge of the sofa, the apoplectic neck falling into great rolls of flesh, the humid eyes, the skull covered with short stubby hair.'

Moore became his Boswell, Martyn claimed; but Martyn had been given the role of Moore's Sancho Panza, and their journeys together, as the novelist described them, might well have been subtitled 'Travels with a Donkey'. Martyn naturally deeply resented this treatment by a friend. Not that his case was unique. Moore sacrificed all his friends on the altar of his autobiographical art. In doing so, he took care to diminish them. Yeats suffered, but not to the same extent as Moore. Only A.E. emerged less than ludicrous from the ordeal.

Martyn suffered somewhat at Yeats's hands as well. A lofty paragraph failed to give credit to Martyn's invaluable support of the Irish literary theatre enterprise before Miss Horniman came forward as the Abbey's fairy god-mother. It was he who brought Yeats and Lady Gregory together. He was a wealthy man and he provided the money that was required to run the theatre. In retrospect he seems to have been a sound judge of art. His Impressionist paintings, now in the National Gallery in Merrion Square, show that he had an eye. When Yeats was cold about Ibsen, and Synge presumed his plays dead, Martyn was saying that Ibsen was the greatest writer of plays that had ever lived. He fell out subsequently with Yeats and Lady Gregory over theatre policy and gave his support to another venture in which Pearse and MacDonagh—the 1916 leaders—joined him. But they did not emulate Ibsen. Martyn led, in literary terms, a second eleven when he broke with his Abbey colleagues.

His political career was more eccentric. A Catholic member of the Martyn family that traced its descent back to a companion of Strongbow, Martyn was educated at Beaumont, the Jesuit School in England, and at Oxford. During his minority a great deal of income accumulated, and he expended £20,000 in turning Tulira, the family home, into a Gothic mansion. Martyn's mother came from a Catholic family that had become rich by buying up property in the Encumbered Estate Court after the Famine. She introduced a strain of peasant blood, which did not have the predictable effect. It usually leads to social unease; but Martyn developed, to an extraordinary extent, contempt for the world's opinion. He was always a very strict Catholic, so scrupulous that he even wrote for official permission to read books on the Vatican Index that were in his own large library.

In his early years he was a confirmed Unionist. He urged Sir William Gregory and other local landlords to stand firm against the Plan of Campaign instituted to reduce tenants' rents and, at the same time, to protect them against eviction—the landlord remedy. He was hostile to Gladstone and refused to give any countenance to Home Rulers. He thought the demand was insincere—the people didn't really want it—and he refused to help in any way that would make him feel 'more or less responsible for the inevitable result of boycotting and murder which are certain to ensue upon the restoration of the League to its former vigour'.

At that time he had dreams of literary fame—he was composing an epic poem—and his closest friends were George and Maurice Moore. He hoped, perhaps, to follow George on the high road to Parnassus. He published a book, inspired by Rabelais, called *Morganate*, as later he was to write a play *The Heather Field*, but he was not a writer of genius, and as he lacked diffidence, he was continually at odds with men who were, and from whom he must have thought he got less than his due. To some extent his philanthropy in the theatre can be put down to a desire to push his own fortunes.

How he suddenly became an uncompromising nationalist can only be explained by reference to his self-sufficiency. He began to read Irish history. He became increasingly religious. Quite suddenly he emerged as a politician. He took part in the demonstrations in 1898 with Yeats and Maud Gonne. When exception was taken to the absence of 'God Save the Queen' from the proceedings at a local glee club Martyn retorted by resigning his commissions as a magistrate and Deputy-Lieutenant of his county. Martyn had in fact no responsibility for the omission of the anthem. He was away when the concert took place, and the local rector, an Englishman, had been responsible for the arrangements. But Martyn was in this respect rather like Parnell; having taken a certain course, he obstinately pushed forward on it, and took a perverse pleasure in downfacing his opponents.

There was still a belief among all sections of the people that national leaders should come from the class that led by hereditary custom. An ambitious, self-made follower of Parnell—Frank Hugh O'Donnell—aspired to high place but was bluntly told by an old Fenian, Matt Harris, that the Irish people would never accept as a national leader such as he.

From many sides invitations came to Martyn to stand for Parliament as a Nationalist. He refused; but he began to make political pronouncements. He developed that itch which can only be relieved by writing letters to the newspapers.

Perhaps through his literary interests Martyn met Arthur Griffith. They became close friends. Griffith worked out a philosophy of home rule agitation based on the example of Deak in Austro-Hungary. It involved abstention from parliament and, in a way, anticipated Gandhi's Indian campaign. Martyn contributed support and, when the Sinn Féin movement was founded officially, was elected President. His support was being given at the same time to the Gaelic League, to the founding of a national music festival (Feis Ceoil) and to the Palestrina Choir in the pro-cathedral in Marlborough Street. Martyn was deeply fond of music and a pioneer of Church music reform in England as well as in Ireland.

While so busily engaged, he lived in two rooms over a tobacconist's shop in Nassau Street, in ascetic discomfort, but used the Kildare Street Club, hard by, during the day. Like many celibates, he enjoyed food. His views were uncongenial to the members; but nobody complained until Martyn wrote a letter to *The Freeman's Journal* when a visit of King Edward VII to Dublin was about to take place. Martyn's letter ended, 'By this move England has once more thrown down the gauntlet to Nationalist Ireland. It is for Nationalist Ireland to take it up and to tell the Government with one voice that if they bring the King here under any other guise than a restorer of our stolen constitution they will regret their rashness.'

The ancestors of some of Martyn's fellow members, had they known it, would not have taken exception to the sentiment, even if they disliked the tone, of Martyn's letter; but in 1903, the voices of Grattan's supporters in 1782 sounded like Griffith's friends in Sinn Féin and more aggressive than Redmond's or Dillon's in the Irish parliamentary party—all equally anathema to Kildare Street Club at the time.

Martyn hadn't done. He wrote again: 'The only explanation I can find for all this absurdity is that such is the pitiful spectacle to which a disloyal people are reduced when their inherent passion for grovelling before visible pomp has once been aroused. Some want to grovel for the sake of grovelling itself. Some want to grovel for filthy lucre. The best of them are paralysed and stand aside [a foreshadowing of Yeats's mighty lines]. On the other hand I see the so-called Loyalists of what Mr Goulding, of the manure, calls the English Garrison in Ireland, united and determined to crush Home Rule and the National spirit with their greatest political trump card, the King of England . . . This is the way the situation strikes a person like me, who am in the somewhat odd position among my fellow-countrymen of always meaning what I say.'

Following this letter, Martyn was written to by the secretary of Kildare Street Club stating that in the opinion of the committee his letters to the press were derogatory to his station in society and asking for an explanation. The matter was to be referred to a general meeting of the Club. He wrote back at once to say that he considered his political opinions to be 'in no way derogatory' to his station of society or to that of any other Irishman and he awaited 'with perfect equanimity' the decision of a general meeting on 'a political matter in a club which is strictly non-political in its constitution'.

Here he put a finger on a feature of Irish life which, in retrospect, I can see was in evidence in my own home. My father always professed that he had no politics, disliked politics, and advised his family to keep clear of politics. But he was himself in favour of the status quo, and must have nourished what is now seen as a delusion that by taking no active part and expressing no opinions in public about politics a man is entitled to call himself a-political. What was disliked was controversy. In a way the situation was not unlike that which operates in Communist and other totalitarian states today, where prison sentences are imposed for criticising the regime. Martyn belonged to a club which was non-political on the assumption that all its members were of one mind on political questions. The committee argued with him. Exception had been taken, not to his political opinions, but to his suggestion that 'under certain circumstances disrespect should be manifested to his Majesty the King in the event of his visiting Ireland'.

Martyn replied that the Sovereign was 'unconstitutional in this country' and came 'in the guise of, and with the assumption of the authority of, a constitutional Sovereign', therefore he had a perfect right to show him disrespect.

Martyn's point was not one which was likely to be taken. It was in keeping with Griffith's doctrine. Griffith wanted to restore the pre-Union legislature with a King, Lords and Commons of Ireland. If the club members at the time had realised it, this was the way to anticipate what was in little more than a decade to become the demand for a republic. But political prescience is exceedingly rare; and it must be granted that Martyn was in a false position. Members of a club can have political differences, but if one finds himself so completely at loggerheads with his club mates as

Martyn was, the obvious course is to join another club. At that time he might have found himself in difficulties in any Dublin club that he would have cared to join. His views were more extreme than those of the Irish Parliamentary party.

In the event the Club took counsel's opinion and changed the rules to be in readiness if Martyn transgressed again.

Unperturbed, he invoked the new rules to complain of a communication to the press on club writing paper by Colonel Hutchinson Poë. A conflict was inevitable; it came when Martyn was reported in Griffith's newspaper, *The United Irishman*, subsidised to some extent by Martyn, as having said in public that 'the Irishman who enters the Army or Navy of England deserves to be flogged'. He was written to by the club secretary to know if the report was correct. He replied that 'on the whole' it was.

Events moved in the expected direction after that, and ended with a ballot decision to expel him. The servants were told not to allow him to enter the club, and I have been shown a brass bar which, legend has it, was attached to the door to effect this purpose. Martyn went to court; and employed Tim Healy as one of his barristers. Lord Gough, a very dear friend of Martyn, wrote to remonstrate with him from the British Embassy in Dresden, reminding him that, until recently, he had shared the views of his fellow members, who considered loyalty to the Sovereign as part of their religion. Supposing a member of a Gaelic League Club were to speak in public of the Pope as Martyn had spoken of the King, how distressing that would be for the other members! Martyn filed the letter.

The trial proceeded; it lasted for five days. The Master of the Rolls ended his judgment, 'I decide that, though the defendants, the Committee of the Club, acted in a manner which cannot be assailed by any right-minded person, though their integrity and honesty can never be called in question, yet the rules, or the particular rules under which they purported to act, did not give them the jurisdiction they assumed in this particular case, and the plaintiff must succeed in his action.'

Martyn had won. Back he came to the club, and from that time onward seemed to take a peculiar pleasure in inviting Sinn Féiners, priests, and monks to dine with him. It is said that he used sometimes to kneel down in the reading room and say the Rosary.

He had struck up a friendship with D. P. Moran, who, in his newspaper, *The Leader*, kept up a weekly diatribe against every aspect of Protestant ascendancy, criticising even Yeats, whose poetry he regarded as an unsatisfactory half-way house between English and Gaelic proper. 'Sour-faces' were what Moran called Protestants, and he was equally rude to individuals. A.E. was 'the hairy fairy'. Moran was justified in attacking a great deal that was a mere shoddy import to Irish life, and uncovering jobs; but his own views were narrow. His ideal was a holy Ireland, Catholic and Gaelic. Would it have been as uncharitable as he was? A.E.'s contributions to national debate make more inspiring reading than Moran's now. Rancour never keeps. It has always a bad spot in it that ultimately rots the whole crop. But Martyn's obstinacy and Moran's abusiveness were certain signs that a new spirit was abroad. The ice of ascendancy was cracking.

Martyn was not a comic character; but a man of very definite and obstinate ideas, combining the self-confidence of a man of family with the tenacity of a peasant. Whatever allowed him to remain a member of a club in which he had surrounded himself with enemies bore him up in other contests. He probably nourished secret grievances about his plays and failed to distinguish between his very just admiration for Ibsen and his failure to emulate him. His vanity must have been hurt when his neighbour, Lady Gregory, devoted herself to Yeats after he had brought them together. Then he had to endure the mockery of his childhood friend, George Moore. His best point was his liberality with money. He did subscribe to causes he believed in. This is not a conspicuously Irish trait. The Irish prefer, as a rule, to spend their own money.

It was inevitable that Martyn should meet Oliver St John Gogarty, who played a distinctive role in the Dublin of his time. He, too, was destined to survive as a character in someone else's book; and his feelings were mixed about immortality as Buck Mulligan in *Ulysses*. It is not altogether pleasing to find that one's friend has been watching one critically and has made capital out of one's defects. Gogarty was satisfied to say that Joyce was not a gentleman. The disproportion between their means as young men was a part of the disapproval that Joyce so patiently nourished. Martyn hit back at Moore in writings that nobody takes off the shelves. Gogarty makes a brief appearance in Moore's *Hail and Farewell*, and many years later, as the survivor of that epoch, scattered Moore's ashes on the waters of Lough Carra. His name fascinated Moore, who borrowed it for his priest in *The Lake*. Gogarty's final gesture was, therefore, symbolic.

They were both, as archmockers, in rather the same line of business; but the young ebullient Gogarty with his classical bawdiness, his energy, his versatility, was a court jester to the ageing dons in Trinity and to weightier poets, to Yeats and the more saintly A.E. He provided them all with the sauce without which life can be too solemn. Moore's wit was at their expense; he was shamelessly making copy, and if he, too, liked to shock, his was not the daring of irreverent youth; he was a snuffer out of candles, a serpent in Eden.

We meet Martyn again in Gogarty's *As I Was Walking Down Grafton Street*; but it is not a convincing picture and suggests that Gogarty knew Martyn better in Moore's pages than in life. Gogarty, says Martyn, looking up at the silver heads in the windows of his club, likened it to a cod bank, and goes on to wonder why Yeats took pleasure in belonging to an institution in which the only persons of distinction were Lord Dunraven and Horace Plunkett. He might have added Lord Dunsany, Plunkett's nephew; and one wonders if any one of these had offered to make Gogarty a member whether he would have refused. He would have not, in any case, denied himself the right to mock at what he found there; he had the insatiable need of the acknowledged wit for ammunition. Inevitably he fell back on personalities, the last refuge of the permanent jester. 'A maker of witticisms, a bad character'—Pascal damned the whole race. Supplemented with the aphorism of his countrywoman, 'when you want an enemy, choose a friend: he knows where to strike', it gives you all the warning you needed in Dublin in those days.

I wonder if Gogarty had bad moments when he was alone with himself, as Healy was said to have had. He put no bridle on his tongue, like the Gaelic *fili* of old he was prepared to mock a man to death. If words could kill, de Valera would have been dead, slain by Gogarty. He expressed pleasure when he heard that Childers had been shot. What I can remember of Gogarty persuades me that he would have killed only with his tongue. He would fire that, but not the anonymous bullet that would dispatch the victim in silence. Wilde walked in some of Gogarty's paths a quarter of a century before him. He, too, set about making his fortune with his wits. He, too, was a lover of the classics. He, too, came under the influence of Mahaffy at Trinity College and pushed on to Oxford in search of his rainbow and the pot of gold that is hidden at the foot of it. Admittedly Wilde did it all better. His Greek was better; his jokes were better; his writing was better. At Oxford he won the Newdigate prize, Gogarty failed it. Not that that matters, but it serves as a measuring rod for this occasion. Wilde had whatever genius is; Gogarty only walked in its shadow. Yeats did not subscribe to this. He acknowledged that in conversation one had to put up with a great deal of clay before Gogarty produced a nugget worth cherishing; but it was found if one waited. And when he compiled his *Oxford Book of Modern Verse* he gave Gogarty lavish space, to the chagrin of other Dublin poets.

'Twelve years ago Oliver Gogarty was captured by his enemies, imprisoned in a deserted house on the edge of the Liffey with every prospect of death. Pleading a natural necessity he got into the garden, plunged under a shower of revolver bullets and as he swam the ice-cold December stream promised it, should it land him in safety, two swans. I was present when he fulfilled that vow. His poetry fits the incident, a gay, stoical—no, I will not withhold the word—heroic song. Irish by tradition and many ancestors, I love, though I have nothing to offer but the philosophy they deride, swashbucklers, horsemen, swift indifferent men; yet I do not think that is the sole reason, good reason though it is, why I gave him considerable space, and think him one of the great lyric poets of our age.'

And A.E. who was the one indisputably *good* man of that generation of talented people—admittedly in a preface to Gogarty's poems—said: 'I take so much pleasure in my friend's poetry because it is the opposite to my own. It gives to me some gay and gallant life which was not in my own birthright. He is never the professional poet made dull by the dignity of recognised genius. He has never made a business of beauty; and because he is disinterested in his dealings with it, the Muse has gone with him on his walks and revealed to him some airs and graces she kept secret from other lovers who were too shy or too awed by her to laugh and be natural in her presence.'

Yeats, as we know, justified his aristocratic preferences by claiming to belong to a master race. But what of Gogarty? He entered the Anglo-Irish world, like Tom Moore, a century before him, when he came through the front gate of Trinity College. He had been to Stonyhurst, the Jesuit school in England, something he had in common with George Moore, also a Jesuit pupil. But his talents were his only claim to distinction, and this led to a curious ambivalence in his attitudes. He admired Arthur Griffith and wrote of him with deep respect. So far, therefore, he was a nationalist. But yet he seemed to despise his own people, as in the poem.

> Dervorgilla's supremely lovely daughter,
> Recalling him, of all the Leinstermen Ri,
> Him whose love and hate brought o'er the water
>   Strongbow and Henry;
> Brought rigid law, the long spear and the horsemen
> Riding in steel; and the rhymed, romantic high line;
> Built those square keeps on the forts of the Norsemen,
>   Still on our sky-line . . .
> Brought the implacable hand with law-breakers,
> Drilled the Too-many and broken their effrontery;
> Broken the dream of the men of a few acres
>   Ruling a country . . .

The full significance of the poem can only be understood if it is remembered that Devorgilla was the wife of Diarmuid, King of Leinster, who invited Strongbow to Ireland, and promised him the hand of his daughter.

As I copy out the verses I recall a sunny morning in 1938 and meeting Gogarty in Ely Place, outside his house. He invited me in; and I can see him in his study, writing in the fly-leaf of the book, then turning to correct a misprint. He radiated good spirits

—it must have been the morning the author's copies had arrived from the publisher and he wanted to share his pleasure. It was very kind of him to give a mere youth—whose identity he was not always sure of—"Hello, Pearson", he used to say sometimes—a precious book when he had a legion of better acquaintances. Even if he sometimes thought my name was Pearson, he was always friendly and without pomp or conceit. And yet he could be so scathing; it was as if nature had equipped him with a weapon for defence without fitting it with a safety catch.

When I think of that sunny morning in Gogarty's study looking into the garden, I am reminded of Moore in the same garden:

'A light breeze rustled the lilacs, and I stood for a long time, forgetful of my idea, seeking within the long, pointed leaves for the blossom breaking into purple and white. It seemed to me that the tranquil little path under the bushes was just the one Pater would choose for philosophic meditation, but, feeling that the sunlight beguiled my mind into thought, I wandered round the garden, thinking, while noticing the changes that had come into it within the last few days. "The great ash by the garden gate seems to be making some progress. The catkins are gone, and in about three weeks the plumy foliage will be fluttering in the light breeze of the summer-time. The laburnum blossom is still enclosed in grey-green ears about the size of a caterpillar," I added, "with here and there a spot of yellow." And pondering on Nature's unending miracles, I walked under the hawthorns, stopping, of course, to admire the hard little leaves "like the medals that Catholics wear," I said, on my way to the corner where the Solomon-seal flourishes year after year, and the blooms of the everlasting pea creep up the wall nine or ten feet, to the level of the street, hard by the rosemary, which should perfume the whole garden, but the smoke from Plunkett's chimney robs the flowers of their perfume. The little blossom freckling the dark green spiky foliage held me at gaze. Above the rosemary is thick ivy; it was clipped close a few years ago, but it is again swarming up the wall, and Gogarty, the arch-mocker, the author of all the jokes that enable us to live in Dublin—Gogarty, the author of the Limericks of the Golden Age, the youngest of my friends, full in the face, with a smile in his eyes and always a witticism on his lips, overflowing with quotation, called yesterday to ask me to send a man with a shears, saying, "Your ivy is threatening my slates." A survival of the Bardic Age he is, reciting whole ballads to me when we go for walks; and when I tell him my great discovery he will say, "Sparrows and sweet peas are incompatible as Literature and Dogma; and you will cut the ivy, won't you?"'

One day I met him in Fitzwilliam Square. He asked me where I was going, and when I told him, said, 'The Jellets. Oh, Jellets and Pursers! I know them. Invest in Guinness, and then get conscientious scruples when the shares are at the top of the market; sell out and invest in tobacco, which happens to be low.'

The Jellets, whom I was going to visit, were most unjustly treated in this sweeping condemnation of two worthy families. I wonder if Gogarty had crossed swords with Sarah Purser, who had said of Moore, 'Some men kiss and tell; George Moore tells but does not kiss.'

Sarah Purser kept a salon in Dublin in those days. She had been poor as a girl—the father deserted the family. But the Pursers and poverty were certainly incompatible; and when I came to know her she had the reputation of being enormously rich. This was given point by her ostentatious economies. Her entertainment was strictly limited to tea and scones, and she is reputed to have said after one of her Thursdays—'a record this month, four hundred people for four and six.' She had a formidable wit and had been a good painter in her day. I do not remember Yeats or Gogarty at those gatherings. Jack Yeats used to attend, and Miss Purser's biographer said that these two were devoted friends; but when she died he expressed dislike of her to me.

How all these people managed to get along together in a small city remains a mystery. Their friendships were dotted with minefields. A.E. emerges as the one who consistently helped others, loved and was loved in return. But one of his protégés, Frank O'Connor, told the world that he was, in the end, rather a bore; and Sean O'Casey had the same to say. Perhaps the Irish are too articulate, must say everything. No man is a hero to his own valet; and the roles of hero and valet are not always kept distinct and separate. Gogarty played both.

He came into his own after the Treaty, with the setting up of the *Irish Free State*. His friend Arthur Griffith led the delegation to London that signed the treaty. His friend Yeats was in the first Senate. He was much in evidence on State occasions and he, also, was in the Senate.

His witticisms—sometimes scurrilous—at the expense of de Valera (whom he hated) and de Valera's followers, had this justification: they opposed the Treaty. In doing so they led Ireland into Civil War. Michael Collins was shot; Griffith died—the strain cannot have been a help to his heart. Gogarty revered Griffith and respected Collins; and he had unconcealed contempt for a group of men who were undistinguished by birth and education and signally devoid of verbal brilliance and any feeling for the arts. His condemnation was too sweeping. De Valera had a gift for leadership, and impressed the world; and this gave Gogarty's incessant sneers a boomerang effect.

CHAPTER XIX

The Optimists

BUT WE HAVE now left the Anglo-Irish behind. Gogarty is a distraction. Seeming to typify one aspect of them, he had, in fact, nothing to do with them. He acknowledged as much when he echoed Martyn that the only people of distinction, as well as Yeats, in Kildare Street Club, were Dunraven and Horace Plunkett. Both of these men had taken a very prominent part in public life, and in so doing had been criticised by the hard core of Unionism which found its apogee in Ulster's 'Not an Inch'.

The Dunravens were an unusual family for Irish peers. Windham Thomas Wyndham-Quin, the fourth Earl in a line that had advanced in the peerage at and after the Union, as a child, when asked to make a speech, and lifted on to cottage tables for the occasion, confined his remarks to the simple assertion, 'I am an Irishman bred and born'. Quin is an old Irish name, even if the Dunravens take their title from the place of that name in Glamorganshire. The fourth Earl was brought up at Adare in County Limerick. This village, Enniskerry, Westport, and the town of Birr, spring to mind as advertisements for the noblemen who created them. There are others; but they are exceptions; they show what could have been done in Ireland if all landlords had lived up to Drummond's precept and done their duty.

Dunraven's father had some reputation as an archaeologist; and he supported that group in the Royal Irish Academy which did so much that has never been recognised adequately in Ireland, their work having been overshadowed by the more popular and less arduous campaigning of the Gaelic League.

His father became a Catholic, caught up in the enthusiasm of the Tractarian movement at the same time as Aubrey de Vere—a neighbour—and Dunraven's brother-in-law, William Monsell. Before that he had been, with Monsell, one of the founders of the

College of St Columba at Rathfarnham, now a public school, but endowed in 1841, like Trinity College, as a proselytising enterprise. At that date it was calculated that in Ireland 3,740,217 of the population spoke English, 3,061,610 Irish. And there was a movement to bring the bible in Irish among the people and get them away from their priests. Lord Farnham in Cavan was one who depended on soup kitchens to achieve this end. Neither expedient was successful; but the language was to fall away. And it is hard now to believe that so comparatively recently it held an equal place with English. Many of those Irish speakers were to emigrate to America in the next thirty years.

Dunraven's uncle was Sir Michael Gore-Booth, father of the lovely daughters, whom Yeats was to immortalise. The Gore-Booths were English, descended from a celebrated explorer, but one of them—Constance Markievicz—was a leader in 1916, a member of the Irish Citizen Army. What is one to call such a family? I heard one of the present generation of Gore-Booths, when being racked by a television interviewer, say that she was regarded as English in Ireland and Irish in England, and did not know what she was. Several generations of residence in Ireland, devotion to the people on the estate, an exemplary record during the Famine years—did this make them Irish? Anglo-Irish is the label that sticks. But only because the class to which the Dunravens and Gore-Booths belong no longer exercise any power. It means that they have the accents and bearing of a former ruling class, and because there was a Union with England and that Union was dissolved they are left on the beach, castaways. If a Dunraven were now to say 'I am an Irishman bred and born', he might be indulged, but he would not be believed. But it is only a matter of class in a restricted setting. Why should latter-day revolutionaries —Mr de Valera or Cathal Brugha or Patrick Pearse—be better entitled to say that, when their fathers drew the first air into their infant lungs in Cuba and in England?

A collapse of family fortune and a decline socially would be the necessary purgation. In the case of the Gore-Booths it can be said that no effort has been spared by the current establishment to hasten their apotheosis. Petty's voice can be heard down the centuries. 'English in Ireland, growing poor and discontented, degenerate into Irish; and vice versa; Irish, growing into wealth and favour, reconcile to the English.' It was only another way of saying that flowers turn to the sun.

Because of his peculiar heredity the fourth Earl of Dunraven was not restricted in his ideas by the prejudices of his order. After the Boer War, he said that he wanted to devote what remained of his life to his country; and he was one of the chief negotiators in the conferences of the next few years between representatives of the landlords, the Irish Party and Government, represented by George Wyndham, the Chief Secretary and an Irishman, Sir Anthony McDonnell.

The result of the meetings was the Land Act of 1903, which enabled tenants to buy their holdings from the landlords by instalments. The Government put up the necessary capital. The business had the blessing of the Church and, less enthusiastically, of the Irish party. But it was bitterly opposed by John Dillon and Michael Davitt—by Dillon because he nourished an unquenchable hatred of the landlord class, and thought they were being too well done by and were inflating the price of land, by Davitt because he believed in the nationalisation of the soil.

Emboldened by this success, Dunraven put his finger into the Home Rule pie with a scheme for Devolution. It was furthered by McDonnell, the under-secretary, an enthusiast for reform. As I related previously, Wyndham did not read his letters right through and, unwittingly, committed the government to the scheme by sheer inattention. When the mistake was discovered Wyndham had to resign. McDonnell was sacked. That was the end of the attempt by the Conservative Government, under Balfour, to solve the problem of Home Rule. After that, it became, once again, the Liberal party's headache.

While Dunraven and his friends, in the teeth of the Landowner's Convention, were pushing forward their reforms, Horace Plunkett was devoting his times and money to agricultural reforms. He established the co-operative movement in Ireland. The Irish Agricultural Organisation Society (a clumsy title) is still in operation. Plunkett, as we saw, enlisted A.E. in its services, to the detriment of his poetry and his painting. But he had more ambitious plans. He persuaded Gerald Balfour, Wyndham's predecessor, to get his brother, Arthur, to set up a Ministry of Agriculture, with a substantial income. Plunkett was put in charge of this with, as an assistant, an Irish Londoner, T. P. Gill. When Plunkett lost his seat in parliament, he had, reluctantly, to resign his office. He refused to commit himself to the Nationalists and remained an improving Conservative; as a result he fell between two stools politically. Moore seized on Plunkett as a character for his book. As Bouvard and Pécuchet, he made merry at the expense of Plunkett and Gill, making wonderful copy of the disasters that attended their effort to import asses to Ireland from Spain. Plunkett never showed any ill-will in return, and shamed Moore by his magnanimity.

Plunkett built himself a house at Kilteragh in Foxrock on the south side of Dublin. It became an intellectual centre where Bernard Shaw and every Irishman of distinction might be found at one time or another. Plunkett had an immense and thoroughly un-Irish genius as a catalyst. After a lifetime of effort, his reward at the hands of his countrymen was to see his house and its contents burned to the ground. His offence: he agreed to serve as a Senator in the Government of the Irish Free State. In his memoir of A.E. John Eglinton referred to Plunkett as 'certainly the most attractive figure of his time, in Irish public life, the only one whom it was "good to think of".'

The lighter side of this life is told in the artless memories of Daisy, Countess of Fingall, who acted as Plunkett's hostess at Kilteragh. Lady Fingall, as Daisy Burke, was to serve Moore as a model. Her husband spoke little but is credited with an original definition of a gentleman, one who tells the truth and takes a bath every day.

Lady Fingall, at shooting parties with King Edward VII, out driving with Douglas Haig, presiding over Plunkett's table, accompanying Lady Lavery to the lying-in-state of Michael Collins, floated gaily over many an abyss into which more committed folk foundered. In her latter days she kept a smaller salon than Sarah Purser's, at which the young met survivors of what seemed more splendid days.

As a Burke from Galway, Lady Fingall, a Catholic, could hardly be described in strictness as *Anglo*-Irish, any more than the

Fingalls—Plunketts, like their cousins the Dunsanys, lawyers for the first Norman conquerors, with a genius for survival, which has never deserted them. Lord Dunsany was a more eccentric being than his uncle, Horace Plunkett. His talents as a writer were considerable, overrated once, now unduly neglected. He was encouraging to young writers. His last protégée, Mary Lavin, is one of the writers who filled the vacuum left when the Anglo-Irish disappeared from Irish literature.

Of all these people Lady Fingall was, intellectually, much the slightest. Had she not been pretty and gay and a Countess she would not have come into the story at all. But these attributes recommended her to some women and all men, and gave her access where a sterner sister might have been denied. When government employ women as spies they choose attractive, not intellectual ones. Lady Fingall's gaiety, courage and appetite for life were considerable. She was like a child, and a spoilt child; but one determined to make the best of whatever was available without being deceived for a moment.

Their photographs tell us that Arthur and Gerald Balfour and George Wyndham were favoured by nature to a greater extent than the Ministers of State whom she sometimes met in the new Ireland. She did not dwell on this; but I sometimes saw her glancing at a photograph of Gerald Balfour on her desk when she was talking to some new arrival, his equivalent in office, and I could not help surmising that she was noting a contrast. Once or twice she said so; and I remember on one occasion she complained that the only subject of conversation the new Ministers had was their prison experiences, and she was weary of them. Her butterfly disposition was very different from Sarah Purser's more massive qualities. Miss Purser was resolutely plain, and she spoke with a deep brogue, a sort of voice which has quite disappeared—a Protestant Dublin accent, of which the best model was Shaw's. This way of speaking was a survival. None of these people went to school in England, any more than Burke, Swift or Grattan did. At one time because it meant a sea voyage of uncertain duration; as a result the Arnold tradition was well established before it touched Ireland. When I was young most of my contemporaries, Protestant and Catholic, went to English schools, following, in most cases, in their fathers' footsteps; but not, as a rule, in their grandfathers'.

Lord Dunraven's experiences were unique. His father wanted him to become a Catholic, his mother was determined that he should remain a Protestant. He refused to go to Oscott, a Roman Catholic School, and was educated by tutors until he went to Oxford. For members of the Dublin professional class, a day school or one of the Irish boarding schools was deemed sufficient, hence the glamour of English officers for their sisters in the Dublin season.

Miss Purser and Lady Fingall (who had no accent) were alike in their passion to have people around them. The motive was creative. Jane Austen wrote of 'the company of clever, well-informed people who have plenty of conversation'. These ladies were for ever trying to collect such people for their mutual pleasure. And the effort necessitated a certain watchfulness for new recruits. Lady Fingall had to be more careful because her room was small. Both women took a genuine interest in their friends; they tried to help them, encouraged them, introduced them to people who could be useful. It has always been the fashion to rail against the superficiality and essential hardness of 'society'; but these hostesses were genuinely concerned for the welfare of those whom they approved of, or thought promising. Of the two, Miss Purser was probably more impressed by solid worth. But Lady Fingall had an instinct for quality which women sometimes have, the instinct that some people have for picking out valuable objects in a junk store without any technical training.

Nowadays the idea of salons is probably repulsive; a waste of time; but they had a value which is possibly being eroded from life. I greatly admire the novels of Solzhenitsyn and the man who shines out of them; but it came as a shock to find him writing a story about a school building as if it were identified by a personality. It gave me a depressing look into a future where, instead of Hamlet, Emma Bovary or Anna Karenina, we shall be asked to contemplate a psychiatric ward, a gymnasium, a community school; and be satisfied to learn at the end that they lived happy ever after. Miss Purser was interested in things of the mind; Lady Fingall was out for entertainment; but both were interested in people as individuals, and when that is replaced by an exclusive sympathy for social organisations the world will be a drabber place.

Neither Miss Purser nor Lady Fingall had anything approaching the significance of Lady Gregory; are not to be mentioned in the same breath. Through her literary curiosity she developed a concern for the dignity of the peasantry. But hers was a harsh family history, and she had little of the active philanthropy that marked Maria Edgeworth and her father. Their family origins were much the same. Lady Gregory was probably sterner about 'the rights' of landlords because she was brought up in a rougher county—Galway in the west—than the sleepy midlands where the Edgeworths had settled. The Persses were a family of Cromwellian origins, not at all the type of improving landlord, on the English model, that the Edgeworths were. Augusta Persse was a twelfth child in a family which had all the unpleasing characteristics of Protestant ascendancy. They were harsh with tenants and their piety took the form of proselytising. But a good fairy put into this rude blood two charms: a Huguenot ancestor and an O'Grady mother. From the O'Gradys Lady Gregory got her literary gift. She married a distinguished man, when she was twenty-eight and he sixty-three. And they had that one son—Robert Gregory—whose death as an airman Yeats was to immortalise.

She always had literary talent, but only as a widow did she find the form in which to exercise it; and deliberately obscured her own fame by contracting cerebral liaisons with men—first Hyde, then Yeats. In one respect she was Hyde's feminine counterpart; they both found their inspiration in the untapped sources of Gaelic speech, legend, and literature. One of Lady Gregory's better short plays, *The Workhouse Ward*, is her own later version of a play that she helped Hyde to write.

With Yeats, Moore and Martyn she brought to birth the first Irish literary theatre; but of the four she was the only one endowed by nature with a true dramatic gift. Moore and Martyn were to be disappointed in their ambition and Martyn embittered by his failure. Yeats, with an overpowering will and a noble purpose, driven on by his daemon, but always a coldly calculating man, tried Moore first, and then turned to Lady Gregory to supply him with the help he needed to give his poetic gifts a dramatic form. His genius is incontestable, and Lady Gregory recognised it, devoting herself to its development and not obtruding her own smaller gift. A man would have jealously guarded his own identity and removed himself from Yeats's shadow; he would not have subordinated his own achievement in order to supply what the other lacked.

A woman—Elizabeth Coxhead—has been the first to do justice to Lady Gregory and in the process to expose Yeats's limitations. Lady Hanson, Moore's 'pretty, witty, Deena Tyrrell', cousin of George Tyrrell, the last survivor from that era, said to me, 'Lady Gregory used to write the plays that kept the Abbey going when Yeats's plays were performed to almost empty houses. He was always there himself with a handful of devotees.'

Miss Coxhead got herself into hot water with critics for proving that Yeats's only popular play *Cathleen ni Houlihan* was largely written by Lady Gregory. Gogarty was one of the worst offenders in spreading the rumour that the boot was on the other leg, that Yeats wrote Lady Gregory's plays. Synge was sufficiently magnanimous to acknowledge that she preceded him in the use of what is called 'Kiltartan' speech, the English of people whose first language is Irish. Lady Gregory was, in fact, the first to use it. Synge had more genius than she; I am sure she acknowledged it; but if Synge had written some of her plays they would receive a critical approval which is not accorded to them. And I agree with Miss Coxhead that she has been the victim of her own heroic self-sacrifice.

Like most great women she was rather formidable. Because she was keeping the estate at Coole Park for her son during the years of his minority and because her husband had been a great gambler on horses in his day—she developed strict habits of economy. She pinched in small things and was generous in great. For instance, she looked for no financial reward for the plays she wrote with such profusion to keep the doors of the Abbey open. There is in her diaries an account of a tea party at the Standard Hotel, given to bring some people she was interested in together. She deemed it a success; but, somehow, the picture conjured up of that respectable, moderately-priced (then), temperance hotel and the inevitable afternoon tea, strikes a chord of chilling sobriety. She had no time at all for nonsense; and the gifts of barmbrack (bread-cake with currants) to the Abbey cast were sometimes sneered at. It was so very *Protestant*. Irish Catholics, on the whole, are more given to lavishness, sometimes a foolish lavishness, and it is not always accompanied by a strict discharge of monetary obligations. There is often behind it a desire to cut a good figure. It is partly the result of years of social suppression, but it also springs from a cheerful indifference to prosaic considerations, a belief that—in the last resort—God will provide.

The Protestant God practises the rule of double entry. His accounts are strictly kept. And there are other reasons: an awareness of priorities in which the substance precedes the shadow. School bills—for good schools—must be paid, buildings and capital investment kept in repair. All this is true: but Protestants, when they die, are usually richer than they appeared to be; Catholics, not so well off.

If Lady Gregory had thrown lavish parties and looked only after her own interests and told Yeats to write his own plays—she would have been more highly regarded by her countrymen when she was alive, and she could not have been more neglected by posterity. She had no Irish gush. She was stern. But she always extended a helping hand to merit. Sean O'Casey owed his initial success to her help; when he discarded her influence his plays became a tedious mockery of those first three upon which his claim to lasting fame depends.

Her sense of chivalry, her nobility, was of a higher order than that of the men she helped. Yeats in a recently published diary revealed that she thought he failed her when he talked himself out of reprimanding Gosse for a slight to her family. Yeats had to consider many things, including the fact that Gosse was instrumental in getting him a pension on the Civil List. Lady Gregory did not understand; and when, later, Moore attacked Yeats and herself, she employed a solicitor to defend her wounded pride, leaving Yeats to take what course he pleased. Moore and Gogarty did not relish the sort of woman she was; she made it quite plain that they were less important than Yeats, for one thing. Her standards were high. 'Her eyes', Moore wrote in *Ave*, 'were always full of questions, and her Protestant high-school air became her greatly and estranged me from her.' And elsewhere he remarked that her husband was 'more at his ease, more natural'.

She must have recognised at once the flaw in Gogarty, refused him by instinct a place in the Pantheon. As a rule men and women see through their own sex and are taken in by the other. But Lady Gregory's eyes that were 'always full of questions', would have asked Gogarty some that he might have preferred to leave unanswered. She offended Moore by not inviting him to sign a fan on which she collected autographs; she was probably keeping him in his place; but eventually she did invite him. Edwin Arnold, Henry James, Theodore Roosevelt, Lecky, Froude, Morley, Orpen, Bourget, Twain, Mancini, Plunkett, Hardy, Ellen Terry, John, Kipling, Nansen, Shaw, Jack Yeats, Martyn, Synge, John Eglinton, Sean O'Casey and George Moore. A constellation!

Gogarty was not admitted to that company, and he took his revenge; but there were probably other slights and snubs to pay off. The prude in her was possibly disapproving of Gogarty's reputation as a creator of bawdiness; and she may have resented the attention Yeats paid to him. If she had lived long enough to read Gogarty's reminiscences, her sure instinct for the first-rate would have told her that they were Moore again, with less malice and less art. Gogarty did not attempt any revenge against Joyce, whose sessions in bars he found 'far pleasanter and simpler than the ritual of Yeats or A.E.'. Joyce was then beyond his range: and he may have been grateful, after all, for the Mulligan picture in *Ulysses*. Worst fate of all to be left out of the story!

Miss Coxhead is right in laying principally at Gogarty's door the injustice to Lady Gregory, not only does he say that Yeats wrote her plays, he adds that they were infernally dull. It was said of Johnson that when his pistol misfired he knocked you down with the butt of it; Gogarty aimed the barrel at Lady Gregory and hit Yeats with the butt.

Lady Gregory's insistence on the first-rate was only equalled by her loyalty to family; both combined to make her a tireless fighter in the cause of her nephew, Hugh Lane. When the National

Gallery of England—with strict legal correctness—refused to give back the pictures that he had offered to Dublin, then taken away, then left back in an unexecuted codicil to his will, Lady Gregory enlisted Yeats, and anyone else she could, to plead the Irish claim. They took a high and mighty line in London—always a mistake when you have no case in law—and did more harm than good. A compromise was arrived at after many years, when Yeats and Lady Gregory were dead.

Lane could have stayed in London, where he was able to make a fortune, but he preferred to come back to Dublin and work for a pittance in the National Gallery in Merrion Square. He gave to it lavishly in his short lifetime; and I look around among those who speak of the Anglo-Irish as aliens for deeds of equal note. But this type of activity has been replaced by laying on Government the duty of answering every national need. Shaw's will gave the Gallery funds of which it has always been starved by Government.

The National Library and the Museum, both the creation of a group of Anglo-Irishmen, are in such disarray in Government keeping that they provide a perennial theme for newspaper articles when less chronic topics fail. The last great gesture to Ireland was made by Sir Chester Beatty, a naturalised citizen of American origins, who left his priceless oriental collection to the Nation. But the tycoons, who benefit by the system of protective duties which Mr de Valera introduced in 1932, have not so far given anything away. Some of them have invested in companies to pull Dublin down and replace it by concrete office blocks, in which the only consideration is maximum return on the money invested. The contemporary Irish patriot likes to regard the artistic achievements of the Anglo-Irish as marks of servitude and memorials of social injustice. He plans to replace them with a brand new city, looking like Chicago.

CHAPTER XX

The Approach of Home Rule

THE SMALL SIZE of Ireland is a factor which has to be taken into account in every speculation about her—it becomes apparent at once when names are juggled with. Looking for someone less distinguished to carry on my survey I bethought me of Canon Hannay (George A. Birmingham), a clergyman who won considerable popularity with *Spanish Gold*, a funny book about the West of Ireland, raised above the commonplace by shrewd observations and knowledge of the people. Hannay also wrote a successful play in which Charles Hawtrey, the most polished comedian on the London stage at the time, appeared. *General John Regan*, as that play was called, was Hannay's version of a story which was also given to Lady Gregory. She made of it her best long play *The Image*. When I leave the Abbey circle to look at the Ireland outside it, a coincidence like this draws me back. And I am drawn back further in my narrative when I read that Hannay married a Miss Wynne and that she was a distant cousin of Lady Ferguson, 'a most hospitable old lady' who 'established during her widowhood a sort of salon in Dublin. One of her great delights was to collect in her house as many Guinness cousins as she could.'

Mrs Hannay helped Lady Ferguson with her writing of her husband's career, and had been injected mildly with enthusiasm for the Young Irelanders of whom her cousin used to speak. It was possibly his wife's influence that encouraged Hannay to take an interest in the Gaelic League—he was rector in Westport when he met Douglas Hyde. It followed a disastrous evening when Mrs Hannay read a paper to a literary society on the Young Irelanders. The result was a break between the Hannays and their Church of Ireland congregation. One of his parishioners asked him if he were still a member of the Gaelic League, and when he admitted as much, slammed the door in his face.

The Hannays followed Hyde's precept, their interest in Gaelic was literary and strictly non-political. When war broke out in 1914, Hannay, no longer a young man, volunteered at once for chaplain duty with the army at the front. But to his parishioners there was no distinction between Gaelic culture and anti-British leanings. They shared, in a less articulate way, Mahaffy's instinct that one led to the other. In the event they were right. Their political instinct was sound. The Gaelic revival was giving Ireland an idealism to set off against Empire, flag, the Royal family and the symbols of Unionism. Before it began, there had been only apathy, punctuated by seasonal violence stimulated by agrarian grievances.

A country parson in the west of Ireland, at odds with his flock, was in an awkward position; nor had he the comfort of support from those who might have been expected to see him as a martyr. His novels excited disapproval; they seemed frivolous or worse. A local priest insisted that he had been libelled, and the fact that he had arrived in the parish after the book was published left him unconvinced.

The sad story had the happiest of endings. *General John Regan* brought in so much in royalties, Hannay was able to escape from Westport. His parochial life ended in the milder atmosphere of Mells.

Hannay was born in Belfast and educated at Haileybury and Trinity College. I recognise the world he describes, and it must have resembled that in which my father grew up. Hannay was third generation Scottish on his father's side, and Anglo-Irish on his mother's. His mother's grandfather, Rector of Moira, was of the opinion that the Number of the Beast in the book of Revelation, representing Anti-Christ, worked out, if the figures were properly understood, to the name of William Ewart Gladstone. In any family with such a clerical heritage, Gladstone as the man directly and solely responsible for disestablishing the Church of Ireland was anathema.

My own parson forebears probably shared this opinion—Lord Salisbury was the favourite Prime Minister in Church circles—but I cannot remember hearing any strictures against Gladstone in my youth. But I have to admit that my father was not a religious enthusiast. He took a rather cynical view of the sincerity of the vocations for the Church that drew some of his relations and acquaintances into its service. Not long before he died my uncle, a rural Dean, having read in the morning newspaper that a Catholic, F. H. Boland, had been appointed Chancellor of Dublin University, remarked that he had been looking forward to some such outcome ever since the Government had given a large subsidy to the Trinity Library. 'I knew then that they had sold out to your *party*,' he said. I remember another member of the older generation telling me that he always wrote 'Church of Ireland' when asked to give his religion for census purposes. He believed in nothing but wanted to make it quite clear that he was not a Roman Catholic. I therefore recognise Hannay's account of his own family's attitude in these matters.

'It must always be remembered that in the north of Ireland, indeed throughout the whole of Ireland, the word Protestant in those days meant strictly churchman. The prevalent religions were divided into Papists, Protestants and Presbyterians; the Presbyterians not being regarded as Protestants in our numeration of faiths. The Church of Ireland was the Protestant Church and alone had the right to use the word Protestant. On the one side of it were Papists and on the other side Presbyterians and Methodists. In the middle were what in England would be called Anglicans which we called, and still do call, simply Protestants, meaning by the word, members of the Anglican Communion. But our Protestantism was different in quality from anything of the kind which exists in England. We pronounced the word as if its third consonant was a D, thereby giving it an explosiveness and an obstinacy which no religion in England has possessed since the days of Cromwell's Ironsides.'

Hannay was too pleasant and versatile to become rooted in stone age prejudices. His talents helped him to escape from Irish protestantism as he experienced it in Westport. His wife, to whom he was deeply devoted, was another influence. Lady Fingall, who met them with Horace Plunkett, thought that she was the cleverer of the two, and the humour left his work when she died.

Canon Hannay never came back to Ireland after the First World War. The Ulster troubles on its eve, the 1916 rebellion in the middle of it, 'the troubles' at its close, concluded by the Treaty but reopened in Civil War, created a chasm into which Protestant ascendancy fell never, in spite of Yeats's prophecy, to rise again.

We get a glimpse of it in its last phase in the recollections of Maurice Headlam, who was on the Viceregal staff from 1912 to 1920. When he came to Ireland Lord Aberdeen was Viceroy. His predecessors, Lords Dudley and Cadogan, had cut a tremendous dash in Dublin, spending lavishly. A chef from the Viceregal Lodge stayed on to open the best restaurant Dublin ever had—Jammet's. It was a very appropriate memorial. The Aberdeens were an appointment of the Liberal government. Their Chief Secretary was Birrell, a literary man, who saw himself as marking time until the inevitable coming of Home Rule. His undersecretary, Sir Robert Nathan, was instructed to keep in close touch with the Nationalist leaders, Redmond and Dillon. By this device Birrell believed he could keep by proxy his fingers on the Irish pulse. He disliked politics, particularly the Irish variety, and preferred, when in Ireland, to go to the Abbey Theatre or visit the West of Ireland. Unknown to all these distinguished people a revolution was in preparation. It blew up under their noses.

The Aberdeens cultivated Nationalists; an innovation at the Viceregal Lodge, it was not quite unprecedented. There was for people with very long memories the Drummond time, when O'Connell dined at the Viceregal Lodge with Lord Mulgrave and *The Times* and *Dublin Express* raged at how the lowly had risen. More recently an ordeal had been endured by Lord Houghton, son of Monckton Milnes. He had been sent by Gladstone during his last administration and final effort to carry Home Rule. A conviction that the House of Lords would defeat the measure kept national expectations at a modest level and there was no enthusiasm for Lord Houghton among the populace. Moreover his demeanour suggested more sympathy with the hereditary house than the government he represented, and Unionists boycotted the Viceregal entertainments to register their disapproval of Gladstone.

Lord Cadogan and Lord Dudley—who were the nominees of the Salisbury and Balfour administrations—put on a great show and restored the castle to social favour. Their gay spending and fashionable display was also popular with the unpolitically-minded masses. Lord Aberdeen told Maurice Headlam that he never spent less than £6,000 a year in addition to his official salary of £20,000. When Headlam told this to one of Aberdeen's critics in Dublin, her reply was that he ought to spend another £20,000, as his predecessors had.

When Aberdeen came back in 1906 for his second period of office he carried an olive branch once again; it might give a truer picture to say, several olive branches, which he and his progressive wife distributed wholesale. They were in a position to do so, a Liberal Government had returned, Home Rule was on its way again. To Lady Aberdeen, Dublin tram travellers owed the injunction not to spit 'in or on the car'.

The olive branches were received, on the whole, with a poor grace. Stauncher Unionists kept away from the Aberdeens' parties and contrasted the splendour of the entertainments given by the Dudleys and the Cadogans with what they sneered at as 'tea-and-bun fights'. The harshest criticism of the Aberdeens may be read, not in Unionist publications, but in the files of *Gaelic American*, edited by John Devoy, a newspaper that carried scurrility towards opponents to unsqueamish lengths.

In the light of what happened it may be worth asking what difference, if any, it would have made if the Aberdeens' well-intentioned efforts had met with a sympathetic response from Irish Unionists. The Wyndham Act of 1903 which enabled the landlords to sell their estates, following the Local Government Act of 1898, was the prepared exit for the former Ascendancy from Irish life. If some chose to remain, it was as citizens with no privileges save such as came from local and family associations and social prestige. Very different was the lot of the Protestant Unionists in the cities, in Dublin especially, who had family businesses or professional practices. There was no Wyndham Act for them.

'The Court Balls', Headlam admits, 'were perhaps not "smart", as the big Irish peers, all Unionists, did not attend the court of the Home Rule Aberdeens. There were only, therefore, a few of the Irish peerage and their daughters, the rest of the company being judges, officials, doctors, etc., and soldiers who were commanded to go. But there were plenty of people to dance with. I liked dancing to a good band, and did not know or care whether they were "the right people".'

Headlam discovered Jammet's and went there when he was too late for dinner at Kildare Street Club where the oysters were much cheaper and Pommery 1900 eight shillings a bottle as compared with twelve-and-six in Pall Mall.

He found the members much friendlier than in his London club, The Travellers, where nobody spoke to strangers. 'It was a most tolerant club, and many Roman Catholics belonged; though it had not always been so, and I believe that the Sackville Street Club was formed of those who seceded when Kildare Street decided to admit Roman Catholics.'

There he used to see Edward Martyn, crippled with arthritis, dining regularly, and liked to hear him talk about Irish literature, although he found Martyn's play not a particularly good one. He received kindness and hospitality from Percy La Touche, Horace Plunkett, O'Conor Don, Anthony Maude, Colonel Lindsay, John Bagwell, and others. They had him to stay, lent him horses to hunt on and invited him to shoots.

He adventured where the conventional club member would not have dared—to the Arts Club, where he met Countess Markievicz, who had lost the looks Yeats had admired and was 'a haggard witchlike creature'. He only recalled one unpleasant incident. Susan Mitchell, A.E.'s devoted secretary, author of a very tart little book on George Moore, sang a song of her own composing called 'God of the Irish Protestant'. Headlam registered disapproval and she came across the room to ask him why. He said that he did not care for people who fouled their own nest. As she was very deaf he had to repeat himself and shout.

St John Ervine was there. He was then manager of the Abbey Theatre and had pronounced nationalist leanings; but he reacted violently after Easter Week of 1916, joined the Household Cavalry and lost a leg. Thereafter he was the most savage critic of happenings in the South and a champion of the Carson and Craig regime in his native province.

Headlam's contacts were confined to social clubs, the academic society of Trinity, the coteries of Plunkett House and of Guinness's Brewery. He never went anywhere connected with the National University. 'Nationalist M.P.'s were completely out of the picture.'

He was not a penetrating critic, and like many of his countrymen ready to accept people at their face value. The Irish are more feminine and conduct a rapid character-analysis at the most casual meeting. Headlam was pleased that Gogarty did not think it necessary to emphasise the brogue in his speech as most Irish people did who lived in England. 'For instance, the poetess, Katherine Tynan, who wrote the most beautiful English in prose and verse, cultivated a tremendous brogue. Like most other poets she was naïvely proud of her poetry. I remember the first time I met her, sitting next to her at the Tyrrells' and being interrogated at length about her readers: "D'ye know Lorrd Kilbracken? He reads me pomes"—and so on. But that was only at the beginning—perhaps nervousness; and her great personal charm, and a less obtrusive brogue, were soon apparent.'

Headlam did not know that Gogarty had been at an English school, unlike Katherine Tynan; but if he was too facile an observer he had what is going out of fashion—a habit of loyalty to official superiors. While he worked under Lord Aberdeen, he declined to criticise his entertainments or the policy he stood for. This put them both on the wrong side of the more intransigent Unionists; but Headlam, as an English official, was able to get by where an Irishman might have been asked to account for his company.

After 1916, however, everything changed. Yeats said that 'a terrible beauty was born'. Attitudes certainly hardened. From that time on Headlam became disenchanted with some of his Irish friends, whenever they sounded what he called 'a Sinn Féin note'. A.E. was included in the number.

'The weakness of Plunkett and those whom he had gathered round him was that they *were* "decent people"—and that they entirely underestimated the determination of Sinn Féin. In vain I suggested to Horace Plunkett that, even if Sinn Féin agreed to an Irish Government with greatly extended powers, it would only be a stepping-stone to the independence on which the extremists now encouraged by Sinn Féin success at some by-elections, had set their heart; it seemed to me that it was impossible, as I told him, to stop half-way down a precipice, and such a concession would only be used as an excuse for more. And the release of the Sinn Féin prisoners, which Mr Lloyd George announced as a "Christmas present" in 1916, in order to introduce "a new atmosphere", was only considered by Sinn Féin as an encouraging proof of "England's weakness".

'The "atmosphere" was to be created for the purpose of surrounding a conference—which became the Irish Convention of 1917—and I had an amusing letter from Dr Robert Murray, the Irish historian, saying, among other things, that he remembered so many new atmospheres that he was quite tired of them, that the atmosphere of conciliation was now more removed than ever, and that the word "conference" was nearly as magic as Mesopotamia used to be, though he doubted if the results would be blessed. I entirely agreed, as soon as it was clear that Sinn Féin would take no part in the Convention. But it was set up, and a considerable amount of money was spent on its organization and on visits of its some hundred members, at the public expense, to the chief cities of Ireland . . .

'A significant feature of the Convention was the presence on it, as representing the Southern Irish Unionists, of Lord Midleton (St John Brodrick). He had been elected to this post very much against his will, as he says in his book, *Records and Reactions*; and his election was a disaster to all who believed in the English connection with Ireland, for he was a defeatist from the beginning. He condemns in his book the Unionists of the South who would have stood firm for the Union. He was not an Irishman, as he admits, though his family had been Irish, and he had property in Cork. And though, through that Irish connection, he had more sense of the danger of Sinn Féin than most Englishmen, he did not realise that it is the *premier pas qui coute*, and he entered the Convention on the basis of acceptance of Home Rule. Thereby he split the Irish Unionist Alliance in two. For though he had a following of moderates in the Alliance I think that the "diehard" party was the stronger. Yet, because he and a few others, notably my old colleague Desart and Dr Bernard, the Archbishop of

Dublin, had agreed to the principle of Home Rule, Mr Lloyd George was able to say that the Irish Unionists Alliance had given up the Union, and to disregard the other wing of the Alliance.

'As I have said, I thought at the time that, in the absence of Sinn Féin, the Convention did not matter; whatever they decided the Government would have to deal with Sinn Féin.'

The Irish Convention of 1917, over which Plunkett presided, and during which Mahaffy succeeded in trampling on everyone's toes, brought into Irish affairs the tragic figure of Erskine Childers. The Irish do not always realise his significance outside the Civil War context in which he met his end. Because of a best-selling novel, *The Riddle of the Sands*, written long before his Irish experiences, Childers was widely celebrated. His book, *The Framework of Home Rule*, published in 1911, was a blue-print on the subject for the Liberal party. There had been talk about Childers standing for parliament as a Liberal candidate, and nowhere in that book would it appear that the writer was other than a Liberal writing from the enlightened British point of view. His family had distinguished connections with Gladstone's Irish policies.

When Redmond said, 'We, as Irishmen, are not prepared to surrender our share in the heritage (that is, the British Empire) which our forefathers created', Childers remarked 'That is sound sentiment and sound sense. Indeed we miss the significance of that support if we do not realize that Irish Home Rule is an indispensable preliminary to the closer union of the various parts of the Empire. The claim for the total separation of Ireland from Great Britain is now no more than a sentimental survival among a handful of older men of the fierce hatred provoked by the miseries and horrors of an era which has passed away.'

Childers was an idealist. One of the first acts of a native government, he prophesied, would be an assault on the licensed trade. The proliferation of public houses in Ireland was one of the results of English misrule. He also saw an Irish government lowering the old age pension. 'Ireland where the wages and standards of living are so much lower than in England does not need pensions on so high a scale, and already suffers too much from benevolent paternalism.' There was nothing inconsistent in

Childers' gun-running for the Irish Volunteers in July 1914 and then sailing away to join the British forces. He did not land the arms to help a revolt, but to strengthen the defenders of the Liberal Government's Irish policy against Unionist rebels.

The Convention was a last despairing effort by Lloyd George to give the Irish people an opportunity to agree among themselves about their own future. As Sinn Féin refused to attend and the Ulster Unionists came to watch, determined not to get involved in any government centred in Dublin, the success of the experiment was doomed from the start. Between the two implacables we can see many of the actors in the drama of that twilight time in their familiar roles. Horace Plunkett, all goodwill, indiscreet, over-impressed by the power of persuasion, too civilised, too much the political amateur, unimpassioned in the Chair. Mahaffy, *terrible*, but at seventy-eight no longer *enfant*, revelling in the opportunity to raise every hackle in sight, strong in contempt, but understood and given a jester's privilege. An outspoken and consistent reactionary is always more popular in Ireland than a seeker of the middle way. Mahaffy presented no problem; he could be discounted. One knew where one was with him.

The Southern Unionists—led by Lord Midleton—were much more constructive than their northern brethren, who came to suspect them of willingness to compromise. The Northerners differed from Southern Unionists in this—they had no feeling for Ireland.

Griffith had demanded as a condition precedent to taking part in the Convention that it should be elected by adult suffrage and then empowered to set up a Government. His attitude seemed intransigent; but it was logical. Plunkett, for one, believed that if any group of reasonable men sat round a table they could hammer out an agreement between them. He had astonishing faith in ideas. But almost anyone in Ireland could have told him this was fantastic optimism.

The history of the Convention has been written by R. B. McDowell: it is an essay in exasperation. But what could anyone have expected? Lloyd George was at least justified in saying that if the Irish could not settle their own affairs how could any British

Government hope to accomplish it? Carson, who did not take part in the Convention, had agreed at one stage to a scheme which would enable Ireland to be self-governing with a Council in which North and South could safeguard local differences. He was, at heart, Irish, and not so intransigent as the typical Belfast businessman who was convinced that in a southern-dominated parliament business would be badly done. Ulster was the only province that had flourished under the Union; it was natural that its beneficiaries were reluctant to put their fortunes to hazard for an ideal which they did not share. Sinn Féin and Northern Unionism were totally opposed. There was no solution satisfactory to both. There is none yet. Both regarded with suspicion the men of good will in the middle. The Convention proved to be a talking-shop and it broke up eventually with nothing accomplished, and at a drastic moment in the fortunes of war in Europe. The crisis of imminent conscription raised a ferment in the country. In comparison with this issue the Convention seemed like a pageant. Events moved so quickly that it seemed to belong to ancient history at once. It left no impact. One is reminded of intellectual discussions in pre-revolutionary France, in Dostoievsky's Russia.

Rather than examine these death pangs in detail, it might help to understand the position to study the opinions of a run-of-the-mill Unionist, one of those who might have slammed the door in Canon Hannay's face for belonging to the Gaelic League, one who most certainly would not have attended Viceregal entertainments under the auspices of Lord Aberdeen. Chance let fall into my hands the autobiography of a typical member of the class of silent Unionist, and if ever there were a tomb to the 'Unknown Unionist' I cannot think of a more suitable candidate than Lt.-Colonel Charles O. Head, DSO.

CHAPTER XXI

The Unknown Unionist

I SAID THAT Colonel Head might have slammed the door in Canon Hannay's face. On reflection I withdraw that observation. His book has the tone becoming 'to an officer and a gentleman'. He calls it *No Great Shakes* and introduces himself with a modesty which, as the narrative proceeds, proves misleading if modesty means an awareness of unfitness. The Colonel was one of those men—is it not a Tory characteristic?—who is enthusiastically uncritical of everyone and everything he approves, eager to defer to any authority of his own way of thinking, but unshakeable by any arguments coming from an unapproved source. These are the men who write to newspaper editors to withdraw their subscriptions when they cease to reflect their own views. They are invariably praisers of the past, critics of the present, prophets of future doom. They are not any different from their kind in Britain or in Britain's former colonies; but they may sometimes throw up a sport, an eccentric rebel, such as Captain White, the son of Sir George White of Boer War fame. I met Captain White—he trained the Irish Citizen Army that took its notable part in Easter Week—he heard me speaking in Trinity and sought me out, because he thought he saw the making of a socialist. He was tall and rather nice and rather dotty, I thought. He advised me not to marry a Catholic. 'You won't be marrying a woman; you'll be marrying an institution.'

But Colonel Head was of the parent tree—a man whose every opinion could be anticipated, even his reading of Irish history. Irish hostility to England arose from 'untruthful history'. False and perverted history was taught to the young.

As the Colonel gives a quick résumé of this complicated subject to his readers one is able to glean from that what, in his opinion, the young should have been taught. 'There is no necessity to take readers far back in Irish history.' As Ireland 'missed the Roman occupation her early standard of civilization could not have been high . . . From all impartial accounts they were a wild, lawless people, and nothing in their early history justifies their being accorded favoured or privileged treatment.' The various invasions and plantings of population in Ireland were 'the natural rule of colonization, and it should be remembered that the Irish themselves had not the smallest scruple in dispossessing their own fellow-countrymen of their lands whenever they had the strength to do so'. The Irish overlooked the fact that most of the English invasions were protective measures. He lumped together Spain, France, Lambert Simnel, Perkin Warbeck and the dethroned Stuart Kings. 'England had some justification for her oft repeated forceful action in Ireland.' One of the crimes of the Irish, then, was their failure to drop loyalty when it was bad for business.

England had to find somewhere to settle her troops after each of her periods of military activity. The dispossessed Irish 'were not unnaturally resentful'. But the colonists often gave more trouble than the Irish, because they married Irish women. 'Irish soil and climate quickly convert alien bodies into native type.' That was Bernard Shaw's theory; but the Colonel would not have thanked me for finding confirmation from that source. 'There is always a tendency to lapse into Irish sentiment when British influence (the reformed religion, etc.) grows weak.'

The Colonel then turned his attention to the land question. The titles of Irish landlords were as good as any title anywhere. (Two and a half centuries before this was written, Archbishop King, in the course of a lengthy tract, observed an Irish characteristic to regard land as still the property of the descendants of the original owners regardless of whether it had been taken away by purchase, mortgage or Act of Parliament. Perhaps it is the influence of the clan system. In my early days as a solicitor I was called upon by a Mr O'Toole and instructed to take proceedings to evict Lord Powerscourt from the demesne occupied by the Wingfield family since the reign of Queen Elizabeth.)

Colonel Head was aware of the congestion on estates that led to the policy of eviction; but he acquits the landlords from any responsibility for the condition of affairs on their estates. Landlords depended on the rents for the upbringing of their large families. The absentees whom writers from Swift to Maria Edgeworth had deplored, 'except for a few notorious specimens' existed only in the imagination of English writers 'imbued with political prejudice and careless of the facts of the subject'.

Colonel Head came from one of the smaller landlord families. It is not surprising to learn—a Cromwellian officer. They did live on their properties. And it is not the fashion to speak up for them. Butt—of whom Head would have greatly disapproved—a tireless pamphleteer on this question, admitted that the landlords who behaved badly were a minority. But after the Encumbered Estates Act of 1849, the new men, 80 per cent Irish, and very many of them Catholics, were the most ruthless landlords of all. It was the system that was wrong. Colonel Head could not see this. He put in a special word for land agents; very often poor relations of the magnates, they were as a class—in Head's time—pleasant, as the country gentleman is as a rule, and dependent on a system which was historically calamitous.

From the land Colonel Head turned to the Parliamentary Union, admitting that the Irish Parliament 'by its mishandling of affairs . . . brought about the Irish Rebellion of 1798, and loaded the country with a debt far beyond the means of repayment. It had been distinguished more for eloquence and elegance than for practical efficiency.' Nobody could have said fairer than that; but to Irish minds the natural development was a reform of that parliament as the British parliament was shortly to be reformed and the admission of Catholics to the legislature.

The Colonel thought otherwise. It was the argument for Union. Pitt had to 'clear up the mess'. And he proceeded, 'Bribery of some of the more influential members of the Irish Parliament is said to have been one of his instruments, but there is no proof of it.' There were, he admits, Union peers, but this form of persuasion had persisted up to modern times. Colonel Head wrote without the knowledge of Lloyd George's traffic in peerages, since disclosed. But if the people whom he called perverters of Irish history were to represent their side of any argument in such misleading terms he would have exposed them. In fact only about £10,000 for five years was supplied in cash to bring about the Union. But if Colonel Head, ignoring his despised National schoolmasters, had opened Lecky he would have read in those unruffled pages of 'the whole force of Government steadily employed' in patronage in all its branches to bring over a majority to the Union. Dismissals of the unpurchasable in high office and hope was 'a more powerful agent of corruption than fear, and it is, I believe, scarcely an exaggeration to say that everything in the gift of the Crown in Ireland, in the Church, the army, the law, the revenue, was at this period uniformly and steadily devoted to the single object of carrying the Union.'

Colonel Head, assuming that his readers would never have recourse to Lecky, carried valiantly on. The Union was 'a great ideal' and 'on the whole' an 'equitable, practicable system of government, under which Great Britain passed through the nineteenth century with credit and profit. Pitt, for his action, deserves well of his country.'

Colonel Head was writing in England to which he had removed himself—he was one of those whose houses were burned down in 'the troubles'. This might have been expected to colour his views; but he never sounds bitter, to his credit. What he does reveal— and in this I believe him to be typical—is more regard for England's interests than Ireland's, and an amazing absence of any historical sense.

It is very rare in Ireland: the Irish mind hops back to the Flood when discussing a leaking tap; the Anglo-Irish mind regards history as an untactful obtrusion on present enjoyment, like a reference to death at a wedding, a skeleton at the feast. Colonel Head was not far wrong about the Union if it had come about in 1900 instead of 1800.

Writing in 1943, he can be seen giving utterance to the final expression of Unionism, an unshaken belief that it was a great idea that went wrong; not because less than justice was done to the weaker partner; not because the undertakings given at the time were not carried out, as I had supposed, but because of breaches of another kind. The first, he says, was Catholic Emancipation, then the Disestablishment of the Church of Ireland (when as a *quid pro quo* the number of Irish representatives in the House of Commons should have been reduced). Gladstone was wholly unsuitable, in

Colonel Head's view, to legislate for Ireland. 'He was totally unqualified by up-bringing, education or experience.' He had no Irish friends, no Irish sympathies, no Irish interest, had only been in Ireland, knew nothing of sport, horses, agriculture . . . 'was void of humour, intolerant of light-hearted wit, and quite incapable of comprehending Irish character'. And, of course, 'all his labours lay under the grave suspicion that their main purpose was to procure his own political eminence'. In all this criticism may be read an oblique tribute to the qualities with which the Colonel considered that he was endowed.

In his version Gladstone's plans were eventually destroyed by the Irish priesthood. His Home Rule Bill of 1886 was 'a hopeless affair. It took no account whatever of Ulster—the determined resistance of a vigorous, hard-headed community of nearly a million souls is a factor of some importance.' His second effort in 1893 was little better. That disposed of Home Rule and Gladstone with it, the country was enabled to get on with its business undisturbed. Home Rule seemed to be dead and buried. But it revived when the Liberal party found itself dependent on Irish votes in 1910. 'No more lamentable exhibition of incompetent, selfish government had ever been displayed in England.' The outbreak of war averted disaster.

Coming down to later times Colonel Head must be quoted in his own words. He reveals a spirit which was, I believe, the dominating one in Unionist circles, but it is not usually appreciated. There was no fight left in them in the South by then. That found its headquarters in Belfast.

'Small nationalities are an unmitigated nuisance all over the world, and deserve no encouragement. In the interests of the peace and welfare of humanity they should subordinate their nationalist pride to the claims of geography, expediency and common sense, and should place themselves under the protection of their big neighbours, while retaining any local characteristics and privileges that are not injurious to their protectors.'

In a glowing tribute to Carson, Colonel Head reveals some more of himself. Carson was one of the very few 'great' men of his period—the Colonel reserved this tribute for Unionists: Pitt, Castlereagh, Wellington and, 'greatest' of all, Lord Salisbury.

'Heroically fearless, honest, wise, and unselfish', Carson jeopardised the highest employments and emoluments 'by unconstitutional action on behalf of the great political ideal which he loved with rare intensity'.

I, too, believe that Carson was sincere, but Colonel Head's admiration for his methods recalls his condemnation of the Irish for their loyalty to Stuart monarchs whom the English had deposed. The Loyalists at the time of Carson's campaign inherited a loyalty that had betrayed two Kings and had emerged on the winning side in two revolutions.

Colonel Head tells us about himself and his family, descended from the Cromwellian who (or it may have been his son), became Mayor of Waterford in 1680. On his mother's side he had connections with the peerage, his father married a Biddulph, whose mother had been one of the La Touche family. His strictures on Gladstone reveal his own idea of what his own sort were like. They had wit and humour—it appears nowhere in his writing, and I cannot trace it in the photographs of himself with which his book is generously endowed. Horses, of course, came into it. Lord Salisbury, I believe, rode a tricycle, Balfour a bicycle—in these respects they had an advantage over Gladstone, who was a tireless walker. If skill with horses was the test, none of them was qualified to rule the Anglo-Irish.

Colonel Head tells us that his father was sent to an Irish school, as 'in those days of difficult travelling was often the way'. I am sure the old gentleman had a slight brogue and his son, I am equally convinced, had none. The father had inherited 300 acres in Tipperary; but after marriage (at the age of fifty) he purchased another, in King's County (now Offaly). The Irish gentry, the Colonel says, were affluent in those days—about 1859—because heaps of money had been made in the cattle trade in the Crimean War. The Colonel's father was one of the lucky ones who had not been broken by the Famine. Here, the writer, an only son, grew up with donkeys and ponies to ride, with shooting and fishing when he was older. 'No doubt', he admits, 'it was a snobbish community. The landed gentry looked down on the townsfolk, though many of the latter were their own stock and breeding. And even among the landed classes there were grades of distinction, measured by acreage, family antiquity or aristocratic connection... a drive or approach was always an avenue, though no trees may have bordered it.'

In Ireland it was not uncommon, if the house was near the road, to make the drive wind across country before coming up to the house, for the sake of appearances. W. B. Yeats in his *Reveries Over Childhood and Youth*, remembering his grandfather's house, admits to this. 'The avenue, or as they say in England, the drive, that went from the hall door through a clump of big trees to an insignificant gate and a road bordered by broken and dirty cottages, was but two or three hundred yards, and I often thought that it should have been made to wind more, for I judged people's social importance by the length of their avenues.'

Colonel Head supports this view. Avenues doubled or trebled the distance from road to house. 'Ponds or pools were always lakes, and streams were rivers.' He might have added that hills were mountains and what English people call cottages were houses. Sometimes what English people call houses were castles.

The Head's butler was a Nationalist, the gamekeeper a fervid Orangeman; he inclined to the views of the latter, as more natural for a landlord's son. 'It is usually only cranks or ultra-egoists who dispute the views of their own class.'

He tells us about Birr—one of the most attractive county towns in Ireland. A distinctive feature were the two 'malls or rows of comfortable, commodious houses, occupied by retired army officers, or the best, socially, of the professional practitioners. These houses belonged to the Earl (of Rosse); and his agent had strict orders to enquire carefully into the qualifications of the prospective tenants. So a little society of some class and distinction was collected, with wider tastes and proclivities than is usually found in small provincial towns. Wild-fowl shooting and gossip were its chief recreations, and its pro-British sentiment was always strong and unquestionable.'

But dominating the scene, second only to the Castle, was the barracks. 'Nothing I enjoyed more, when driving into Birr, than seeing the red-coated soldiers walking along the road in or out of the town. They looked such gentlemen compared with the local inhabitants. And the officers that I came in contact with always appeared to me to be veritable gods from Olympus.' The Colonel admits that Birr may not have seemed so wonderful to the visiting soldiers whom the local gentry did their best to entertain. 'To dispose advantageously of a girl of the house or a horse was a useful *quid pro quo* for generous hospitality.'

The Colonel went to a boarding school 'near Bray'. Born twenty years later his parents would have almost certainly sent him to England. He asked to be sent there, but his father refused. At sixteen he was to go to Woolwich, and to pass the entrance he was sent to Dublin, to Strangway's, a crammer institution for the Army and Royal Irish Constabulary examinations. 'This was a hateful time.' Strangway's had then been taken over by a Mr Crawley, and when the present writer went there it was officially St Stephen's Green School, but always called 'Crawley's'. It was, even in the Colonel's time, a gentle sort of place; one did as much or as little as one pleased. And there was no corporal punishment.

We need not follow the Colonel in his subsequent career—in India, South Africa and, finally, the Great War. The conclusion of the last found him a civilian once again, returning to an Ireland greatly changed from that of his boyhood. He painted what might seem a far too idyllic picture of landlords and their like, but it is probably accurate in its context. Round Birr would have been a settled district in comparison with what was to be found a few miles away, across the Shannon. At first he thought life could be resumed where he left off in 1885 but . . . 'As time elapsed it became clear that this optimistic view was not justified. Farmers, it was true, were nearly content, but the lure of acquiring the ownership of their farms, without paying further instalments of rent, was attracting many of them. The old Unionist class were growing impatient of high taxation, and were talking hopefully of an income-tax of sixpence in the pound under an Irish Government. Many of their leaders, led by an Anglo-Irish nobleman, Lord Midleton, had withdrawn their support from the Union, and were advocating schemes of compromise, distinguished principally by lack of practicability. The four hundred Unionist members were proving themselves very broken reeds, and some of their numbers were unconscious abettors of Sinn Féin. But most serious of all factors was the large number of young farmers, labourers and shop-boys, wishing to justify their non-participation in the war, ignorant, conceited, and easily manipulated. Behind all were the ferocious, bitter, fanatical haters of England, scheming, plotting, and working ceaselessly, not for the good of Ireland, but for the mortal injury of England. These have always existed, but not for a long time previously under conditions so favourable for their designs.

'Though certainly ominous, the situation yet, from a Unionist point of view, was by no means hopeless. The great bulk of the people were peaceful, sensible, and easily ruled. The police force was excellent, the army behind it capable and sufficient; only firm government was wanted, if it were possible to get it! That soon was the obvious difficulty. Chief Secretaries succeeded each other, each weaker and more futile than his predecessor. A Government of Ireland Bill was passed without the intention of enforcing it, or the necessary courage and determination. The myriad and highly paid officials of Dublin Castle contributed variegated services to the Executive, with or without regard to the published policy. With the advent of that famous body, the Black and Tans, it did look at one time as if the physical resistance of Sinn Féin would be crushed: and such undoubtedly was nearly and easily within reach, in spite of the obstruction and interference of these Castle officials: but on the eve of that desirable result a truce was arranged between the opposing forces, followed six months later by an agreement, out of which has resulted the Irish Free State with its present conditions.'

He describes the life at the time. He shot without interference; but others were not so lucky. He never advertised his plans in advance. 'In dealing with Irishmen that was an important point to bear in mind. Crime and violence however congenial, were not a spontaneous, impulsive production, but required much crafty plotting for their contrivance.' Life became in many ways less pleasant. There were frequent strikes. Public transport broke down. The blocking of roads began, and trenching made them extremely dangerous. Motor-cars were raided. The Colonel's view was that though some form of self-government would be necessary 'disorder should first be suppressed so that something of British character should be preserved'. The magistrates failed in their duty, either from caution or sympathy with the popular trend. The Colonel usually found himself sitting on the bench alone. 'Our court-house at that hub of the world, Borris-O'Kane, a substantial imposing building, was destroyed by incendiarism; but we sat in its ruins with the majority of the law represented by a bodyguard of the Black and Tans, smart, clean-looking young fellows to whom my instincts and sympathy were freely extended. It is a delicate subject, the employment and methods of the Black and Tans. Nothing seemed to me meaner than the outcry raised against them by superior people in England, perfectly safe themselves, and giving no assistance whatever in procuring a settlement of the horrible and perplexing situation in Ireland. The old Irish police, as kindly and serviceable a body of men as ever existed, had been intimidated by a series of outrages of cold-blooded ferocity, and had either retired from the force, or had ceased to do any work. The army was confined to barracks, as the Government refrained from proclaiming martial law, though exhorted to do so by some of their most expert advisers. If the British Government was to preserve any semblance of authority in Ireland, no course was left open but the creation of a special body of police. The means were readily available in all the demobilized officers and men stranded by the termination of the war and eager for employment. And the quality and capabilities of the material were entirely suitable for the disagreeable work in hand. These ex-soldiers were hailed as heroes in the war, and they are now, many of them, highly respected members of the British Legion at Armistice services, but when they were discharging duties of the most dangerous and unpleasant character in Ireland, they were one and all denounced as unmitigated blackguards. I saw many of them in Ireland and saw in them only the usual type of good-mannered, plucky young Englishmen, affected more or less by the looseness of morality engendered by the war. Undoubtedly some of the first recruits were men of bad character, but these were soon got rid of; and as discipline tightened, the Black and Tan became a very efficient force indeed for its peculiar purpose; though not unnaturally, with its growth in efficiency, there swelled correspondingly the vociferation of those with whom they had to deal. No one can defend—or wants to—

some of their earlier actions, which were the acts of a wild lot of undisciplined men, exasperated by incidents and methods to which they were unaccustomed; but their later conduct was mild in comparison with what police methods would have been in any other country under similar conditions. And after the truce was declared, not a single instance was noticed of misconduct on their part, which was in very marked contrast to the proceedings of their opponents.'

It is not surprising to discover the end of the Colonel's connection with the country to which his ancestor had come with Cromwell. The house suffered the same fate as Horace Plunkett's and others who had worked tirelessly for the betterment of the country. Colonel Head confined his thinking to the interests of his own class and defended them against the charge of cruelty to 'the natives'. For the country he seems never to have had a thought. His wife showed spirit when the inevitable occurred—she was English—and shot a fire-extinguisher into the face of one of the raiders when he set about burning down the house.

Off went the Colonel to Shropshire, where he beguiled his time as District Head of the Soldiers' and Sailors' Help Society, Vice-Chairman of the local branch of the British Legion, Local Commissioner for Income-Tax, Churchwarden, Chairman of the local branch of St John Ambulance, Chairman of the local Conservative Association. But he admits that he found it all a bore; and he gradually slipped out from under his obligations to concentrate on shooting pheasants, the main attraction of Shropshire. But it had been fun to live in Ireland. When he returned there in 1937, he thought that he observed a very great improvement in the conditions of the towns, in Dublin especially; but 'an Irish gentleman of discernment and experience' was at hand to assure him that appearances were delusive.

His own property, which had been divided among seven or eight local men now 'in a state of abject poverty' was sub-let to better-equipped neighbours. The pair fortunate enough to get the farm-buildings of the burnt-down mansion alone prospered. For the others it was 'a change of masters, which they did not greatly appreciate'.

Was Head a typical Anglo-Irishman? He had none of the gifts

that legend attaches to the race; and he shared the views that one might expect retired Army officers in any part of England to hold. He found life among them dull; but that was because in Ireland he had always had a large playground, and if he was contemptuous of the people, he was not insensible to the charm of the country and the influences which Shaw claimed the climate had on everyone who lived in it.

The gods he worshipped were not the gods of Ireland. Patriotism meant love of England. Duty meant duty to England; loyalty, loyalty to the King of England. Even after three hundred years he regarded Ireland as a lawful prize—a land, as Africa was, which the benighted natives were unfit to develop. He did not even inherit the tradition of the Indian Civil Service, which worked sincerely for the betterment of India. Head belonged to a class that felt it owed nothing to Ireland; England commanded its service. His ancestors never acquired in Ireland the self-sufficiency of aristocrats. They never forgot their place, which was over the Irish peasant and under English Government in perpetuity. This provided the equilibrium which they required. Imagination never troubled them. They retained all the aspirations of their class in England. Red coats on Irish roads were the happiest recollections of young Head. And when he surveyed his Irish home in ruins and no red anywhere to contrast with the prevailing green, he comforted himself. 'Though the flag is lowered in Dublin it still flutters in Delhi, where it is not yet too late to nail it to the mast.'

It was later than he thought. The collapse of the world of the Anglo-Irish of Head's stamp was not confined to one country. Even if there had been no political change in Ireland things would never have been the same as in the days when the Mall in Birr was 'Quality Street' in an Irish setting, and the peasants knew their place.

CHAPTER XXII

The End of the Anglo-Irish

THE LAST APPEARANCE of the Anglo-Irish on an Irish stage was in 1922. In the five years that had elapsed since the Convention, there had been guerrilla warfare conducted with the approval and so far as possible under the direction of a Sinn Féin Government. Griffith got his way in 1918. The Sinn Féin party emerged from the 'khaki election' with 75 per cent of the Irish seats and 47 per cent of the votes of the Irish people. Instead of going to Westminster they stayed in Ireland and sat, as a self-appointed government, in the Mansion House in Dublin until they were proscribed and forced to go underground.

Then began what used to be called 'the troubles' and is now officially the Anglo-Irish war. It ended when a Treaty was signed in December 1921. In the Constitution which was framed under the Treaty there was a Senate, and in this body Mr W. T. Cosgrave (Griffith was dead) gave a generous representation to the Anglo-Irish. The decision was not the result of any sudden impulse. In all the negotiations the interest of Irish Unionists had been considered. True, they regarded themselves as deserted by Lloyd George and his colleagues; but Griffith and, indeed, Collins—the leading spirits in the new government—sincerely wanted to draw this element into the service of the State.

Before the Treaty was signed, Griffith, with de Valera's consent, had given the assurance to Lord Midleton, Mr Andrew Jameson, and the Provost of Trinity College, that in an independent Ireland they would be represented, and their interests safeguarded by a second chamber in the legislature. Griffith was attacked by Countess Markievicz—one of the few of that class in politics then—for trucking with the Unionists, but he was not perturbed. 'I met them,' he said, 'because they are my countrymen . . . and as far as I am concerned they will have fair play.'

When Kevin O'Higgins was defending this policy while the Constitution was going through the Dail, Countess Markievicz and Maud Gonne were among the loudest protesters, an interesting sidelight on feminine psychology. 'These people,' O'Higgins declared, 'are part and parcel of the nation, and we, being the majority and strength of the country ... it comes well from us to make a generous adjustment to show that these people are regarded, not as alien enemies, not as planters, but that we regard them as part and parcel of this Nation, and that we wish them to take their share of its responsibilities.'

Noble words, on which it would be refreshing to let the curtain fall, but unfortunately they were still-born. In the Civil War fought between the Government for which Griffith and O'Higgins had spoken and the followers of Mr de Valera who refused to accept the oath of loyalty to King George V in the Treaty, the houses of the Anglo-Irish who accepted the invitation were, in many cases, burnt to the ground by Mr de Valera's followers.

Many of these decent people stood their ground; but those who were not prepared to help—the type of Colonel Head—took this as the final blow and said 'good-bye' to Ireland. These were landowners. In Dublin, and Cork to a lesser extent, there were professional and business folk who were not at all anxious to leave the source of their livelihood. Nor was there any reason except sentiment to make them wish to go. They were not, as it were, in the front line as were the owners of conspicuous houses. They stayed on and many prospered exceedingly when Mr de Valera introduced a policy of protective duties for industry. In time he, and not the party of the Treaty, was to win the support of what remained of the Protestant ascendancy. As they had had the foresight to back Cromwell and William III, they saw, in this conflict (which was none of theirs) the right horse to put their money on.

Lennox Robinson wrote in his attractive way about one of those who accepted the invitation of the Irish Free State to play a part in the making of a new State.

Bryan Cooper had the same background as Colonel Head. He, too, came of Cromwellian stock. He, too, enjoyed a privileged childhood, at Markree in County Sligo—wilder country than the Colonel's. An ancestor had met Arthur Young on his travels and had favourably impressed that inquiring traveller with his methods of husbandry. He had sat, as others of the family, in the Irish parliament, and voted against the Union. But later Coopers represented Sligo at Westminster, 'in touch again with the class from which they had sprung'. The Coopers did rather better than the Heads. They were probably more intelligent and more attractive. Bryan Cooper was destined for Woolwich, but not by way of Miss Haynes's establishment in Bray. It was Eton for him after a preparatory school in England. He was being kept—one would think—further away from Ireland than Colonel Head, but he was never so far away from ideas; and he had a political ancestry. In 1910 he stood for South County Dublin as a Unionist and won the seat, defeating the Nationalist candidate by sixty-six votes. It hardly seems credible now. He had made typical ascendancy speeches (Colonel Head would have endorsed every word) and was described in his native Sligo as 'a scallywag from Collonney, the spawn of Orangeism, landlordism and every other ism which has been working against this country'. He was soon to lose his seat; but he spoke against Home Rule on every available platform. Then came the war. He returned to Ireland in 1919 as Press Censor. But the war had changed him. Instead of reacting bitterly to the changed scene, or shrugging Ireland off, he looked deeper, and he was far ahead of his class in his time, when he wrote of James Connolly, who had been shot after 1916: 'Connolly was probably the greatest man whom Ireland has produced in the present generation . . . His great soul gave to the Dublin labourer a noble inspiration and a hope of better things.'

As Press Censor Cooper exhibited perfect fairness, leaning towards leniency; but the political climate hardened and his office was abolished. It was fortunate for him. He stayed in Ireland and wrote letters to the newspapers complaining of the unjust way the nationalist press was being treated under the Defence of the Realm Act (DORA). He resented the decision of the Ulster Unionists to break with their party in the South and thus sabotage the possibilities of an Irish State in which Unionists would have real influence.

Colonel Head went to Shropshire, Bryan Cooper (who was much younger) settled down in Kyber Pass, a house on top of Dalkey Hill. There was plenty in Dublin to interest him, which an average landlord might not have taken much comfort from—theatre especially (he wanted to write, and did, without much success). His marriage had ended in divorce. He was at a crossroads in life. He took a turn that he may have been contemplating when he stood for his old constituency in the Dail election of 1923. But not this time as a Unionist—there was no Unionist party. He stood as an Independent. On one of his platforms he had Andrew Jameson, a moderate Unionist, who had accepted the invitation to become a member of the Senate, W. B. Yeats, former Sinn Féiner, but now representing the eighteenth-century Anglo-Irish, and Stephen Gwynn, once a member of the Irish party, one of a family that had given lustre to Trinity College in scholarship and in the playing field. Gwynn and Cooper had both fought in the Connaught Rangers.

The election was on the system of proportional representation, and of the eight available seats, Cooper won the seventh. The poll was headed by Kevin O'Higgins. In the 1927 election Cooper came second. Within a few weeks O'Higgins was murdered by IRA gunmen; and this led to a radical change in the constitutional framework. Mr de Valera, whose party had stayed out of the Dail because of the Oath of Allegiance, was forced to find a way round it, because abstention from the Dail was now made illegal. He discovered a suitable formula. Would that he had done so before the Civil War! Bryan Cooper in the ensuing reshuffle now offered his services to Mr Cosgrave; but his health began to deteriorate. He died in 1930.

The career of Bryan Cooper proves that the way lay open to any Unionist who was prepared to play a part in the new Ireland; but certain qualifications are necessary. He sat for almost the only constituency in which a man with his background could have hoped to win a seat. His was a charming personality—he was a very 'nice' person—and not every public-spirited individual is blessed with such a happy temperament, such an open mind, such a talent to please, such a generous heart.

Colonel Head was, I fear, a more representative figure than

Bryan Cooper. He would have regarded the latter as 'a traitor to his class'. A taste for literature was part of the trouble. There were so many cads at the game. Look at George Moore! It led to certain temptations—the Abbey Theatre, for instance, the Irish language... God knows where it might end.

When Yeats was proposed for Kildare Street Club by Andrew Jameson there was some opposition. It was explained to me twenty years later by Raymond Brooke, then the father of the Club. 'It was not so much Yeats himself that anyone objected to, but the sort of people he was likely to bring in. Members wouldn't like them.' Birrell had gone soft when he came to Ireland as Chief-Secretary. He had found Abbey play-bills more interesting than reports from the Royal Irish Constabulary. Literary ambitions had been the social downfall of Edward Martyn. Bryan Cooper went the same way. He even cherished hopes of having a play acted in the Abbey.

Raymond Brooke was a cultivated man with a knowledge of furniture and pictures. He was a cousin of Lord Brookeborough—all the family were descended from a Sir Basil Brooke who came to Donegal in Queen Elizabeth's time, and the present branch retains its large estates in Fermanagh, awarded them for adhering to Cromwell after 1641.

Raymond belonged to a junior branch which had been in the wine trade for a few generations. At the time of 'the troubles' he was himself the head of a well-established wine business. And he stayed in Ireland as did most of his family. 'I think I may claim to be Irish', he writes in the pleasant volume of recollections published not long before he died. In Dublin he was held in affection by anyone who knew him. He was full of active kindness and without rancour. Everything he believed in politically had been defeated in Ireland; and he refused to distinguish between the varying shades of green that covered what had once been red, white and blue. His object in life was to avoid controversy and help to keep alive what he believed in for so long as possible. In his last years, in declining health, he was sometimes tearful.

As Grand-master of the Masonic Lodge in Ireland he was a person of considerable influence; and the average Catholic would have regarded him as being in league with the devil. Less so now than when I was young. It would be ingenuous to believe that freemasonry was not often a source of jobbery; but this aspect of it was not present to Raymond's mind. I met him when I was a young solicitor acting for the Monck estate, and he was a trustee for some members of that family. I know that he recommended me—a Catholic as my predecessor had been—to Lord Monck, and I had many other proofs of his friendship. He sometimes demurred when I praised Michael Collins in my writings. 'What would you feel about him if you knew that he stood downstairs in Westland Row Station while one of his men was upstairs murdering your cousin in his office?' he asked. I admitted that it would not have endeared him to me. But Collins was the only one of the political figures whom he ever mentioned in this way, and I think it was on this very human ground. Raymond was one of those people who did not care for politics or politicians—except at given moments; Churchill in war-time, for example. He liked an ordered, civilised life against a background of religious belief, and with a lively consciousness of the obligations of charity. It was a sort of life that had taken root in favoured places before the First World War, a temporary foothold in the whirlpool of unrest that constitutes human existence. Such an attitude is not admitted now. Raymond would be expected to feel guilty about the way the family turned up trumps after 1641, even though he saw all round him people in business who had turned up trumps after 1922, and regarded it as the reward of virtue. It is always best, if you can manage it, to come in on the last wave.

His private means were modest and had been acquired by honest work in the wine trade; he had no landed estates, and there was no reason at all why he should have felt guilty. Nor did he. He had relations in England, and if his world had contracted it had by no means disappeared. By marriage the Brookes were related to Moncks, Cobbes, Beresfords, Martins of Ross, McCalmonts, Bartons, Graces (Le Gros), Parnells—families who have played prominent parts in Ireland's history. They had been in Ireland for four hundred years. After a similar lapse of time, Normans in England had been assimilated, as had Gaels in Ireland (whose right of conquest is never questioned) and Raymond must have felt entitled to claim that he was Irish. Unlike Colonel Head, he had not gone to England when the break with Britain came to take up boring appointments on charitable committees or shoot pheasants. He remained because he had always been happy in Ireland, and he still had his niche. Had he married his children might not have stayed. His nephews lived in England. I wish I had thought of asking him about Bryan Cooper. There was an Irish Unionist who had wished to represent his country in parliament at Westminster; but when that was impossible, reverted to the practice of his eighteenth century ancestors and took a place in an Irish Parliament. Perhaps an historical connection with Grattan's parliament had an influence in Cooper's case.

Raymond Brooke had none. He was related to the Beresfords, who had been firmly and advantageously connected with the *Executive* in that parliament. They had nothing to do with Grattan or those who sought to widen its scope or enlarge its powers and liberties.

Once in Raymond's house I commented on the likeness to Gladstone of the face in a portrait on his wall; he was not pleased and said his ancestor would not have been complimented either. Trying to extract my foot, I made a reference to the disestablishment of the Church. Raymond snapped his fingers at that. Gladstone's offence, it appeared was the Land Act of 1881. He was an enemy of 'our lot'. He remembered as a child being taken away from the window by his nurse so that he would not have to see Parnell go by.

His published reminiscences are happy and free from any controversy. Nowhere is to be found a more faithful description of the disfavour in which Lady Aberdeen was regarded in Unionist circles. There is a detailed account of a controversy at the beginning of the First World War over the Red Cross. Lady Aberdeen took up the cudgels for an Irish Branch—of which she was a patron, and offended Unionist opinion. It must be said that she comes out of the controversy looking sly and without much grace. There is also in these pages the only account I know of the procedure at the Castle during the Viceregal season, the drawing-rooms and the presentations.

The young Brookes were sent to an English preparatory school to cure their brogues—the family all have singularly pleasant speaking voices. Raymond's sister acted in the West End with Gerald du Maurier in Barrie's *Dear Brutus*, before her marriage to 'Atty' Persse, a horse-training relation of Lady Gregory. William Smith O'Brien, it will be recalled, was shocked on returning from banishment to find what brogues his children had acquired during his enforced absence. Raymond's father's anxiety on this point marks a dividing line between the Anglo-Irish of the landlord class and the Dublin Protestants with whom he was connected by reason of having a wine business (the idea had shocked the family when first mooted in 1806). Raymond belonged to Kildare Street Club as did every landlord in Ireland. The Sackville Street Club, more exclusively Protestant, was a city club. I can remember as a child, shortly before it closed, hearing the old hall porter in the latter tell my father that he remembered the day when no member of the Jameson family would have been considered eligible for membership.

Proust would have found a happy hunting ground in Dublin, lifting layers of snobbery, always to find another underneath. I suggest that a brogue was rarely heard in Kildare Street, sometimes in Sackville Street, and more frequently in the University Club. When an amalgamation between Kildare Street and the University was under discussion some years ago, the principal opposition came from older dons nourishing a resentment of the way land had looked down on learning in the past. One recalls the antipathy in which Mahaffy was held by many of his Trinity colleagues for his shameless pursuit of game—birds and the lords who raised them.

It is too broad a view that sees the Anglo-Irish as a race—they were a class. As landlords they suffered (with compensation) the fate of their kind in Russia, Central Europe and the Balkans. The difference between them and other Irish is not indifference to Gaelic culture. Many of the enthusiasts for that were from Anglo-Irish ranks. The greatest enthusiast of all—Patrick Pearse —was the son of a man of Devon. Religion marked the dividing line. The Reformation put an end to the tendency to become more Irish than the Irish themselves. By becoming Protestants, Irish families became indistinguishable from the English in Ireland.

Religion is—in spite of what Miss Bernadette Devlin says—the dividing line in Northern Ireland. Next to colour, it is one of the most potent divisive forces in the world. And in Ireland it has nothing to do with the gospels, nothing to do with the Sermon on the Mount, or the Virgin birth, or any point of doctrine. In the minds of Mr Paisley and his followers it is firmly connected with the career of William of Orange, a tolerant man for his time. To Irish Catholics, Protestantism conjures up every injustice that England has ever inflicted on Ireland. In Southern Ireland, because the minority is so small, it is tolerated; but bigotry is plain to be seen in all its ugly nakedness in the Northern counties.

The issue was resolved in the South half a century ago when, as Lady Fingall records, 'the country houses lit a chain of bonfires through the nights of late summer and autumn and winter and early spring . . . People whose families had lived in the country for three or four hundred years, realised suddenly that they were still strangers and that the mystery of it was not to be revealed to them—the secret lying as deep as the valleys in the Irish hills, the barrier they had tried to break down standing as strong and immovable as those hills, brooding over an age-long wrong.

'It was those who tried to atone for that wrong and to break down this barrier, who did most of the paying.'

APPENDIX

A Potted History of Ireland

THE 'DANES' IS the word used colloquially to describe the Norsemen whose unwelcome attentions made all Ireland unhappy from 795 until 1014. The word does not distinguish between the Vikings from Norway, who in Irish idiom are called 'the fair strangers', and the Danes, properly described as 'the dark strangers'. It fails to note that these people were of the same stock as those Normans who invaded Ireland in 1170. Edward Bruce, who came to Ireland from Scotland in 1315 and supported the Irish against the English, was also a Norman, though he had both Scottish and Irish forebears.

Once and once only was Ireland a single kingdom—when Brian Boru overcame all his rivals. After the conquest it was unified again, its freedom lost.

The Danes founded towns—Dublin, Wexford, Waterford, Cork, Carlingford and Limerick. Here they were unassailable. From time to time they went up the rivers upon which these towns were built, raiding and plundering. History ignores their creations and makes them scapegoats for the ruins, when in many instances the Irish were responsible.

The Danes who were driven away at Clontarf by Brian Boru were parties from the various Danish dominions, summoned to the conquest of Ireland by Gormflath, sister of the King of Leinster, widow of King Olaf and King Malachy and Brian's repudiated wife.

Another of the women who brought disaster to Ireland was Devorgilla, wife of O'Rourke, King of Breffni (in the northwest of Ireland). She was carried off, at forty, by Dermot Mac Murrough, who was King of Leinster. Dermot, although a notable Church patron, was ruthless and ambitious, and tried to suppress a revolt of petty chiefs. The revengeful O'Rourke joined and rallied them and forced Dermot to flee.

To defend himself against the chiefs of Dublin, north Leinster, Waterford and Ossory, Dermot sought out Henry II of England in 1166 and enlisted the Normans and Welsh adventurers, promising to Richard Strongbow, Earl of Pembroke, the hand of his daughter Eva and the succession to his kingdom. Three invading parties came in successive waves. The last on 23 August 1170 was led by Strongbow, who captured the Danish town of Wexford and married Eva. Henry followed and received the submission of Irish princes. Pope Adrian IV (the only English Pope) had already commissioned Henry II to invade Ireland and reform its church, and had issued a bull *Laudabiliter* (1155), but nothing seems to have been known about the bull in Ireland. In 1172 Pope Alexander III issued three letters of approval of the Norman invasion.

One of Henry's first acts was to give the city of Dublin to the town of Bristol. The Danes left the city and moved to what is now called Oxmantown on the north bank of the River Liffey. Near the mouth of the river is the district called Irishtown.

In Strongbow's train came FitzGeralds, de Courcys, de Lacys, de Burgos (Bourke), Gautiers (the king's bottlers, who under the name of Butler were to found the house of Ormonde).

A fatal tendency to split and its concomitant, inability to sink differences, rendered futile Irish opposition to the Norman invasion.

O'Connor, the last Irish king, retreated behind the Shannon, which cuts the province of Connaught off from the rest of Ireland; the Normans took over the old Irish forts and put in their place impregnable castles, the ruins of which stud the country. A few, added to and altered, are still in use today.

By 1341 English influence in Ireland had dwindled to such an extent that even the Anglo-Irish Parliament complained about the loss of revenue and land to the Irish. Finally Lionel, Duke of Clarence, was sent by Edward III to rule as viceroy. During his tenure of office the Statutes of Kilkenny were passed in 1367 which bore a striking resemblance to the modern apartheid law of South Africa. The Statutes preserved as large an area as possible for English sovereignty, and the 'Independent Irish' were henceforth treated as enemies 'outside the pale of English law'.

Curiously enough, when Edward III was occupied with France and the English writ ran so lamely in Ireland, it was in Ulster that the Normans not only took most to Irish ways, but let power slip into the hands of the Irish in the person of the O'Neills.

If the Statutes were observed more in the letter than the spirit they were renewed as Poyning's Law in 1495. This decreed that no bill could be initiated in Ireland until it was approved by the King and his Council in London. As a result the Irish parliament never became an autonomous body, even in its palmiest days at the end of the eighteenth century. Moreover, the two dominating Norman houses after the fourteenth century, the Butlers and the FitzGeralds, lived in constant rivalry. If they had combined, and if the Butlers had not cared so much for their English properties, an Irish-Norman independent kingdom might have been established. It never was. England continued to rule through Dublin and inside what was called the Pale except for the period of the Wars of the Roses when the FitzGerald family virtually ruled Ireland. The Pale as an expression has passed into English as an idiom. It was an elastic area. The strict Pale was in Leinster, and it was protected by certain castles—Leixlip and Dunsany are two of them still in use; the ruin of Dunamase in County Leix, fifty miles from Dublin, is another.

In a parliament held in Trim and Drogheda in 1465, the Irish living in the counties of Meath, Louth, Dublin and Kildare were ordered to take English names, to go as English, and be known as lieges within a year. This is the first recognition of the Pale of four counties as the only true English land, and the fact of the legislation indicates that the native Irish were beginning to obtrude upon it. Queen Elizabeth began the attempt to subjugate the native race, disastrously with Essex, ruthlessly and efficiently with Mountjoy. In the short reign of her sister Mary, plantations were effected, the old Irish driven out of what are now called Leix and Offaly (and after her campaign, Queen's County and King's County). The chief towns in each were Maryborough and Philipstown (Portleix and Birr).

With the dissolution of the monasteries by Henry VIII a new class sprang to fortune and influence in England; in Ireland the centres of learning were destroyed and the monks scattered. Had the Irish more readily accepted Protestantism, there would have been a different story to tell, but their fidelity to the older form of the faith gave to the people a solidarity and coherence that they had previously lacked. However this solidarity was to prove a bedevilment in interpreting Irish history. Henceforth it would be increasingly difficult to distinguish between religious, nationalist, social and economic problems.

The return to Catholicism in Mary's reign did not alter relations between Ireland and England. We have seen that King's County and Queen's County were shires created by Mary, and given their new names after her husband Philip and herself. The process of plantation was begun. But it was in Elizabeth's reign that the most earnest effort to subdue Ireland began with the general destruction of Gaelic and feudal Ireland.

Life in Ireland when Elizabeth initiated her campaign of expropriation may be seen from the account given by Lord-Deputy Sir Henry Sidney when he made a tour of Connaught in 1575. The Norman Prendergasts called themselves Mac Morris, the Nangles had become Costellos, the de Burgos were Mac Williams. Some of these families spoke only Gaelic.

Gaeldom was making one of its last efforts to assert itself, its chief agent the two great Ulster families of O'Neill and O'Donnell. Hugh O'Neill charmed Elizabeth and proved himself an accomplished courtier, having lived six years in England as ward of the Earl of Leicester, Elizabeth's favourite. Moreover, he was a man of great cunning; and much of his behaviour is hard to explain unless one puts it down to ambition and a desire to survive. 'Red Hugh' O'Donnell was more the typical warrior. The alliance of these two men between the years 1594 and 1603 was the last stand of the old Gaelic world in the province which the English had never settled. The Battle of the Yellow Ford on the Blackwater in 1598 was an Irish victory, when a third of the English army was destroyed and the remaining troops were driven back upon Armagh. In 1601, however, Elizabeth's deputy, Lord Mountjoy, at the Battle of Kinsale defeated the combined Irish and Spanish forces. It could be said that on that day, with 'the flight of the Earls' in 1607, Gaelic Ireland died as a political possibility. Gaelic culture went underground, although Gaelic continued to be the tongue of the majority of the people until about 1800.

The system of planting begun by Mary was accelerated by Elizabeth. The Earl of Desmond, a FitzGerald, and his supporters of the Munster Rising, were suppressed. They had expected help from Philip II and the Pope; but the forces landed at Smerwick in Kerry were wholly inadequate, and Sir Henry Sidney and Sir Walter Raleigh put down the rising with customary and appalling severity. In 1586 Elizabeth approved the confiscation and plantation of Desmond lands in Munster affecting 210,000 acres. Grants of from 12,000 to 4,000 acres were made to Undertakers, who were to plant English tenants under them. Raleigh and the poet Edmund Spenser were among the beneficiaries; Nicholas Brown, ancestor of the present Earl of Kenmare, was another. However, the experiment was not a success and Elizabeth received little revenue from her plantation scheme. In Ulster, Hugh O'Neill had managed to stall until he was able to revolt; and we have already read what happened to him. After this the plantation of Ulster became the principal concern of English policy. To the disappointment of Catholics who had hopes of James I when he succeeded to the throne in 1603, there was no relaxation of government policy. In his reign the greater part of the plantation of Ulster took place. The City of Derry, for example, was given to the City of London—hence its name, Londonderry, not used, as a rule, by Irishmen.

Sir Arthur Chichester, who ruled Ireland as Lord-Deputy from 1604 until 1616, was a man for strong measures against the Irish and the Catholics. He wrote complacently on one occasion of a general slaughter of Irish families in a centre that was giving trouble to the authorities. In 1609, 500,000 acres of profitable land, confiscated from the Irish, was given out to English settlers. Some of the Irish landlords contrived to hang on; but they became a permanent minority.

The counties of Monaghan, Antrim and Down were not planted; but two Scots, Sir James Hamilton and Sir Hugh Montgomery, got possession, by skilful bargaining, of North Down and South Antrim, where they introduced a colony that brought Presbyterianism to Ireland and formed what is now the hard core of resistance to a united Ireland under native government.

After the departure of Stafford in 1639, who had conferred benefits and made exactions during his period of office, the Irish were left with the Earl of Ormonde as Viceroy. He might have held Ireland solidly behind the Royalist cause, but he was recalled. Thus the war between the King and Parliament in England was reflected in Ireland, and with additional local complications.

In 1641 took place the greatest rebellion in Irish history. The 'old English' and the Catholic Irish made common cause to recover their lost lands. They originally intended only to displace the planted English and to leave the Scots alone. Dublin was to be captured and the government displaced. Because of informers the plan miscarried. Dublin was not taken and a rival Catholic parliament was set up in Kilkenny. There was great loss of life among the Protestants, thrown out of their homes. Milton wrote of millions murdered—more than the total population! Nobody recorded the barbarities that accompanied the attempts at re-establishment of law and order, even before Cromwell arrived.

For eight years the Irish held out. Owen Roe O'Neill crushed the army of General Monroe at Benburb in 1646. Ormonde in Dublin was prepared to make peace with the Catholic Confederation in Kilkenny; but the arrival of the Papal Nuncio defeated this. He insisted that the war should go on. Thus Ireland was prevented from forming a solid block in the Royalist cause, and after Ormonde's departure, Dublin decided that it was prudent to keep on terms with the forces of Parliament.

A scheme to reconquer Ireland was worked out in England. The 'adventurers' who financed it were to be rewarded with confiscated lands. One of these was Oliver Cromwell; and he eventually led the expedition when it landed in Dublin at Ringsend, in 1649.

Cromwell carried out a ruthless, efficient, celebrated and swift campaign.

There were mass confiscations of land on a scale which put Elizabethan measures in the shade. Henry Jones, Bishop of Clogher, was partly responsible. By exaggerating the massacres of 1641, he confirmed Cromwell in his view that he had fought a religious war and had to punish the Catholic murderers. He held all Catholics responsible for the excesses of some. When he had subdued the country 30,000 Irish soldiers were sent to the Continent, and thousands of Irish were deported as slaves to the Barbadoes. (The population in 1652 was about half a million.) Phelim O'Neill and fifty other leaders were executed for their part in the rising. Nine counties were confiscated to meet arrears of army pay. 'To Hell or Connaught' is said to have been Cromwell's maxim; it was certainly his policy. To Clare and Connaught the Irish gentry were sent. The Down Survey, by Sir William Petty (nowadays an invaluable document of historical reference) was compiled to facilitate the Cromwellian plantation.

Before an appointed day every Catholic landlord had to transport himself and his family beyond the Shannon. There were inevitable haggling and delays, but a few executions expedited the tardy. The need for a labouring class left the workers on the land, and some landlords stayed on in that capacity. Others were taken on as tenants by the new proprietors.

In defiance of the laws, not less harsh than those of Edward III's reign, some of the settlers married Irish girls and became Catholics. (In Aran there is a rich mixture of Cromwellian blood among the Irish-speaking population.) There were, therefore, some cracks in the surface.

When Charles II came to the throne one of his first acts was to send Ormonde back to Ireland as Viceroy in 1662. Dublin benefited by this step because a city plan was worked out by Ormonde, and Phoenix Park was given to the people. Nevertheless there was intense disappointment at the measures he introduced for reinstatement of the dispossessed. This was really due to the failure to establish a Royalist front in Ireland when Ormonde was unable to make peace in the previous reign between the Dublin and Kilkenny Parliaments. When James II sought refuge in Ireland in 1689 and ruled in person, there was surprise and disappointment that he refused to disestablish the Anglican Church or to reverse all Cromwellian grants. James considered Ireland a stepping-stone to his recovery of the English crown and would do nothing to jeopardise his reputation in Protestant England.

The Revocation of the Edict of Nantes in 1685 was to help

Ireland indirectly. Huguenot refugees established the linen trade in Queen Anne's reign—names such as Delmege and Switzer are evidence of their continued presence; the Quakers also came, and brought lace-making and milling to the midlands.

James's refuge in Dublin and the presence of an Irish Catholic Viceroy, Richard Talbot, Earl of Tyrconnell, terrified the Protestant settlers. In Derry and Enniskillen they held out against James's Irish army until William's commander, Schomberg, landed in Bangor in 1689 with 20,000 men. When Louis XIV sent 7,000 soldiers under Lauzun to stiffen James's resistance, James exchanged 5,000 of his best men for the French contingent.

On 1 July 1690 (12 July, new style) King William III, having landed at Carrickfergus a fortnight before, was joined by Schomberg and routed James's forces at the Battle of the Boyne.

The real importance of this battle was that it marked the end of the Gaelic order, and the suppression of the old English loyalist aristocracy. Gaelic peers like Iveagh, Mountcashel, Clare and Clancarty, lost their power to the Protestant Anglican crown. James II had proved that he had no real interest in Ireland, and Louis XIV was only interested in his Continental strategy. In spite of the gallantry of General Patrick Sarsfield, the Irish hero of the campaign, a treaty was eventually signed at Limerick. Under this the Irish soldiers were granted free passage to France; and William undertook to secure such freedom for Catholics as they had enjoyed during the reign of Charles II. Ginkel, William's Dutch commander, acted for him in these arrangements. The military terms were carried through—'The Flight of the Wild Geese' is what the Irish call the departure of Sarsfield, his officers and men—but the Irish Parliament—to which William was subject, it being the creature of the Parliament at Westminster—not only refused to make any concession to Catholics, it proceeded to pass what are known as the Penal Laws, forbidding Catholics to exercise their religion, to hold land or own a horse over £5 in value, to bear arms, hold army commissions, exercise the franchise, sit in Parliament, or to become counsels at the inner bar. Priests, by one law, were liable to be castrated.

These were the laws of Ireland until a native parliament in

which the chief character was Henry Grattan obtained a measure of self-government and an English acknowledgement that the Parliament of Westminster could not make laws for Ireland. But as all laws of the Irish Parliament had to be sanctioned by the King in London, this was not an independent government, and Grattan was never a Minister of the Crown. Nevertheless, Grattan's Parliament, as it is called, was an inspiration to Irish life. It was backed by the Irish Volunteers, a body founded by Lord Charlemont in Armagh when the poverty of the government prohibited the organising of a regular militia and the country found itself defenceless. There was a rush to arms. In Dublin the Duke of Leinster took command; in Mayo, Lord Altamont. In most counties the principal landlords appeared at the head of their tenants. Catholics were not enrolled. The Viceroy, Lord Buckingham, while acknowledging that these public-spirited men had supplied a necessary defence force when a French threat was very real, came to realise that the Volunteers could be a serious challenge if they remained under arms. This proved to be the case: in the same spirit as the American colonists, the new-found strength of the Protestant settlers encouraged them to insist on a measure of autonomy. What is called Grattan's Parliament, although he never led an administration, owed the concessions made in 1782—amounting to a modified form of Home Rule—to the backing of the Volunteers.

In 1793 Catholics were allowed to vote, but not to sit in Parliament. If Grattan was to some extent inspired by revolutionary unrest in America, a younger generation in Ireland fell under the influence of Jacobinism in France, and found common cause with the dispossessed native Irish. The United Irishmen, as they were called, had firm adherents among the Presbyterians in Belfast as well as the Catholics in the South. Their leader, Lord Edward, was the last of the FitzGeralds to revolt against English rule. He was the son of the Duke of Leinster, a first cousin of Charles James Fox, and was married to Pamela, daughter of Philip Egalité. With him was associated Thomas Addis Emmet, whose younger brother, Robert, was destined to lead an abortive rising in 1803, and die on the scaffold.

The most honoured name among the United Irishmen is that

of Theobald Wolfe Tone. A Dublin barrister of humble Protestant stock, Tone was a man of persuasive charm with good address, military ambitions and a pellucid English style as his diaries show. In Paris he made such an impression on Carnot that he was made an adjutant-general in the French army and succeeded in persuading Napoleon to send shiploads of men and arms to Ireland on two occasions.

Once again in 1798 the familiar pattern repeated itself. Treachery led to FitzGerald's capture; and French help was tardy and inadequate. The Irish refused to rise *en masse* as had been expected. Tone was captured and cut his throat to avoid the indignity of being hanged.

The revolution which FitzGerald was to have led in 1798 resolved itself into a series of local outbreaks. These were to a considerable extent—in County Wexford especially—provoked by the cruelty of the yeomanry allegedly keeping law and order and by a rumour of an Orange plot to massacre all Catholics. In Wexford the most effective leaders were priests. There the rising resulted in some spectacular rebel victories; but in the end it was put down with terrible severity. In Westmeath, Carlow and other counties there were skirmishes followed by mass hangings. In Belfast and Dublin, floggings led to the surrender of arms. There was no general rising as in 1641.

Under a promise of Catholic Emancipation, the Catholic bishops were led to support the idea of a Union with Britain. Bribery on a vast scale brought about a parliamentary majority for the destruction of the Irish Parliament. The chief agents of the transaction were John Fitzgibbon, the Irish Chancellor, and Viscount Castlereagh, the Chief Secretary. Grattan, John Philpot Curran, and other patriots orated in vain. In 1801 the Parliament in Dublin moved to Westminster; the premises on College Green became the headquarters of the Bank of Ireland. The fact has a cynical appropriateness.

From the Union until the treaty of 1921 Ireland was governed from Westminster; and the century saw Daniel O'Connell's campaign for Catholic Emancipation and against tithes, his agitation for a repeal of the Union, the great Famine, the emergence of the Young Irelanders and the rising of 1848, the Fenian Rising of

1867, the Home Rule movement, led first by Isaac Butt, later by Parnell, the Gladstone reforms and his own Home Rule efforts, enlightened Conservative government, the emergence of Sinn Féin, the decline of landlordism, the Ulster crisis. Finally, 1916, Partition and the Anglo-Irish struggle from 1918 until 1921.

Biographical Notes

Persons mentioned incidentally in the text

Birrell, Augustine (1850–1933). Man of letters. Chief Secretary for Ireland when 1916 Rebellion took place.

Brugha, Cathal (1874–1922). Born Charles Burgess, of English parentage. Secretary for Defence in the first Dail Cabinet. Killed in the Civil War.

Burke, Thomas Henry (1829–1882). Under-Secretary for Ireland, 1869–1882. Murdered in Phoenix Park by 'The Invincibles' with Lord Frederick Cavendish.

Cavendish, Lord Frederick Charles (1836–1882). Chief Secretary for Ireland, murdered 6 May by 'The Invincibles' in Phoenix Park.

Childers, Erskine Robert (1870–1922). Son of an eminent scholar, Robert Caesar Childers; his mother was one of the Barton family of Co. Wicklow. A great-uncle was Gladstone's Chancellor of the Exchequer. Author of *The Riddle of the Sands*. Ran guns on his yacht *The Asgard* for the Irish Volunteers in 1914, then served in Naval Intelligence in the 1914–18 War. Attended the Irish Convention of 1917. Secretary to the Treaty Delegation of 1921. Executed by the Irish Free State Government for being in possession of a firearm during the Civil War.

Duffy, Sir Charles Gavan (1816–1903). Close friend of Thomas Davis. Co-founder and proprietor of *The Nation*. Imprisoned for articles published in 1848 when Editor. Emigrated to Australia in 1852 and became Prime Minister of Victoria. Knighted by Queen Victoria.

Duffy, George Gavan (1882–1951). Son of above. London solicitor. Employed by Roger Casement. One of the signatories of the Irish Treaty, 1921. Later a Judge of the High Court.

Emmet, Robert (1778–1803). Son of Dublin doctor of English origin. Member of The United Irishmen. Organised a rebellion in 1803, which miscarried. He was executed. His love for Sarah Curran has been immortalised by Thomas Moore.

Emmet, Thomas Addis (1764–1827). Robert's elder brother. A leader of the United Irishmen. Pardoned on the instigation of John Fitzgibbon on condition he emigrated. He became distinguished and prosperous at the New York Bar.

Gwynn, Denis Robertson (1893–1970). Historian, biographer and journalist. Involved in the organisation of the Davis Commemorative Ceremony in 1913, which Mahaffy forbade in Trinity College on account of the presence of Patrick Pearse.

Gwynn, Stephen Lucius (1864–1950). Father of above. Essayist, biographer and man of letters. Served in 1914–18 War. Nationalist MP for Donegal.

Kettle, Thomas (1880–1916). First Professor of Economics in University College, Dublin. Nationalist MP. A brilliant lecturer and essayist. Served in 1914–18 War. Killed in action.

Martin, Violet (1862–1915). One of the two brilliant women who collaborated as Somerville and Ross. Their fame rests on the *Irish R.M.* stories; their best book is a novel, *The Real Charlotte*.

Moore, Thomas (1779–1852). Son of a Dublin grocer. At Trinity College. His poems and songs made him a celebrity. He was one of Byron's closest friends, and his biographer. Responsible with John Murray, Byron's publisher, for burning Byron's diaries. Rather unfairly criticised for his popularity in society.

O'Brien, William Smith (1803–1864). MP for County Limerick. Overcoming an early disapproval of Daniel O'Connell, threw over his conservative politics, and joined O'Connell's Repeal Association. From this he retired and became titular head of 'Young Ireland'. He led the abortive rebellion of 1848.

O'Higgins, Kevin (1892–1927). Minister of Justice in the Irish Free State Government. Murdered in 1927.

O'Leary, John (1830–1907). Prominent in the Fenian Movement of 1867. His influence brought W. B. Yeats into Irish politics. He introduced Yeats to Maud Gonne.

Pearse, Patrick (1879–1916). Son of an English tradesman who settled in Dublin and an Irish mother. Gaelic Revivalist. Founder of the first Irish school. Signatory of the Republican Proclamation of 1916. Shot after the Rebellion by the British.

Somerville, Edith O'E. (1858–1949). Collaborator with Violet Martin (q.v.).

Stokes, William (1804–1878). A leading physician in Dublin; one of a family which distinguished itself in several generations in medicine and scholarship.

Stokes, Whitley (1763–1845). Father of the above. Originally a United Irishman. But he resigned when that body advocated violence. Tone described him as the best man he had ever known. Regius Professor of Medicine in Trinity College.

Stephens, James (1880–1950). Author of *The Crock of Gold* and other books and poems.

Tyrrell, Robert Yelverton (1844–1914). Professor of Latin and Regius Professor of Greek in Trinity College, Dublin.

White, Captain J. R. DSO (1871–1945). Son of Sir George White, the South African War general. An eccentric. He trained the Irish Citizen Army of 1913 which formed the spearhead, under James Connolly, of the Rebellion of 1916.

Yeats, Jack Butler (1871–1957). Artist brother of W. B. Yeats.

Bibliography

General

A History of Ireland Edmund Curtis (Methuen).
History of Ireland in the Eighteenth Century W. E. H. Lecky, 5 vols (Longmans).
The Cromwellian Settlement of Ireland J. P. Prendergast (Longmans).
History of the Family of White John Davis White, Cashel, 1887.
The English in Ireland in the 18th Century James Anthony Froude (Longmans).
The Ordeal of Richard Feverel George Meredith.

In Search of Identity

A Fretful Midge Terence de Vere White (Routledge and Kegan Paul).
The Senate Speeches of W. B. Yeats edited by D. B. Pearce (Bloomington, Indiana).
An Irish Gentleman Maurice Moore (T. Werner Laurie).
John Bull's Other Island G. B. Shaw (Constable).
Hail and Farewell George Moore, 3 vols (Heinemann).
Reflections by W. B. Yeats transcribed and edited by Curtis Bradford (Cuala Press).
Autobiographies W. B. Yeats (Macmillan).
The Parents of Oscar Wilde Terence de Vere White (Hodder and Stoughton).
Mahaffy. A Portrait of an Anglo-Irishman W. B. Stanford and R. B. McDowell (Routledge and Kegan Paul).
Of One Company Essay on Mahaffy by Walter F. Starkie (Icarus. Trinity College, Dublin, 1951).
The Film of Memory Shane Leslie (Michael Joseph).
A Lady's Child Enid Starkie (Faber).

Jonathan Swift vols X and XII in collected works (The Shakespeare Head Press).
Autobiography and Correspondence of Mary Granville (*Mrs Delany*) edited by Lady Llanover, 3 vols (Bentley).
Life of Skelton Burdy—account of Madden—(London, 1824).
Letters of Lord Chesterfield (vol. II) edited by J. Bradshaw (Swan, Sonnenschein and Co).
Letters of C. W. Hamilton in the National Library of Ireland.
The Story of the Royal Dublin Society Terence de Vere White (Kerryman).
Thomas Prior A memoir by Desmond Clarke for the Royal Dublin Society.
Adventures of an Irish R.M. by E. O'E. Somerville and Martin Ross (Nelson).
The Absentee Maria Edgeworth.
Some Considerations for Promoting Agriculture and Employing the Poor Viscount Molesworth (in the National Library).
The Querist George Berkeley, edited by J. M. Hone (Maunsell) and by Joseph Johnston (Dundalgan Press).
Personal Sketches Sir Jonah Barrington (Colburn).
Ireland Her Agitators W. O'Neill Daunt (Dublin, 1867).
Memoirs of Richard and Elizabeth Shackleton Mary Leadbetter (Harvey and Dalton, 1822).
The Journals of John Wesley edited by N. Curnock, 8 vols (Standard Edition).
The Life of James Gandon James Gandon and Thomas Mulvany edited by Maurice Craig (Cornmarket).
Henry Grattan, His Life and Times Stephen Gwynn (Browne and Nolan).
Dublin Maurice Craig (Allen Figgis and Co).
Life of T. W. Tone by himself and continued by his son, 2 vols.
Theobald Wolfe Tone Frank Mac Dermot (Macmillan).
Some Fitzgibbon letters from the Sneyd muniments in the John Ryland's Library by R. B. McDowell (Manchester).
Life of Sir Edward Carson E. Marjoribanks and I. D. Colvin (Gollancz).
Byron Leslie A. Marchand (Murray).
John Philpot Curran Leslie Hale (Cape).

Studies in Irish History and Biography H. L. Falkiner (London, 1902).

Decline and Fall

Life and Letters of Thomas Drummond R. Barry O'Brien (Routledge and Kegan Paul).
Sixty Years Experience as an Irish Landlord John Hamilton (Digby Long).
The Nineteenth Century W. E. Gladstone on Daniel O'Connell.
The Road of Excess Life of Isaac Butt. Terence de Vere White (Browne and Nolan).
A Plea for the Celtic Race Isaac Butt.
The Irish People and The Irish Land Isaac Butt (Falconer).
Young Ireland Charles Gavan Duffy (Unwin).
Sir Samuel Ferguson in the Ireland of his Day 2 vols, Mary, Lady Ferguson (Blackwood).
Aubrey de Vere A Memoir. Wilfred Ward (Longmans).
Coole Lady Gregory (Dolmen Press).
The Real Charlotte E. O'E. Somerville and Martin Ross (Nelson).
Memoirs Major-General Sir Hugh McCalmont (Hutchinson).
Bowenscourt Elizabeth Bowen (Gollancz).
Diaries of George H. Lamb in the National Library of Ireland.
The Kellys and the O'Kellys Anthony Trollope (Oxford).
Wild Sports of the West W. H. Maxwell (Bentley).
A Patriot's Mistake E. M. Dickinson (Hodges Figgis).
Life of Charles Stewart Parnell R. Barry O'Brien, 2 vols (Smith Elder).
George Tyrrell Autobiography and Life M. D. Petre (Arnold).
The Anglo-Irish Predicament Perry Curtis, Jun. (University of Kent).
Edward Martyn and his Revival Denis Gwynn (Cape).
Newman's University. Idea and Reality Fergal McGrath (Browne and Nolan).
Collected Poems Oliver St John Gogarty (Constable).
As I Was Walking down Grafton Street Oliver St John Gogarty (Rich and Cowan).
George Moore Susan Mitchell (Maunsell).

Lady Gregory Elizabeth Coxhead (Macmillan).
Past Times and Pastimes Windham Thomas Wyndham Quin, 4th Earl of Dunraven (Hodder).
Seventy Years Young Daisy, Countess of Fingall (Collins).
Pleasant Places George A. Birmingham (Heinemann).
Irish Reminiscences Maurice Headlam (Robert Hale).
With Horace Plunkett in Ireland R. A. Anderson (Macmillan).
The Irish Convention R. B. McDowell (Routledge and Kegan Paul).
A Framework for Home Rule Erskine Childers (Arnold).
A Memoir of AE by John Eglinton (Macmillan).
No Great Shakes Lt.-Col. C. O. Head (Robert Hale).
Things Past Redress A. Birrell (Faber).
'Mahaffy, the Anglo-Irish Ascendancy and the Vice-Regal Lodge', Terence de Vere White in *Leaders & Men of the Easter Rising, Dublin, 1916*, edited by F. X. Martin (Methuen).
Bryan Cooper Lennox Robinson (Constable).
Kevin O'Higgins Terence de Vere White (Methuen).
The Brimming River Raymond Brooke (Allen Figgis).
The Irish Free State and Its Senate Donal O'Sullivan (Faber).
Patrick H. Pearse Louis Le Roux (Dublin, Talbot Press).

Index

Abercorn, Duke of, 168
Abercromby, Lord (Viceroy), 99
Aberdeen, Lord and Lady, 238–43
Addison, Thomas, 33
A.E. (George William Russell), 41, 47, 50, 189, 199, 204–11, 219, 227, 240–1
Austen, Jane, 20, 27, 229

Bagenal, Beauchamp, 74, 75
Bagley, Captain, 117–19
Balfour, Arthur, 202–5, 226, 228
Balfour, Gerald, 203–5, 226, 228
Barrington, Jonah, 68, 69, 73, 74, 86
Barton, Richard, 19
Beatty, Sir Chester, 234
Behan, Brendan, 17
Benson, Dr, 182, 208
Beresford, Lord William, 171
Berkeley, Bishop George, 37, 50, 54, 58–62, 97, 139
Bernard, J. H., Provost, 242
Birmingham, George A. (Canon Hannay), 190, 235–46
Birrell, Augustine, 238
Boland, F. H., 237
Bowen, Elizabeth, 35, 38, 172
Brooke, Raymond, 262–5
Browne, Denis, 68
Brugha, Cathal, 225

Burke, Edmund, 26, 27, 37, 46, 50–2, 75, 84, 86, 89, 97, 109, 139, 228
Burke, Richard, 89
Burke, Thomas Henry, 154
Byron, Lord, 25, 33, 101–3
Butt, Isaac, 135, 160, 153, 155–61

Cadogan, Lord (Viceroy), 238–39
Carson, Edward (Lord), 94, 96, 110, 202–5, 245, 250–1
Castlereagh, Viscount, 94, 205, 250
Cavendish, Lord Frederick, 154, 202
Charles II, King, 22, 55
Chesterfield, Philip Stanhope, Earl of, 63–5
Childers, Erskine, 19, 219, 243–4
Clare, Earl of, *see* Fitzgibbon, John
Clare, Lord (2nd Earl), 101, 102
Connolly, Lady Louisa, 99
Collins, Michael, 223, 227, 263
Connolly, James, 260
Cooke, Alistair, 22
Corkery, Daniel, 17
Cooper, Bryan, 259–61
Cosgrave, W. T., 44, 258–61
Craig, Maurice James, 69
Cumberland, Duke of, 115, 116
Curran, John Philpot, 24, 58, 69, 93, 102–6

Curtis, Perry, 48

Davis, Thomas, 134, 135, 144–54, 188–9, 198–9, 204
Davitt, Michael, 165, 226
Delany, Mrs, 56, 67, 76
de Valera, Eamonn, 218, 223, 225, 234, 258–9, 261
de Vere, Aubrey, 139, 141, 179, 180–1, 224
Devoy, John, 239
Devlin, Miss Bernadette, 266
Dickens, Charles, 18
Dillon, John, 165, 226, 238
Donoughmore, Earl of, 120–1
Drummond, Thomas, 113–38, 156, 157
Dufferin, Lord, 156–61
Duffy, Charles Gavan (Sir), 135, 144, 152, 204
Duffy, George Gavan, 19
Dudley, Lord (Viceroy), 238, 239
Dunraven, 4th Earl of, 205, 224–9
Dunsany, Lord, 210, 228

Eden, William (Lord Auckland), 72, 98
Edgeworth, Maria, 38, 70–1, 127–9, 230
Edward VII, King, 214–15, 227
Eglinton, John, 207, 209, 227
Emmet, Robert, 37, 45–6, 104, 125
Emmet, Thomas Addis, 86, 89
Ervine, St John, 240

Farquhar, George, 24, 37
Faucit, Helen (Lady Martin), 179
Faulkner, Brian, 42
Ferguson, Sir Samuel, 18, 25, 93, 152, 153, 146–54, 178, 187

Ferguson, Lady, 147–54, 177, 235
Fingall, Daisy, Countess of, 168, 227–9, 237
FitzGerald, Lord Edward, 99
FitzGerald, George Robert, 68
Fitzgibbon, John (Earl of Clare), 14, 15, 72, 90, 94–110, 191, 192, 205
Fox, Charles James, 86–7, 109
Froude, James Anthony, 13, 71

Gandon, James, 79–83
George, Lloyd, 19, 44, 242–4
George V, King, 259
Gibbon, Edward, 39
Gill, T. P., 227
Gladstone, W. E. G., 33, 136–7, 153, 156, 165, 202, 203–4, 213, 236, 238, 249–51, 264
Gogarty, Oliver St John, 49, 189, 192, 210, 217–23, 233–4, 241
Goldsmith, Oliver, 24, 34, 37
Gonne, Maud, 44, 204, 207, 213, 259
Gore-Booth family, 139, 225
Gough, Lord, 216
Goulding, Cathal, 36
Grattan, Henry, 13, 37, 45, 54, 94–5, 108, 153, 228
Gregory, Lady, 25, 43, 50, 180, 207, 211–13, 230–5, 265
Griffith, Arthur, 204, 206, 213, 215, 220, 244, 258, 259
Gwynn, Denis, 189
Gwynn, Stephen, 191, 193, 199, 261

Hackett, Professor Earle, 157
Hamilton, Sir James, 20
Hamilton, John, 139–43
Hawtrey, Charles, 235

INDEX

Head, Lt.-Colonel Charles O., 245–61
Headlam, Maurice, 238–43
Healy, T. M., 164, 216
Henry VIII, King, 14, 60
Hervey, Bishop (Marquis of Bristol), 78
Hill, Sir George, 92
Hogarth, William, 18
Hone, W. P., 175
Houghton, Lord (Viceroy), 238
Hyde, Douglas, 32, 50, 185–96, 204, 235

Ingram, John Kells, 146, 178

Jameson, Andrew, 258, 261
James I, King, 21
Johnson, Samuel, 63
Johnston, Francis, 78–83
Joyce, James, 207

Keogh, John, 89
Kettle, Tom, 189
Kildare Street Club, 43, 190, 211–23, 240, 262, 265
Kitchener, Lord, 31

Lamb, Lieut. George H., 171, 172
Lane, Sir Hugh, 233–4
Larcom, Captain Thomas, 148–9
Lawrence, Sir Thomas, 103
Leadbetter, Mary, 75
Lecky, W. E. H., 13, 21, 57, 71, 249
Leslie, Shane, 183–4, 195
Lifford, Lord, 156–61

Macaulay, Thomas Babington, 33, 135, 145

McCalmont, General Sir Hugh, 170–1
MacDermot, The, 36
MacDonnell, Sir Anthony, 205, 226
Mac Neill, Eoin, 204
Madden, Samuel, 62–5
Mahaffy, John Pentland (Sir), 23, 52, 178, 185–96, 204, 236, 243
Mangan, James Clarence, 145
Markievicz, Countess, 240, 258–9
Martin, Mrs Richard, 87–8
Martin, Robert, 173
Martin, Violet, 26, 35, 38, 68–71, 169–70, 174
Mary I, Queen, 21
Martyn, Edward, 47, 211–23, 230, 240
Mathew, Father, 114
Maxwell, W. H., 176–7
Meagher, Thomas Francis, 138
Meredith, George, 24, 25
Midleton, Lord, 242, 244, 253, 258
Mitchel, John, 135, 144, 145
Mitchell, Susan, 209–10, 240
Molesworth, Lord, 65–6
Montgomery, Lord, Field-Marshal, 31
Montgomery, Sir Hugh, 20
Moore, George, 38, 45–51, 168–9, 176, 209–11, 217, 227–34, 240
Moore, George Henry, 156, 160
Moore, Henry, 18
Moore, Sir John, 99
Moore, Thomas, 24, 49, 58, 102, 104, 206, 220
Moran, D. P., 217
Morpeth, Lord, 115, 125, 130
Mulgrave, Lord (Viceroy), 130–1, 238
Murdoch, Iris, 21

Murray, Dr (Archbishop), 129
Murray, Dr Robert, 243

Napoleon Bonaparte, 91
Nelson, Lord, 31
Newman, Cardinal, 35, 107, 181, 184

O'Brien, William Smith, 132-8, 145, 150, 153, 155, 265
O'Casey, Sean, 44, 222, 232, 233
O'Connell, Daniel, 13, 85, 113-37, 144, 156, 160, 163, 206, 238
O'Donavan, John, 23, 148, 149
O'Higgins, Kevin, 210, 259, 261
O'Leary, John, 43, 45, 204
O'Neill, Terence (Lord), 42
Osborne, Charles E., 182

Parnell, Charles Stewart, 45, 144, 161, 162-6, 204, 213
Parsons, Sir Lawrence, 89
Pearse, Patrick, 84, 188-91, 206, 225
Petrie, George, 148, 149
Petty, Sir William, 36, 225
Pitt, William, 88, 109, 250
Plunkett, Archbishop, 146-54, 178
Plunkett, Sir Horace, 204, 207-11, 226-34, 237, 240-3
Plunkett, Luke, 173
Pöe, Colonel Hutchinson, 216
Prior, Thomas, 61-3
Purser, Sarah, 222, 228-30

Redmond, John, 162, 189, 214, 238
Reynolds, G. N., 99
Robinson, Lennox, 259
Robinson, Private, 78-83
Ross, *see* Martin, Violet

Rosse, Lord, 156-61, 174
Royal Dublin Society, 63, 127-38
Ryder, Archdeacon, 117-19

Salisbury, Lord, 202, 236, 250
Shakespeare, William 18
Shaw, George Bernard, 31-7, 50, 181, 189, 197
Sheares brothers, 99, 101, 103
Sheridan, R. B., 22-7, 37, 41, 93, 103, 105
Somerville, Edith O'E., 22, 26, 35, 38, 69, 71, 169, 170
Starkie, Enid, 194, 195
Starkie, Walter, 193, 194
Stephens, James, 23
Sterne, Laurence, 22
Stokes, Dr Henry, 178
Stokes, Whitley, 86
Strangway's or Crawley's (St Stephen's Green School), 253
Swift, Jonathan, 33-7, 45-6, 50-66, 72-3, 97, 108, 153, 207, 228
Synge, J. M., 37, 45, 50, 186, 206-7, 231

Tennyson, Alfred, Lord, 180, 190, 207
Tone, Theobald Wolfe, 13, 37, 84-93, 94, 99
Trollope, Anthony, 173
Tynan, Katherine, 241
Tyrrell, Deena (Lady Hanson), 231
Tyrrell, George, 181-4, 231
Tyrrell, R. L., 23, 241

Verner, Colonel, 119-20
Vesey, Mrs, 67

Watson, Joshua, 192

Wellington, Duke of, 31–3, 141–2, 250
Wesley, John, 76–83, 141
Whaley, Buck, 68, 107
White, Capt. J. R., D.S.O., 188, 189
White, John, 72
White, N. J. D., Professor, 183
White, Rebecca, 71
Wilde, Oscar, 23–4, 50, 59, 145, 179, 187, 194, 197–201
Wilde, Lady (Speranza), 145, 179, 197–201
Wilde, Sir William, 179, 197–201
Wilde, Willie, 179, 198
William III, King, 55, 259, 266
William IV, King, 116, 136
Wyndham, George, 205, 226

Yeats, Jack B., 23, 42
Yeats, W. B., 25, 41–52, 179, 186–7, 189, 191, 194, 197–201, 207–11, 217, 230–4, 241, 252, 261–2
Young, Arthur, 67–8, 139, 260